**Karl Kraus 1933**

# Perspectives on Jewish Texts and Contexts

**Edited by**
Vivian Liska

Editorial Board
Robert Alter, Steven E. Aschheim, Leora Batnitzky, Richard I. Cohen, Mark H. Gelber, Moshe Halbertal, Christine Hayes, Moshe Idel, Menachem Lorberbaum, Samuel Moyn, Ilana Pardes, Alvin Rosenfeld, David Ruderman

# Volume 25

# Karl Kraus 1933

---

Citing Violence, Inciting Critique

Edited by
Gal Hertz, Ron Mieczkowski and Ari Linden

DE GRUYTER

ISBN 978-3-11-136437-7
e-ISBN (PDF) 978-3-11-136459-9
e-ISBN (EPUB) 978-3-11-136480-3
ISSN 2199-6962

**Library of Congress Control Number: 2024943046**

**Bibliographic information published by the Deutsche Nationalbibliothek**
The Deutsche Nationalbibliothek lists this publication in the Deutsche Nationalbibliografie; detailed bibliographic data are available on the internet at http://dnb.dnb.de.

© 2025 Walter de Gruyter GmbH, Berlin/Boston
Cover image: The Prussian Minister of Justice Hans Kerr during a visit to the trainee camp in Jüterbog, 1934. https://commons.wikimedia.org/wiki/File:Der_Preu%C3%9Fische_Justizminister_Hans_Kerrl_bei_einem_Besuch_im_Referendarlager_in_J%C3%BCterbog.jpg
Typesetting: Integra Software Services Pvt. Ltd.

www.degruyter.com

# Contents

Gal Hertz, Ari Linden, Ron Mieczkowski
**Kraus 1933 – Citing Violence, Inciting Critique** —— 1

Karl Kraus
**Language** *(Die Sprache)*, **translated and introduced by Peter Winslow** —— 9

Isabel Langkabel
**Karl Kraus's "Language" and National Socialism** —— 19

Ron Mieczkowski
**Die Sprache „der Richter und Henker" und der Genitiv bei Karl Kraus. Vom Paradigma der „grammatischen Methode"** —— 39

Gal Hertz
**Poetry and Truth in the Third Reich – Karl Kraus's Ethical Campaign 1933** —— 55

António Sousa Ribeiro
**Kraus's Poetics of Quotation in Times of Despair** —— 67

Ari Linden
**Jargon, Journalism, and Heideggerese: Adorno and Kraus** —— 83

Björn Quiring
**"A Contest Between Words and Deeds": Karl Kraus and Hannah Arendt on Proto-Totalitarian "Wahrlügen"** —— 107

Galili Shahar
**Karl Kraus: Literature, Halacha, a Jewish Joke** —— 125

Katharina Prager
**„Wir Anhänger des Geistes sind in einer tragisch-komischen Position …" – Biografische Perspektiven auf Karl Kraus zwischen 1933 und 1936** —— 137

Gal Hertz, Ari Linden, Ron Mieczkowski
# Kraus 1933 – Citing Violence, Inciting Critique

Today it has become clear to many scholars and readers that Karl Kraus's analysis of Hitler's first months in power in 1933 is one of the most insightful documentations of its era. Kraus recognized early on the violent nature of the Nazi regime, which aspired to nothing less than total annihilation (*Vernichtung*). As Kraus wrote in May 1933: "For what has happened is truly designed to restore mankind to its condition before the Fall (albeit retaining the apparatus responsible for its degeneracy) and to reduce the life of the state, the economy, and cultural practices to its simplest formula, namely annihilation" (published later in July 1934, 819, 158). Kraus lays out the main features of National Socialist discourse: the ways it blends the theological and the political, the modern and the archaic, the technological and the primitive. Kraus noticed that beyond the pathos, there is another element that must be accounted for: the emphasis on the "final reckoning" (*letzten Endes*) demonstrates Kraus's insight into the fatalistic direction of the regime. Kraus documented the submission of all state and social institutions to the will of one party, demonstrating the force of Nazi propaganda, supported by some of the key organs of the press and prominent intellectuals of the time. He showed how the new regime was effective in dominating public discourse through spreading hate and fear, and how the use of language made it possible to separate words from meaning and deeds from consequences. In this way he was able not only to portray the political and cultural outcomes of the new form of power, but also to closely observe the deportations to concentration camps and the torments of those who were considered enemies of the people (*Volksfeinde*). He juxtaposed the ideological phrases of the Nazis against their actual violence and revealed the relationship between vacuous speech and consequential action.

Kraus's main concern as a satirist was less the burning of books or the demolition of shops and property than the physical harm inflicted on theatre actors, trade unionists and Jews; his critique was motivated by the suffering endured by individuals. Kraus also targeted and denounced those he referred to as the "verbal accomplices of violence" – intellectuals and public figures like Martin Heidegger and Gottfried Benn, among others, who did nothing less than whitewash violence even if they were not "perpetrators" themselves. Their role was crucial to the process of "coordinating" the German mindset, since they elevated the brutality of political force to a spiritual realm. While his readers desperately wanted Kraus to undertake a polemic against Hitler, the vehemently anti-war Kraus thought that only a preemptive war against Hitler could save Europe. Polemic could only do so much, for while collecting, documenting and writing, Kraus realised that separating truth from falsehood was a problematic task at a time when myth and cliché were so effectively integrated into violent action. Kraus's main point was not that the Nazis deceive their followers, but that their lies, as irrational as they may be, actually work; against them, truth stood no chance. The mechanism that the critic should address is thus not *what* they say, but how, to whom and in what forms. But under such conditions, satire, Kraus also sadly confessed, had no redemptive power, for it requires an audience that will recognize the normative backdrop against which the satire obtains its legibility, an audience on which Kraus could no longer depend. This painful acknowledgement led him to the decision not to publish *Dritte Walpurgisnacht* in its entirety, leaving future generations to make of it what they may.

And yet, *Dritte Walpurgisnacht* shows that Kraus did not shy away from the challenge of citing, documenting, commenting and reacting to Nazi discourse. In the original German edition, the polemical essay is over 300 pages long, with no division into chapters. The structure of the text is unique; it can be separated into different themes, yet such themes return and are further developed like a musical symphony. It was composed between May and September 1933 and remained a fragment. The first edition, edited by Heinrich Fischer, was published in 1952 with the Kösel Verlag. The first complete English translation by Edward Timms and Fred Bridghan appeared in 2021 with Yale University Press.

*Dritte Walpurgisnacht* might also be read as an analysis of and warning against modern national populism, a political form that has received more scholarly attention over the last decade on account of its global rise. In an article titled "National Socialism as Populism," Andrea D'Onofrio claims that although the comparison is limited, National Socialism shares similar features with contemporary political populism. This includes the personalisation and emotionalisation of politics, the use of bogeyman enemy figures, and the juxtaposition of the repressed or the unrepresented (the people) against those in control who only seek their own benefit ('corrupt' elites/the 'rigged' system). Nationalistic symbols are mobilised against those who are defined as enemies, while the people are presented as the idealised collective that symbolises a desired moral order. It is then once again the Volk who stands for the idealised promises of liberation and salvation by a charismatic leader who should return their people to a mythical "völkisch" origin. The point here, as Ernesto Laclau claims, is that through the introduction of old symbols and values into the modern political system, a different kind of political formation becomes possible – one in which, like a network, many people believe to have found an echo of their thoughts and beliefs, thereby shaping a "new collective will" (Laclau, 2005).

Kraus does not provide a theory of populism, yet he engages in a discourse analysis of the Third Reich. More specifically, he exposes the ways such public discourse becomes more and more saturated with the dichotomy of the German people and its enemies; with the myth of national destiny and rebirth; and with the attribution of symbolic values to the party and its leader. Such an analysis transcends traditional theories of fascism that are based on coercion or racism, and instead accounts for the processes by which popular and national ideas are fused into a totality defined as the 'German people,' which should then become the main political actor. Kraus was able to presciently identify this belief in a collective identity that is constantly under threat and that is thus able to justify its violent conduct–a tactic that has become all too familiar in contemporary fascist and right-populist discourse.

Unlike Kraus's *The Last Days of Mankind*, *Walpurgis*'s reception is still limited, hence the need for this volume. For the questions it raises about the unbearable lightness of being evil, so to speak, and about discursive and actual state-sponsored violence are relevant once again and demand further investigation. Essentially, this volume seeks to broaden and enrich the study of Kraus in the context of European fascism by offering incisive new readings of *Dritte Walpurgisnacht*.

As intertwined and varied as the areas of critique and thought are in *Dritte Walpurgisnacht*, so are the academic disciplines and approaches represented in this volume. Beginning with the first English translation of one of Kraus's key texts of his later period, "Language" ("Sprache") (1932) – yet to be discovered by a wider audience – we witness the starting point of Kraus's thoughts on National Socialist discourse just a few months before the events of 1933, when Kraus began to occupy himself primarily with *Dritte Walpurgisnacht*. Much of the critical work produced from 1932 onward can be traced back to the language critique of his "Sprachschule," which is still often critically – and wrongly – received as an expression of his grammatical and stylistic purism. "Language" is presented here both in German and in English rendered by Peter Winslow, who also contributed a preface and explanatory annotations. In this short piece, Kraus gives an account of the moral potential of poetic language as well as its problems and abuses, mainly by the press.

Isabel Langkabel's essay further analyses Kraus's "Sprachlehre". Langkabel shows how according to Kraus, the masses are formed and to a large extent also controlled through certain usages of language. Hence, Kraus is particularly interested in the decoupling of speech from signification – what is said from what is meant. Kraus notices an ever more message-oriented language of the press and the "Gestaltungssprache" or "figuration-language" of contemporary poetry. He does this by quoting and juxtaposing flawed newspaper articles, "badly"-rhymed verses and translations. Langkabel points out that Kraus acknowledges how recent linguistics recognizes the importance of creativity, but complains that both the older and the newer linguistics have not adopted from poetry any affinity to the essence of language, which in Kraus's case would mean the syntax *within* language.

Ari Linden's essay offers a comparative reading of the language critiques of Kraus and the Frankfurt School philosopher Theodor Adorno. Both Kraus and Adorno, Linden contends, are attuned to linguistic reification as it was manifested in the distinct though related discursive modes of journalism, the "jargon of authenticity" (Adorno), and National Socialist rhetoric. Linden argues that a common denominator of their critiques emerges in their individual treatments of Martin Heidegger and his recourse to ontology, which Adorno views as the quintessence of modern jargon and thus as reactionary in its orientation toward the "origin." For Adorno, Kraus's more dialectical and avant-garde views on the "origin" provide a necessary antidote to Heidegger's variant thereof. Linden concludes that in thinking Adorno's philosophical polemic against Heidegger and alongside Kraus's satirical response to the philosopher, we can more clearly view the relationship between Kraus and Adorno's respective projects and their implications for a more general critique of language under the regime of reification.

The essay by Ron Mieczkowski focuses on Kraus's grammar as a critical element and significant part of his concept of "Sprachethik". While studies devoted to Kraus's critique of language focus on the word-games and his questioning of the usage of concepts and forms of speech, Mieczkowki shows that Kraus's critique works on the linguistic syntax itself. He shows the ways Kraus problematizes grammatical forms in order to expose what lies behind the interlocutors' communicative strategies. In so doing, Kraus was able to demonstrate the manipulative usage of grammatical forms, particularly the genitive. Ultimately, Kraus was able to criticise the politicisation of such linguistic terms not only in terms of what they state or imply (not as a source of meaning), but, rather, as another attempt of naturalising and blurring the power mechanisms involved with possession, harm, and control.

Gal Hertz's article "Poetry and Truth in the Third Reich – Karl Kraus's Ethical Campaign 1933" continues the discussion about language, citationality and moral critique in Kraus. More than what it says and the arguments it presents, Kraus' satire raises questions regarding the act of using language, an act usually performed without much reflection. This means that beyond analysing the discourse and scrutinizing linguistic manipulations and fake truths, we should consider what constitutes the language of criticism and why it is not intended to communicate content in the regular sense, but instead destabilize the message and thereby providing space for the imagination and thought in a way that its subversive function does not itself become authoritative or dogmatic. Hertz argues that this is what Kraus expresses by way of the phrase "barricades of words against the rule of banality," i.e. words function beyond the logic of their usage and contrary to the regimenting social logic, and it is for such purposes that he invokes poetic language. Words according to Kraus are semantically charged with something that undermines the social order and in place of ratification and representation, enables language to grasp the political unconscious of the discourse. In Kraus's words: "To learn to see abysses in commonplaces – that would be the pedagogic mission."

Another aspect of Kraus's critique of language is examined in António Sousa Ribeiro's elaboration on Kraus's method of "Einschöpfung" – creating and shaping in language. Ribeiro begins by contextualising the famous first sentence of the *Walpurgisnacht* – "about Hitler nothing comes to my mind" – as a satirical rejection of the political discourse. Emphasising the importance of silence in Kraus and linking it to the only option of resisting Nazi propaganda, Kraus brings language to a standstill. Instead of speaking, Kraus invokes a poetics of quotations: speaking through the words of others. This aspect exemplifies the performative character of Kraus's critical-satirical method. Ribeiro shows how by citing Goethe and Shakespeare, Kraus is able to create a new form of expression that changes the relations between author, interlocutor and reader. In this way, Kraus attempts to address the challenging historical moment, not through tones of defeat, but by suggesting an alternative genre.

Bjorn Quiring's essay offers an insightful comparison between Kraus and Hannah Arendt in relation to their respective views of truth, specifically the ability to use truth in order to disseminate lies. The term "Wahrlügen", which has been described by both Kraus and Arendt, aims to capture this paradoxical practice. Kraus and Arendt focus on the relations between the Nazi regime and a discourse of truth; Kraus sees it as more of a chaotic endeavour while Arendt emphasises its orchestrated and planned nature. Both thinkers agree that the Nazi state is not like any other despotic state, but they differ in their reasoning vis-a-vis modernity. Arendt sees the Nazi state as an extremely modern form of government, while for Kraus it's a return to ancient barbaric times. Kraus believed that the Nazis were demonstrating the weaknesses of the project of Enlightenment, while for Arendt it was about a process of modernization going astray. This disagreement also explains the different solutions for the crisis they had in mind, as Quiring shows: while Kraus believed in silence as a mode of resistance, Arendt believed in a politics of communication and in robust engagement with the public sphere.

In his essay, Galili Shahar asks about the influence of the weak but nonetheless latent Jewish roots of Kraus's work. To address this question, he draws on the essays of Walter Benjamin and Franz Kafka on Kraus. For Benjamin, Kraus's writing should be understood as a Talmudic interference in the realm of German court-language, a tension between Halacha (Jewish law) and Agaddah (Midrash). What Halacha means here is not only an act of resistance within the realm of law, but also an interruptive movement in the world. This notion finds an echo in yet another argument by Benjamin, referring to the nature of Kraus's writing. Kraus's writings, Shahar argues, are not only, for Benjamin, manifestations of the essence of language, but rather they refer to the language of the law: every word Kraus writes is meant as an act of judgement. For Kafka, the German pejorative term "mauscheln" marks the German-Jewish body-language, considered as an Eastern, foreign, Yiddish-influenced jargon, and it defines the essence of Kraus's work and (German)-Jewish writing as such. Kafka refers to an opera written by Kraus (*The Mirror-Man*) and concludes: "no one can mauscheln like Kraus." Similarly, Benjamin suggests that the true essence of Kraus's work is liturgical, and that it is really a prayer. He compares Kraus with an angel who is created every moment to sing before God and then disappears immediately thereafter. This angel is made to sing the song of exile, which is a mixture of sorrow and joy.

Katharina Prager ends this volume with an outline of Kraus's biography between 1933 and 1936, the years during which *Dritte Walpurgisnacht* was written. For this she uses archival material of Kraus's close friend and ally, Berthold Viertel. She uses these materials to reconstruct Kraus's personal life in this period, as well as the general feeling and understanding of the events leading to the Nazi seizure of power. Prager describes the friendship between Kraus and Viertel as well as Kraus's friendships with Ludwig Münz, Sidonie Nádherny and others. To make the events of the last years of Kraus's life more comprehensible, Prager presents a comprehensive body of details in relation to the "Dollfuß-Fackel", the *Fackel* issues in which Kraus expressed his sympathies with the Austro-Fascist Engelbert Dollfuß. Prager then points to the complicated relationships to, and the reactions of various friends of Kraus: the admiration, the disappointment, the rejection. This struggle with and over Kraus, she claims, continued long after his death and to some extent still complicates his present-day reception.

What Kraus once named his technique of "Einschöpfung" – a creation ("Schöpfung") that results from the ladling of language out from one text and into another ("einschöpfen") – is, in many respects, in full effect in *Dritte Walpurgisnacht*. And yet his quotations contain a certain lability and frenetic urgency here that is absent from other texts, an urgency that stretches Kraus's satire to its limits. At moments, it still elicits derisive laughter, as in Kraus's evisceration of Benn and Heidegger; the satirist in him, we might conclude, simply cannot help himself. At other times, however, Kraus's satirical voice gives way to the dark and desperate plea of an intellect at wit's end, who can, as in the essay's pathos-laden conclusion, do nothing but invoke the Kaiser from *Faust II*. Though even in this final invocation, Kraus, through the words of the Kaiser, expresses the faint hope that the phantom ("Gespenst") that has risen up against his own people will soon, by his own hand – however we may interpret this line – be banished to the realm of the dead.

Peter Winslow
# Translator's introduction to Karl Kraus's "Language"

Karl Kraus wrote at least part of the following essay between late June and mid-July 1932, while he was visiting Sidonie Nádherný in Janowitz. During the night of Tuesday, 14 June/Wednesday, 15 June 1932, he writes to say his trip will be delayed a bit, because he wanted to finalize "Deine Sprachlehre" (BSN I, 727), a book, which Kraus originally called *Zur Sprachlehre* and which was Nádherný's in the sense that Kraus had considered dedicating it to her (BSN I, 650). This consideration rested on his belief that the book belonged to his lyrical poetry, to *Worte in Versen* (BSN I, 650), whose first five volumes were dedicated to Nádherný, directly or indirectly (BSN II, 252). The "repetition of dedication," he writes to her on 6 January 1923, is "entirely justified" (BSN I, 650). The repetition was also apt, given the title. "Sprachlehre" is a synonym for "rhetoric," characterized, among other things, by repetition. And repetition even came to extend beyond the contents of the book; repetition came to extend to the book itself. For the rest of his life Kraus would return to it time and again. And when he returned to it in the early 1930s, he collaborated closely with Nádherný – seemingly to fruitful effect (Lorenz, 128). In his letter dated 14 June/15 June 1932, Kraus advises the book was just about ready for print, save for the final chapter, "which will have to wait until I'm in Janowitz" (BSN I, 727).

His plan was to arrive in one week's time, on Tuesday, 21 June 1932, which he did (BSN II, 697). Presumably, he stuck to the plan and worked on that final chapter. While we do not know how much of that final chapter Kraus composed in Janowitz, we do know that final chapter became the present essay. A handwritten draft also reveals that, early in its conception, Kraus envisioned this essay as a response to the writings of Karl Vossler (1872–1949), a Romance scholar of the early twentieth century, with a bent for what one might call, broadly, the philosophy of (the German) language.[1] As we shall see momentarily, Kraus knew Vossler's 1923 anthology *Gesammelte Aufsätze zur Sprachphilosophie*. While it is irresistible to speculate that Kraus had access to a copy of that book during his visit, it is speculation all the

---

[1] See, for instance, the Literaturhaus Wien's website (https://www.literaturhaus.at/index.php?id=7961&L=0, retrieved on 19 December 2020). This site contains an image of the first page of Kraus's handwritten draft of this essay, on which the name "Vossler" is clearly visible. Due to the coronavirus pandemic, however, the present translator has been unable to access the Literaturhaus Wien's Kraus holdings (but compare Langkabel, 19).

same. Whatever the case, after Wednesday, 13 July 1932, the day Kraus left Janowitz (BSN II, 697), the record goes silent – until Friday, 7 October 1932.

That evening, Kraus reads "Die Sprache," or "Language," as the essay came to be called, in the Offenbach-Saal in Vienna, as part of his 626th public reading. The flyer announces that "Language" forms the final chapter of a book, no doubt Nádherný's "Sprachlehre," in progress, and now titled *Die Sprache*.[2] The flyer also announces that "Language" will appear in the forthcoming issue of *Die Fackel*, "whose publication is scheduled for October 11th" – that is, in just four days' time. In the event, the forthcoming issue of *Die Fackel* came in "mid-October," but omitted the essay promised. Instead, we find another essay, "Subjekt und Prädikat," in which Kraus dedicates several pages to an explicit discussion of Vossler's "Ueber grammatische und psychologische Sprachformen," an essay, Kraus tells us, he read in Vossler's *Gesammelte Aufsätze zur Sprachphilosophie* (F 876–884, 153–154). From here, the record goes silent – until Monday, 24 October 1932.

That evening, Kraus reads "Language" in the Steinicke-Saal in Munich, as part of his 629th public reading.[3] This time the flyer makes no mention of the essay's publication in *Die Fackel*; it mentions only that the essay will form the final chapter of *Die Sprache*. From here, the record again goes silent – until the end of December 1932, when Kraus publishes "Language" in *Die Fackel*.

But why, one might ask, is this brief, even rudimentary, timeline relevant to the present translation? In her essay "Karl Kraus's 'Language' and National Socialism," included in this volume, Ms. Isabel Langkabel shows that this essay underwent significant changes between the time it was conceived and the time it was published (Langkabel, 19). It went from being an explicit response to Vossler to being a kind of programmatic statement on (the German) language. This movement in conception may or may not have had something to do with Kraus's omitting it from *Die Fackel* in mid-October 1932. We don't know. We do know that, at some point, Kraus purged all explicit mention of Vossler (compare Langkabel, 19). Despite that purge, however, parts of "Language" still point, or allude, to writings published in Vossler's *Gesammelte Aufsätze zur Sprachphilosophie*.

---

[2] The program was reproduced in *Die Fackel* (F 885–887, 11). An original of the flyer itself is part of the Kraus archive maintained at the Wien Bibliothek im Rathaus, which can be reviewed here: https://www.kraus.wienbibliothek.at/content/626-vorlesung-am-07101932 (retrieved on 19 December 2020).

[3] The program was also reproduced in *Die Fackel* (F 885–887, 13). An original of the flyer itself is also part of the Kraus archive maintained at the Wien Bibliothek im Rathaus, which can be reviewed here: https://www.kraus.wienbibliothek.at/content/629-vorlesung-am-24101932 (retrieved on 19 December 2020).

While one can understand Kraus's essay without recognizing those allusions, one cannot translate the former without giving due consideration to the latter. These allusions inform word choice and other decisions, which fall clearly within the purview of the translator. For the interested reader, translator's notes have been added, which address these and other matters.

Karl Kraus
# Language (*Die Sprache*)
Translated by Peter Winslow

The attempt to define language as figuration and the attempt to define it as communication – both invested in the material through the means of investigation – seem to meet at no point of common insight.[4] For how many worlds, encased by the word, won't fit in the space between the auscultation of a verse and the percussion of a linguistic usage![5] And yet it is the selfsame relationship to the organism of language that distinguishes life from death, both here and there; for in every region of language, from the psalm to the local report, it is the selfsame harmony with natural law that imparts sense to the mind.[6] No other element pervades the law, that a particle entails the logical whole, or the secret, how by some-

---

4 Following Timms in translating "Gestaltung" as "figuration" (Timms, 137).

5 In German, the second sentence might give a clue as to how many worlds have room between the auscultation of a verse and the percussion of a linguistic usage. The German reads, "Denn wie viele Welten, die das Wort umfaßt, haben nicht zwischen der Auskultation eines Verses und der Perkussion eines Sprachgebrauches Raum!" Kraus's statement is no doubt rhetorical. But might there be something more to it? What if it is also self-reflective? I mean, what if Kraus hints that an answer can be found in his text? that one should count how many worlds, encased by the word, fit in that space? The count is one – that is, the word "und" – if the question is taken literally. If the question is taken figuratively, the count is sixteen – that is, all the words between "Welt" and "Raum." Sixteen alone does not seem to be the answer, however. Sixteen alone fails to make much sense. The key, it seems, is that sixteen is a factor of four. If one takes Kraus's statement to refer to Vossler, then that reference might be to the four kinds of sense enumerated by Vossler (see note 6 below). Perhaps this is an accident, but nothing in this essay feels accidental. Of course, a feeling is not proof. But if one follows this feeling, one arrives at a pointed answer to Kraus's question, which one might summarize as follows: How many worlds fit in that space? Exponentially more than Vossler believes. In English, I have tried to create a sentence that resembles something like Kraus's sentence. In English, there are eight words – "encased by the word, won't fit in the" – between "world" and "space." It is true that eight is also a factor of four, but eight risks being less forceful than sixteen. With eight, the answer risks falling flat: How may worlds? Twice as many as Vossler believes.

6 In "Ueber grammatische und psychologische Sprachformen," Vossler distinguishes between four kinds of sense (*Sinn*): "induktiv," "spekulativ," "psychologisch," "grammatisch" – literally, "inductive," "speculative," "psychological," and "grammatical" (Vossler 1923a, 118). Whether Kraus has exactly these four kinds of sense in mind here – one can only speculate (compare note 5 above). Whatever the case, Kraus seems to have Vossler's general idea of sense in mind here, that is: the idea that one and the same term, utterance, or sentence can be understood in different ways, to different purposes.

thing more trifling still a verse will bloom and blossom or wither and wilt.[7] Recent linguistics may be up to par insofar as it places creative necessity above regularity: as for the former, it has failed to discern any affinity to the essence of language; as for the latter, it has discerned just as little as past linguistics has, whose promise of essential insight remained unfilled in its meritorious registration of forms and malformations. Is what they call poetic license bound by meter alone or does it owe that license to some deeper law? Does that law differ from the one revealed through linguistic usage, until some rule is owed to it? The responsibility for one's choice of word – the most demanding there ought to be, the most undemanding there is – disavowing this responsibility: no one would wish to impute such to any writer of words; yet, seizing it, seizing it is where even those theorists of language founder, who drum up some psychological grammar wherever it suits them, but who, in the cerebral space of the word, are just as incapable of thinking logically as any school grammarian is.[8]

---

7 First, in light of the second sentence, with its possible allusion to Vossler, and in light of the third sentence, with its actual allusion to Vossler, I read "Norm" as "law" in keeping with Vossler's treatment of "natürliches Gesetz" and "Norm" as synonyms or near synonyms (Vossler 1923a,148). Second, Kraus discusses just such a secret in his 1929 essay "Aus Redaktion und Irrenhaus oder eine Riesenblamage des Karl Kraus," part of which he reworked and included in "Wort und Wert," an essay, which immediately precedes the essay "Die Sprache" in the book *Die Sprache*. In that 1929 essay, Kraus discusses a lyrical poem, "Junge Tänzerin," which was published in *Die Fackel* in June 1928 and subsequently, as Kraus advises, by the *Vossische Zeitung*. The two printings, which Kraus included in that 1929 essay for purposes of comparison, display variations, but each runs sixty-eight words long. In other words, the variations constitute differences not in the number, but in the choice of words. And one of those differences, the one, with which Kraus took the most issue, is the change made to the initial and final refrains, that is: from "Eine große Glockenblume," in the *Fackel* printing, to "Eine zarte Glockenblume," in the *Vossische Zeitung* printing. The story is more complicated than a translator's note allows. Suffice it to say Kraus thought the latter version disimproves, and thereby changes, the poem entirely. In "Aus Redaktion und Irrenhaus oder eine Riesenblamage des Karl Kraus," Kraus writes, in pertinent part:

> And here I say: contrary to those clueless enough to wish to show, by emphasizing the minor disparity between "groß" and "zart" (in the initial and final refrains), that the two poems are really identical – here I say, this very disparity nullifies that very identity. Lyrical poetry [. . .] knows no "identity." A poem is not an inventory of words, which remains invariably complete, whenever one of the sixty-eight words has been switched out for another. Through that one word alone, life can be breathed into, or choked out of, all the words together. In the vision of the "große Glockenblume" culminates the creation that I lauded (111; but compare Kraus's "Wort und Wert," 383).

8 Of course, Vossler is one of "those theorists of language," and the words "psychological grammar" allude to Vossler's "Ueber grammatische und psychologische Sprachformen."

Of a theory concerning language and speaking the practical teaching could never be that one learns the language when one learns to speak, but it can be that one draws closer to grasping the figures associated with a word and, in so doing, to the sphere fruitful beyond the manifestly practical. This guarantee of moral gain resides in a discipline of the mind, which not only sets the highest standard of responsibility for the only thing that can be violated with impunity, for language, but which also is suited like no other to teach respect for that other natural right.[9] Could one conceive of a moral palladium more potent than a skeptical stance toward language?[10] Would not that stance, above every substantive wish, lay claim to being father to the thought? As the epitome of frivolous decisionmaking, all speaking and writing today, including that done by authorities, has turned language into the dross of the times, which takes its events and experiences, its being and justification, from the *Times*.[11] As the great moral gift, which man could receive from language, but has hitherto spurned, the skeptical stance would be a redemptive frustration of a progress that, with perfect certainty, shall lead to the downfall of a civilization, in whose service it believes to act.[12] And it is as if fate had blessed that part of humanity,

---

9 The German term translated here as "natural right" is "Lebensgut," a legal term of art. It is commonly used in contradistinction to "Rechtsgut," or "legal right." A natural right is a right "that is conceived as part of natural law and that is therefore thought to exist independently of rights created by government or society [= legal rights], such as the right to life, liberty, and property" (*Black's Law Dictionary*, 10th Edition). Kraus has precisely these kinds of rights in mind. In his November 1905 essay titled "Kinderfreunde," Kraus even gives a list of *Lebensgüter*; he writes (translated here more or less literally): "If morality should become a legal right, then the natural rights of liberty, peace of mind, and economic security shall be placed at risk" (19). Even though Kraus does not say what the natural right is, one has some reason to suspect the natural right is life, especially when considered in connection with the last paragraph of the present essay.

10 The German term translated here as "skeptical stance toward language" is "sprachlicher Zweifel." In his second volume of *Apocalyptic Satirist*, the late Edward Timms provides a translation of this term as "linguistic skepticism" (Timms, 530). While his translation is not inaccurate, Timms never published a translation of the present essay. If he had, the present translator believes that, ultimately, he would have opted for a different translation – perhaps not exactly the one proposed here, but likely one informed by reasons substantially similar to those discussed in note 12 below.

11 Kraus plays on the words "Zeit" and "Zeitung," translated respectively as "times" and "*Times*" above. Strictly, Kraus does not use the name of a specific newspaper; he uses the generic term for newspaper, namely "Zeitung." In English, however, metonymy is the simplest way to capture Kraus's play on those words.

12 First, to understand why "sprachlicher Zweifel" is better translated as "skeptical stance toward language," one must see its connection to "Hemmung" and this word's connection to "Fatum," or "fate," in the subsequent sentence. The close proximity of "Hemmung" and "Fatum" calls to mind the idiom "den Lauf des Schicksals hemmen," or "to frustrate fate." And, ostensibly, frustrating a (false sense of) fate is what Kraus has in mind. Kraus's "sprachlicher Zweifel" frus-

which believes they speak German, with the language richest in thought, but cursed them to live outside that language, to think after they have spoken, to act before they have taken its counsel. Its speakers make no use of this language's virtue, of its consisting of all the apprehensions that have space between its words. What style of life would unfold, if Germans would swear fealty to no authority, to no arbiter, other than language![13]

Nothing would be more foolish than to suppose, as has been supposed, that aspiring to linguistic perfection is an aesthetic need in want of arousal or satisfaction.[14] Neither would such a thing be possible, given the deep particularity of this language, which in salutary contradistinction to its speakers refuses to be mastered. It resists being mastered, with the ever looming eruptive force of a volcanic floor.[15] Even in its most fathomable region, it resembles but an inkling of the highest peak

---

trates a sense of paradoxical fate by compelling us to stop, not to take language for granted, to think before we speak, to act only after we understand the language at hand. Kraus's "sprachlicher Zweifel" also frustrates a sense of ill-fated progress by compelling us to stop in preparation of further action, to investigate all the apprehensions existing in language, to apply an appropriate level of care to those investigations, to stand ready until it is appropriate to act – until one knows what to do, whether to stand firm or whether to give way, whether to change or whether to stay the course. In a word, Kraus's "sprachlicher Zweifel" represents a stance taken toward language in opposition both to that false sense of fate and to that ill-fated progress. Second, Kraus's idea of a skeptical stance toward language is presumably a response to Vossler. In "Die Grenzen der Sprachsoziologie," Vossler mentions Leonardo Olschki, a contemporary Romance scholar and literary critic, and mildly criticizes him, among other things, for having shown, because he succumbed to, "the frustrating [*hemmend*] and disruptive effects that language has on thinking" (219). Where Vossler believes language can have frustrating and disruptive effects on thinking, Kraus believes the skeptical stance toward language not only can, but certainly will have frustrating and disruptive effects on thinking – on unsound thinking. Where Vossler believes these effects are disadvantageous, Kraus believes they are advantageous.

**13** In part, following Timms in translating "Ordonnanz" as "arbiter" (Timms, 137).

**14** Kraus uses indirect speech, indicating that he is relaying a supposition propounded by someone else. Despite best efforts, the present translator has been unable to locate a likely source.

**15** With volcanic floor (*vulkanischer Boden*), Kraus appears to take aim at the following passage from Vossler's "Ueber grammatische und psychologische Sprachformen":

> [. . .] in the back and forth of everyday speech, one originality is expunged by the one that follows, and the one that follows that, and out of the dead and lifeless bodies and out of the decaying of billions of linguistic blossoms and seeds that homogenous bogland [*Moorboden*] is formed, which is the terrain researched by historical grammar (141).

Roughly put, Kraus does not view language as dead, lifeless, or decaying. Rather, he believes language is like a volcano, at once dormant and potentially active, very much alive with the possibility of fiery recurrence – presumably with all the figurative associations.

that it has reached: Pandora, with the inextricable regularity of natural law, the curious alignment with those airy phantoms emanating from that allegoric box:[16]

> To human hands extended not accessible,
> Now by ascending, now by sudden plunging, they
> For ever slipped away from those pursuing hands.[17]

A more commendable conceit than being able to master language is to approximate the riddles of its rules, to sketch maps of its perils. To teach people to see abysses where commonplaces exist – that would be the pedagogical project befitting a nation borne of sin; would be the deliverance of natural rights from the fetters of journalism and from the fangs of politics. To occupy the mind – guaranteed more through language than by all the sciences, which avail themselves of it – is to exacerbate life in a way that alleviates other burdens. Rewarding the failure to exhaust an infinity, which everyone has and to which no one is denied entry. "Nation of poets and thinkers": its language can elevate cases of possession to those of witness, having to being.[18] For any possibility grander than thinking in it would not be a product of the imagination. What otherwise remains open to imagination is the notion of a veneer encasing the abundance of forgone fortune: recompense for soul and senses, which it curtails. Language is the only chimera, whose powers of illusion know no bounds; is the inexhaustible store, from which life shall be beggared not. Man must learn to serve it!

---

**16** Following Michael Hamburger in translating "Luftgeburten" from Goethe's *Pandora* as "airy phantoms" (Goethe, 221). Compare note 17 below.
**17** The lines quoted by Kraus are from "Night," that is: the opening scene of Goethe's *Pandora*. The German reads:

> Und irdisch ausgestreckten Händen unerreich-
> bar jene, steigend jetzt empor und jetzt gesenkt.
> Die Menge täuschten stets sie, die verfolgende

The English translation given above is Michael Hamburger's (Goethe, 221).
**18** Following Timms and Bridgham in translating the phrase "Volk der Dichter und Denker" as "nation of poets and thinkers" (See, for instance, Kraus 2015, 148). For those interested in Kraus's use of the genitive case in German, please see Mr. Ron Mieczkowski's contribution to this volume titled "Die Sprache "der Richter und Henker" und der Genitiv bei Karl Kraus. Vom Paradigma der "grammatischen Methode".

# References

Goethe, Johann Wolfgang von. "Pandora," Translated by Michael Hamburger. *Goethe: Verse Plays and Epic*. Eds. Cyrus Hamlin and Frank Ryder. New York: Suhrkamp Publishers, 1987. 217–246.
Kraus, Karl. "Kinderfreunde." *Die Fackel*, vol. 187 (1905): 1–28.
Kraus, Karl. "Aus Redaktion und Irrenhaus oder eine Riesenblamage des Karl Kraus." *Die Fackel*, vol. 800–805 (1929): 75–132.
Kraus, Karl. "Subjekt und Prädikat." *Die Fackel*, vol. 876–884 (1932a): 147–192.
Kraus, Karl. "Die Sprache." *Die Fackel*, vol. 885–887 (1932b): 1–4.
Kraus, Karl. "Die Sprache." Die Sprache. Ed. Philipp Berger. Wien: Die Fackel, 1937a: 393–396.
Kraus, Karl. " Wort und Wert." Die Sprache. Ed. Philipp Berger. Wien: Die Fackel, 1937b. 380–392.
Kraus, Karl. *The Last Days of Mankind*. Translated by Fred Bridgham and Edward Timms. New Haven: Yale University Press, 2015.
Kraus, Karl. *Briefe an Sidonie Nádherný von Borutin: 1913–1936, Volume 1*. Ed. Friedrich Pfäfflin. Göttingen: Wallstein Verlag, 2015 (BSN I).
Kraus, Karl. *Briefe an Sidonie Nádherný Von Borutin: 1913–1936, Volume 2, Dokumente & Anmerkungen*. Ed. Friedrich Pfäfflin. Göttingen: Wallstein Verlag, 2015 (BSN II).
Langkabel, Isabel. "Karl Kraus's 'Language' and National Socialism." pp 17–34.
Lorenz, Elke. "Die Widmungsgedichte nach 1918." *"Sei Ich ihr, sei mein Bote" Der Briefwechsel zwischen Sidonie Nádherný und Albert Bloch*. Ed. Elke Lorenz. München: iudicium, 2002. 124–142.
Timms, Edward. *Apocalyptic Satirist: The Post-War Crisis and the Rise of the Swastika*. New Haven: Yale University Press, 2005.
Vossler, Karl. "Ueber grammatische und psychologische Sprachformen." *Gesammelte Aufsätze Zur Sprachphilosophie*. München: Hochschulbuchhandlung Max Hueber, 1923a. 105–151.
Vossler, Karl. "Die Grenzen der Sprachsoziologie." *Gesammelte Aufsätze Zur Sprachphilosophie*. München: Hochschulbuchhandlung Max Hueber, 1923b. 210–260.

Isabel Langkabel
# Karl Kraus's "Language" and National Socialism

At the beginning of 1930, Karl Kraus devoted himself intensively to the subject of language. At the end of 1932, just a few months before the beginning of the National Socialist dictatorship, he discussed his theoretical view of language in his short and programmatic essay "Die Sprache" ("Language"), he explained the consequences of a careless and instrumental use of language, which would end in National Socialism. In the following, the intention and significance of his criticism of language under National Socialism will be discussed, considering the context in which it was written as well as the genesis of this essay, which is central to Kraus' conception of language.

In the summer of 1932 Kraus wrote to his friend Sidonie Nádherný that it was only a matter of a few days, "die es ermöglichen, Deine Sprachlehre druckfertig zu stellen (mit Ausnahme eines Abschlußkapitels, welches dem Aufenthalt in J[ano- witz] überlassen bleiben muß)" (which will enable me to finalize your Sprachlehre ready for printing [with the exception of one final chapter, which has to be left over for my stay in Janowitz]).[1] His frequent and intensive examinations of language, published in *Die Fackel* since 1921 under the heading "Sprachlehre", were supposed to be separately and collectively published as a book dedicated to Nádherný.[2] After almost ten years – in 1923, the book edition of "Sprachlehre" was an-

---

[1] Karl Kraus to Sidonie Nádherný, Wien, 14/15 June 1932, in: *Briefe an Sidonie Nádherný von Borutin*, auf der Grundlage der Ausgabe von Heinrich Fischer und Michael Lazarus new ed. and compl. by Friedrich Pfäfflin, vol. 1 (Göttingen 2005), 727–728. – All translations from secondary literature and Kraus, except for those quotes from "Language" (by Peter Winslow) by the translator. Cf. Footnote 12.
[2] Nádherný spoke German, Czech and English. This linguistic diversity obviously influenced her German writing, in which grammatical and word errors were evident. "[Kraus] interpretiert sie, die unter psychologischen Aspekt zweifellos als sogenannte 'Fehlleistungen' einzuordnen und auszudeuten wären, nicht als solche, sondern, wie es bei Karl Kraus einmal heißt, geradezu als 'Sprachleistung'" ([Kraus] interprets them, which seen psychologically should be regarded as 'failures,' not as such but, as he says in fact, as specific 'language achievements.') Kurt Krolop, *Die Hörerin als Sprecherin: Sidonie Nádherný und "ihre Sprachlehre"* (Warmbronn 2005), 13. Kraus was apparently enthusiastic about Nádherný's "sprachliche[] Fehlerquellen" (linguistic sources of error) and intended to dedicate the planned volume on "Sprachlehre" to her. Ibid., 14.

**Note:** Translated by Johannes Knüchel

nounced publicly for the first time[3] – Kraus continued to work on this publication. This book was now to be based mostly on further "Sprachlehre"-texts from 1923 onward, and therefore the compilation from 1932 likely differs significantly from the original version of 1923, of which no preparatory work has survived.

The "final chapter" mentioned in the letter refers to the famous essay "Language", most likely written in the late summer of 1932 in Janowitz and published in *Die Fackel* in December of the same year. One of the existing preparatory tables of contents shows how Kraus constantly rearranged the respective texts. It also shows that later – after June 15, 1932[4] – he put a text simply referred to as "Manuskript"[5] last: that "final chapter", "Language." Kraus did not manage to finish this publication before his death in 1936. His (literary) executor Philipp Berger most likely stuck to the now lost proofs while editing and publishing the first posthumous work of Kraus in 1937, as he also put "Language" last.[6] Heinrich Fischer and Christian Wagenknecht respectively adhered to this idea. Identifying the text "Language" with the "final chapter" is further justified when looking at the lecture program from October 7, 1932. Here Kraus announces the reading of "Language," which was supposed to be the "Schlußwort zu dem Werk 'Die Sprache'" (final word on the work "Language").[7]

While in the column "Sprachlehre," Kraus critiques, on the one hand, the communication-oriented language of the press, and on the other hand, the *Gestaltungssprache* or figuration-language of contemporary poetry by quoting and simultaneously juxtaposing flawed newspaper articles, 'badly'-rhymed verses or translations, in "Language" he wrote one of his few programmatic texts on language: Instead of exemplifying a wrong use of language, he tries to grasp the subject's relationship to language as well as its effect on reality. Changing its title reflects the importance of the text within the collection: whereas the separate publication in 1923 was supposed to be named "Sprachlehre,"[8] the lecture pro-

---

3 Cf. F 613–621.
4 Kraus travelled to Paris and Munich in the summer, briefly returned to Vienna and only went to Janowitz in September, where he stayed for the whole month. Cf. Kraus, *Briefe an Sidonie Nádherný von Borutin*, 730 and ibid., vol. 2, 697.
5 Cf. Eva Dambacher & Friedrich Pfäfflin, *Karl Kraus. Eine Ausstellung des Deutschen Literaturarchivs im Schiller-Nationalmuseum Marbach* (Marbach a. Neckar 1999), 466–467.
6 Cf. Karl Kraus, *Die Sprache*, ed. Philipp Berger (Wien 1937).
7 626. Vorlesung am 7.10.1932, Karl Kraus-Archiv, Handschriftensammlung, Wienbibliothek im Rathaus. Quote from: Katharina Prager (unter Mitarbeit von Brigitte Stocker): Karl Kraus Online (online). Wienbibliothek im Rathaus / Ludwig Boltzmann Institut für Geschichte und Theorie der Biographie 2015. https://www.kraus.wienbibliothek.at/content/vorlesungsprogramm-karl-kraus-406 [16 October 2019].
8 Cf. F 613–621.

gram from September 29, 1932, lists the title as "Language."[9] Thus, not only do all texts of the collection culminate in the text "Language," but they are at the same time united under the identical title as the title of the book.

When in autumn of 1932 Kraus had finished the manuscript of the essay, it did not just differ significantly in form, but also in orientation from the version that was to be published later on: the proofs offer a version or *Fassung*[10] that did not consist of 3.5 but rather 5 *Fackel*-pages, and was far less programmatic than it was polemical and oriented around a critique of language.[11] In particular, Kraus had studied the work of acclaimed linguist and Romance philologist Karl Vossler; this reading apparently directly led to him writing "Language." This hypothesis can be confirmed by looking at the proofs, but it can also be expanded upon: "Language" was first a polemic against Vossler, and only later did Kraus fully develop the programmatic aspect. How and why this text was subjected to this change of genre – from polemic to programme – will be discussed here as well as its meaning for Kraus' didactic examination of language during the era of National Socialism.

*

In the first sentence, one of the two substantial points of the essay is already named:

> The attempt to define language as figuration [*Gestaltung*] and the attempt to define it as communication [*Mitteilung*] – both invested in the material through the means of investigation – seem to meet at no point of common insight.[12]

Stated are two modes of relating to language, as figuration and as communication, but the statement's subject is the notion that the 'value of the word' depends on these two modes. However, the attempt to define the value of the word according to the respective mode does not in any way lead to a "common insight".

His term 'word value' might seem strange in this context, but Kraus's statement is comprehensible when we relate it to his idea of language and art. This view on

---

9   624. Vorlesung am 29.9.1932, Karl Kraus-Archiv, Handschriftensammlung, Wienbibliothek im Rathaus. Quote from: Katharina Prager (unter Mitarbeit von Brigitte Stocker): Karl Kraus Online (online). Wienbibliothek im Rathaus / Ludwig Boltzmann Institut für Geschichte und Theorie der Biographie 2015. https://www.kraus.wienbibliothek.at/content/vorlesungsprogramm-karl-kraus-405 [16 October 2019].
10  The difference is so substantial that the term *Fassung* should be viewed critically at this point and understood as an auxiliary word.
11  Cf. the proofs to "Language" in Literaturhaus Wien, Signature N1.23 / 1.2.2–1–1.2.2–3.
12  For all translations of "Die Sprache" refer to Peter Winslow's translation within this volume. For the original cf. F 885–887, 1–4.

language and art is explained in the text "Wort und Wert" (Word and Value), also within the volume "Die Sprache."[13] In this essay, referred to by Kraus as a(n) "sprachkritische Untersuchung," (examination through critique of language),[14] he claims a difference in value between two versions of the poem "Junge Tänzerin," (Young [female] Dancer) – falsely attributed to Karl Piehowicz – resulting purely from a one-word difference.[15] First and foremost, he stresses the difference in verse 1: "Eine zarte Glockenblume" (A tender bellflower) (*Scherl's Magazin*)[16] and "Eine große Glockenblume" (A great[17] bellflower) (*Fackel* 781–786).[18] According to Kraus, only the word 'great' expresses the "Belebung" (animation)[19] of the "Junge Tänzerin" and thus brings forth the "große Gedicht" (great poem),[20] whereas the adjective 'tender' leads to a(n) "minderwertig[e]" (inferior) version.[21] He defends a rather daring thesis for its time by claiming that there are actually two different poems, thereby implicitly denying the concept of a version or *Fassung*.[22] From this

---

13 The text was first published in *Die Fackel* in 1929, where it formed part of the essay "Redaktion aus dem Irrenhaus oder Eine Riesenblamage für Karl Kraus" (Editing from the Madhouse or A Huge Disgrace for Karl Kraus). Cf. F 800–805, 108–121. A detailed summary of the events surrounding the poems from the mental asylum and their consequences is given by Sigurd Paul Scheichl, *Eine Czernowitzer Literaturaffäre in der "Fackel"*, in: Dietmar Goltschnigg u.a. (Ed.), Deutschsprachige Literatur der Bukowina (Tübingen 1990).
14 Cf. Karl Kraus, *Die Sprache*, ed. Christian Wagenknecht (Frankfurt am Main 1987), 360.
15 Cf. ibid., 359.
16 F 781–786 (Juni 1928), 98.
17 Translator's note: the translation 'great' was chosen not because it is the most precise translation from the German *große* (which would be *großartig*) but because it adequately reflects the ambiguity of the word (size: tall, large; quality: grand, great).
18 Ibid.
19 Kraus, *Die Sprache* (1987), 366.
20 Ibid., 364.
21 According to Kraus, this increase in value is due to a "Defekt" (deficiency) or "Irrtum" (error). Kraus, *Die Sprache* (1987), 364. Wagenknecht has also referred to this phenomenon when he describes it from the opposite perspective: "Es kann also ein einziger Buchstabe über Wert und Unwert eines Satzes [. . .] entscheiden [. . .]. Dieser [der Gedanke] sei unablösbar von seiner sprachlichen Gestalt [. . .] und könne durch einen Druckfehler zerstört werden." (A single letter can thus decide the value or non-value of a sentence. This, the thought, shall be inseparable from its linguistic form and can be destroyed by a printing error.) Christian Wagenknecht, *Das Wortspiel bei Karl Kraus* (Göttingen 1965), 64. It is from here that Kraus's famous lawsuit about a missing comma in a reprint of his poem "Man frage nicht" (One shall not ask) can be understood.
22 Kraus thus anticipates the much-discussed problem of the concept of *Fassung* in modern editorial philology. For a similar case, cf. also Wolfram Groddeck, *Überlegungen zu einigen Aporien der textgenetischen Editionsmethode am Modell von Georg Trakls Gedicht "Untergang"*, in: TEXT 5 (1999), 27–41.

example, we can see that the "word value" of two poems can differ so much that only one belongs to the domain of figuration.²³

In the second sentence of "Language" Kraus explains this view under the semblance of a justification:

> For how many worlds, encased by the word, won't fit in the space between the auscultation of a verse and the percussion of a linguistic usage!²⁴

By placing the two modes in a medical context and at the same time defamiliarising them, the opposition of figurative and communicative language is specified. Listening (to the body), the "auscultation of a verse", is contrasted with tapping or knocking, the "percussion of a linguistic usage" – both techniques are used to examine the body.²⁵ They interpret acoustic signals in order to make statements about the condition of an organism. Their opposition, however, is based on an important difference: while percussion intentionally produces sounds that are foreign to the respective organ, auscultation focuses on natural sounds that arise from the organ's function itself. The "percussion of a linguistic usage" instrumentalises language for the purposes of communication; the concrete linguistic form is not central as long as the communicative content can be grasped. The "auscultation of a verse", also read as *genitivus subjectivus*, has the sound of language as its object as well as language itself. Therefore, in a verse, language can aesthetically convey itself with its own sound like a working organ. Poetry is thus said to have a natural liveliness that is essentially determined by both the semantics of the words as well as their sounds.²⁶

---

23 In "Sprachlehre für Sprachlehrer", Kraus criticizes Vossler's instrumentalization of poetry, through which Vossler explains his theory of grammar. In the gloss, Kraus also accuses him of lacking imagination. According to Kraus, Vossler's attempt to judge poetry according to its logical character in a journalistic style (or "feuilletonistic confusion," as Kraus calls it in the proof for "Language") fails. He questions Vossler's ability to judge the logic of language, as his imagination and understanding of language is limited. An indicator of this is his use of language, which expresses illogical facts, which Vossler himself remains unaware of. Cf. Karl Kraus, *Die Sprache*, ed. by Wagenknecht (Frankfurt am Main 1987), 442–445.
24 F 885–887, 1.
25 Cf. *Meyers Großes Konversations-Lexikon*, vol. 2, (Leipzig 1905), 142 as well as vol. 15, (Leipzig 1908), 592–593.
26 Scheichl refers to Kraus's concept of lyric poetry as the important and "enge Beziehung zwischen Klang und Inhalt" (close relationship between sound and content): "Mit der Hochschätzung klanglicher Wirkung hängt Kraus' Unterstreichen der Bedeutung des Einzelworts für ein Gedicht zusammen." (Connected to Kraus's high estimation of the tonal effect is his emphasis on the meaning of the singular word within a poem.) Sigurd Paul Scheichl, *Aus Redaktion und Irrenhaus – Literaturtheoretische und literaturkritische Aspekte einer Krausschen Polemik*, in: Scheichl et al (Ed.), Karl Kraus – Ästhetik und Kritik (München 1989), 83–102, here: 93.

By transposing two terms from the medical onto the linguistic domain, Kraus opens up a new level of meaning and potentiates their word value. Terms that normally serve the purpose of common understanding in a scientific context can illustrate the facts stated in the first sentence by means of defamiliarisation: what is still formulated as a statement in the first sentence is expressed in the second through its figurative transposition. This implies that Kraus understands the texts of his journal *Die Fackel* as linguistic design or figuration, "Gestaltung aber heißt: daß 'Stoff und Form verbunden, der Spielraum zwischen Gestalt und Gehalt' geschlossen, die 'Aussage' zum 'Ausdruck' umgestaltet werde." (But figuration means: that 'matter and form are connected, the margin between figure and content' is closed, the 'statement' redesigned as 'expression'.)[27]

Kraus describes the process of conveying meaning as a natural law: what "distinguishes life from death, both here and there" is traced back to "the selfsame relationship to the organism of language."[28] Explicit reference is made to the fact that this legality in all linguistic domains conveys "sense to the mind" (dem Sinn den Sinn). Whether "a verse will bloom and blossom or wither and wilt"[29] – such a juxtaposition can be found in the two versions of "Junge Tänzerin" – consequently always depends on that relationship: not every formulation of a literary text is dominated by the aspect of figuration, and not every newspaper text can be classified as mere linguistic communication.

In what follows, Kraus includes the "[r]ecent linguistics,"[30] which meanwhile recognises a "creative necessity above regularity"[31]. While initially praising the older linguistic science, Kraus goes on to complain that both the older and the newer linguistics have not adopted from poetry "any affinity to the essence of language"[32] and that they thus lack the essential knowledge of their object of study, language itself. Finally, there follows a leap in Kraus' consideration, which, however, in addition to the dependence of the word value, leads to the second core point of the essay: "The responsibility for one's choice of word – the most demanding there ought to be, the most undemanding there is – disavowing this responsibility: no one would wish to impute such to any writer of words".[33] With this "responsibility", the consideration of word value acquires a moral dimension that is central to Kraus's conception of language. It is precisely this awareness

---

27 Wagenknecht, *Das Wortspiel bei Karl Kraus*, 63.
28 Cf. Winslow's translation in this volume, 11 or, respectively, F 885–887, 1.
29 Ibid.
30 Ibid.
31 Ibid.
32 Ibid.
33 Ibid.

that modern language teachers lack; instead, they would "drum up some psychological grammar wherever it suits them", although they are "incapable of thinking logically" "in the cerebral space of the word."[34] This allusive passage remains difficult to access for a large part of the readership without commentary – especially for those who have little familiarity with linguistic positions of the 1920s and 1930s. A glance at the proofs, however, shows that the text at this point had, at an earlier stage, a different wording.

In the published text, a new paragraph follows the end of the sentence quoted above ("thinking logically"), but in the proofs, the first continues for another two to three pages in which Kraus deals with Vossler.[35] He first introduces this polemically and writes: "Untief ist der gelehrte deutsche Sprachforscher Karl Vossler. Er gelangt in die Nähe des Problems aller Probleme 'Ausdruck und Aussage.'" (Shallow is the learned German linguist Karl Vossler. He comes close to the problem of all problems 'expression and statement').[36] By means of this introduction, Kraus now clarifies to whom he refers in the preceding sentences when he includes the new linguistics in his considerations.[37] Vossler had published a paper on grammar in 1919 in which he dealt with the "grammatische[n] und psychologische[n] Sprachformen" (grammatical and psychological forms of language).[38] In the essay "Subjekt und Prädikat" (Subject and Predicate) – published

---

34 Ibid.
35 Cf. Literaturhaus Wien, N1.23 / 1.2.2–1–1.2.2–3.
36 Ibid.
37 Christian Wagenknecht already suspected that Kraus was referring to Vossler in "Language" when he wrote about the "recent linguistics." Wagenknecht had already pointed out several times in this context that the essay "Subjekt und Prädikat" (Subject and Predicate) was published in October 1932, in which Kraus deals with Vossler's "psychological grammar", and that the posthumously published gloss "Sprachlehre für Sprachlehrer" (Language Lessons for Language Teachers) – a polemic against Vossler – must also have been written in this year. Cf. Commentary to "Die Sprache" in: Karl Kraus, *Heine und die Folgen*, ed. Christian Wagenknecht (Göttingen 2014), 440.
38 Cf. Karl Vossler, *Ueber grammatische und psychologische Sprachformen*, in: Logos 8 (1919), 1–29. Karl Vossler (1872–1949) was not only one of Germany's most renowned Romance scholars in the 1920s and 1930s, but also an internationally renowned scholar. Cf. *Karl Voßler*, in: Frankfurter Zeitung (11 July 1937). He studied German and Romance philology in Heidelberg, Strasbourg, Geneva and Rome and was rector of Munich University from 1926 to 1928. In 1938 – two years before his actual dismissal – he was forcibly given emeritus status due to his political orientation. "Vossler berief sich mit Croce auf die von Giambattista Vico u. Wilhelm von Humboldt vertretene Sprachauffassung, nach der die Sprache Schöpfung ('energeia') ist u. nicht – wie bei den Junggrammatikern, die mit ihrer mechanistischen Sprachbetrachtung das späte 19. Jh. beherrscht hatten – Produkt ('ergon')." (Together with Croce, Vossler referred to Giambattista Vico's and Wilhelm von Humboldt's view of language, according to which language is creation ['energeia'] and not – as was the case with the young grammarians who dominated the late 19th

in 1932 in the October issue of the *Fackel* – Kraus refers to Vossler's work in a partly affirmative way. In the proofs of "Language", however, Vossler now tends to function as an object of attack, since he misjudges the essence of language by determining the role of syntax in poetry and prose too antagonistically. The following passage from Vossler's "Grenzen der Sprachsoziologie" (Limits of a Sociology of Language) is quoted:

> Sobald die innere Form, die Meinung und Inspiration eines Autors auf das Logische geht, wird sein sprachlicher Ausdruck eo ipso sich auf die syntaktische Seite stützen; je mehr er dagegen ins Lyrische gerät, desto bedeutungsloser wird sein Satzbau, mag er an und für sich noch so kunstvoll und berechnet sein: er gleicht dann einem Zierpfeiler, keinem Tragpfeiler.
>
> (As soon as the inner form, the opinion and inspiration of an author resorts to the logical, his linguistic expression will be based eo ipso on the syntactical side; the more, on the other hand, he tends toward the lyrical, the more meaningless his sentence structure becomes, no matter how artful and calculated it may be in and of itself: it then resembles an ornamental pillar, not a supporting pillar.)[39]

Kraus opposes the statement that sentence structure hardly plays a supporting role in poetry anymore. On the one hand, he uses the quotation to criticize Vossler's idea of sentence structure in poetry and therefore polemically calls it a "neue Erkenntnis" (new insight);[40] on the other hand, he exposes Vossler's choice of words as a confirmation of his own criticism. For Vossler implicitly refutes his own thesis by claiming that syntax in lyrical language is only an "ornamental pillar", i.e. "nebensächlich" (secondary), although, according to Kraus, every pillar

---

century with their mechanistic view of language – a product ['ergon'].) Klaus Ley, *Karl Vossler*, in: Killy Literaturlexikon. Autoren und Werke deutscher Sprache, vol. 12 (München 1992), 67.
39 Karl Vossler, *Die Grenzen der Sprachsoziologie*, in: Hauptprobleme der Soziologie. Erinnerungsgabe für Max Weber (München und Leipzig 1923), 363–389, here: 371 [the underlining refers to Kraus' letterspacing in the proofs]. Kraus probably did not have the first publication, but the volume "Gesammelte Aufsätze zur Sprachphilosophie" (Collected Essays on the Philosophy of Language) from the same year, but which he apparently only discovered in 1932. In "Subjekt und Prädikat", Kraus explicitly refers to this anthology and points out that when he published the reflection "Es" (It) in 1921, he was unaware of Vossler's first publication in *Logos* from 1919. Cf. F 876–884, 154. The fact that Kraus dealt with Vossler for the first time in 1932 (and in three texts at once) indicates that the texts were only available to him then.
40 With the division of verses into feet, the metrical structure is fixed, „[d]ie größte übermetrisch-prägende Einheit ist die *syntaktische Einheit* bzw. der *Satz*." (The largest unit defining the super-metric structure is the *syntactic unit* or the *sentence* respectively.) Fritz Schlawe, *Neudeutsche Metrik* (Stuttgart 1972), 54.

serves fundamentally as a support.[41] Thus, the juxtaposition of sentence structure as a "supporting pillar" (in prose) and as a "ornamental pillar" (in poetry), meant by Vossler as an opposition, is semantically invalid. At the same time, Vossler's 'choice of words' confirms Kraus's conception of language: the communicated 'insight' proves to be false not only on the level of content, but also on the level of expression. The problem of "expression and statement" introduced by Kraus at the beginning is therefore not directly addressed by the Vossler quotation, but is, rather, exemplified by it. Some examples of poetry effectively prove that even in the case of grammatical or syntactical "Mißformen" (malforms), the importance of syntax or grammar is not less than it is in prose, but that, on the contrary, in poetry such 'rule-breaking' sometimes "erst den Wert ergibt" (only then provides value).[42] With these examples, Kraus finally ends his argument with the Romance philologist.

Interestingly, in the proofs Vossler himself serves as a 'supporting pillar' for Kraus: in order to present the problem of "expression and statement" as well as confirm his thesis introduced at the beginning of the essay, Kraus relies on the Vossler quotation and builds his explicative argumentation on it.[43] Speaking with Michael Thalken, this confrontation, which reveals deficits in meaning, can be understood as constitutive of meaning,[44] because "in Form seiner [i.e. Kraus's] satirischen Darstellung" (in the form of Kraus's satirical presentation) he deconstructs "sinnloses Sprechen" (meaningless speech).[45] Kraus later renounces this function of Vossler, which supports deconstruction, when he deletes the explicit passages on the latter.[46] For this, he hardly changes anything in the remaining passages, merely deleting a few insertions that refer specifically to Vossler. It is remarkable that he can rid the text of any reference to Vossler without having to adapt the content of other passages. These striking changes shorten the text and erase its polemical orientation. As a result, the statements on language presented in the first paragraph are, on the one hand, given programmatic value – Kraus's conception of language is not exemplified any further – on the other hand, the text is noticeably con-

---

41 The word 'pillar' comes from Latin and means "support" in architecture. *Herders Konversationslexikon*, vol. 4 (Freiburg im Breisgau 1856), 514.
42 Cf. Literaturhaus Wien, N1.23 / 1.2.2–1–1.2.2–3.
43 Of course, this approach can be extended to the entire *Fackel*, according to which some of the polemically combated have a supporting function on which Kraus was, to a certain extent, dependent.
44 Cf. Michael Thalken, *Ein bewegliches Heer von Metaphern: Sprachkritisches Sprechen bei Friedrich Nietzsche, Gustav Gerber, Fritz Mauthner und Karl Kraus* (Frankfurt am Main 1999), 311.
45 Ibid., 301.
46 In the proofs, these two to three pages on Vossler were deleted or marked with "bleibt zurück" (remains behind). Cf. Literaturhaus Wien, N1.23 / 1.2.2–1–1.2.2–3.

densed.⁴⁷ And by condensing the language the text becomes more abstract and more difficult to access than it had been initially.

Based on these reflections on the "Wortwert" (word value) as well as the relationship between expression and statement, the second part of the text deals with the already mentioned moral dimension of language, which originates in the "Wortwahl" (choice of word). This dimension plays a significant role in Kraus' confrontation with National Socialism and influences his didactic considerations.

With the question whether one could "conceive of a moral palladium more potent than a skeptical stance toward language," Kraus sets the starting point of his ethics of language. He derives from linguistic doubt the possibility of the "great moral gift," which, however, has been "hitherto spurned" by mankind – while it could be the "redemptive frustration of a progress that, with perfect certainty, shall lead to the downfall of a civilization, in whose service it believes to act". Crucial to Kraus' choice of words is the critique of the word 'progress', a critique that is not necessarily conservative, but rather demonstrates the connection between language and action. The generally positive and inflationary use of the word – "Fortschritt bedeutet seit der zweiten Hälfte des 18. Jahrh. die allmähliche Vervollkommnung" (since the second half of the eighteenth century, progress means gradual perfection)⁴⁸ – is polemically questioned by Kraus. For what is characterised and perceived as progressive has, according to Kraus, the opposite effect: it does not perfect, but leads to the "downfall of civilization". Responsible speech or the conscious choice of words could avoid erroneous conclusions. Just as on the linguistic level in Vossler's case, what is actually meant is not expressed, and the result now contradicts the originally intended goal of humanity. Kraus demands that the use of language should be appropriate to the facts to be presented. However, if language is not oriented towards the subject matter, the

---

47 Wagenknecht has highlighted Kraus's "Verknappung" (shortening) as characteristic of his linguistic style. What applies to his sentence structure in the chapter "Die Idee der Sprachgestaltung" (The Idea of Linguistic Figuration) in his dissertation can be applied here to the text "Language" as a whole. Cf. Christian Wagenknecht, *Das Wortspiel bei Karl Kraus*, 63.

48 This initially valid meaning was questioned with the rise of mechanisation and its accompanying changes for people and the environment: "Ob die Natur und das Menschengeschlecht bei ihren Veränderungen fortschreiten oder nicht, ist nicht leicht zu entscheiden. Es ist dies ein Hauptproblem der Geschichtsphilosophie." (Whether nature and the human race progress in their changes or not is not easy to decide. This is one of the main problems of the philosophy of history.) Friedrich Kirchner / Carl Michaëlis, *Wörterbuch der Philosophischen Grundbegriffe* (Leipzig ⁵1907), 205–206.

speaker is disavowed by the language. The language turns against him and reveals his actual striving, for domination or social recognition, for example.[49]

The influence of language on actual action is again explained by Kraus elsewhere: Since language can be "violated with impunity", it is precisely language that teaches "respect for that other natural right".[50] That language is at the mercy of man is based on its high degree of vulnerability; its abuse remains unpunished. According to Kraus, a person who consistently exposes himself to linguistic doubts becomes a moral one; conversely, a careless use of language leads to moral decay.[51] Furthermore, "all speaking and writing today, including that done by authorities, has turned language into the dross of the times, which takes its events and experiences, its being and justification, from the *Times*."[52] Careless speech, which represents irresponsible action, thus falls back on its author. The consequent unconsciousness of the choice of words then results in a moral decline, which in turn is reflected in the language of the speaker. If the person writes for the newspaper – the pun "dross of the times" refers to newspaper language – his or her language is often received by the public and the moral decay continues within language. In this way, Kraus names the press as the formative authority responsible for the deficient use of language. As Djassemy has stated, journalistic linguistic devices sabotage the actual message. The violent disposal of language also disregards the power of linguistic association, which results in a loss of imagination and thus of thought in general.[53]

To reinforce this language ethos, Kraus counters the influence of the press with a didactics of language, which was already formulated more concretely in 1924 and is now repeated, if vaguely, in "Language": "To teach people to see abysses where commonplaces exist – that would be the pedagogical project befitting a nation borne of sin; would be the deliverance of natural rights from the fetters of journalism and from the fangs of politics."[54] The column "Sprachlehre"

---

49 Cf. Irina Djassemy, *Der "Productivgehalt kritischer Zerstörerarbeit"*. Kulturkritik bei Karl Kraus und Theodor W. Adorno (Würzburg 2002), 64.
50 Cf. Winslow in this volume, 14; see also F 885–887, 2.
51 Michael Thalken notes that for Kraus "ethisch-moralisches Verhalten und sprachliches Verhalten" (ethical-moral and linguistic behavior) are identical and at the same time points out that this does not mean "Regelverstöße gegen die Gesetze der Grammatik" (breaking the laws of grammar). These would rather refer to a "Abdunklung der Sprachintention zugunsten der Sprecherintention" (obscuration of language's intention in favour of the speaker's intention) such as the instrumentalization of language. Michael Thalken, *Ein bewegliches Heer von Metaphern*, 296.
52 Cf. Winslow in this volume, 14; see also F 885–887, 2.
53 Cf. Irina Djassemy, *Der "Productivgehalt kritischer Zerstörerarbeit"*. Kulturkritik bei Karl Kraus und Theodor W. Adorno (Würzburg 2002), 64.
54 Ibid.

had already pursued this didactic claim to some extent, but the formulation of 1924 suggests that Kraus envisioned his project as more practice-oriented: "Es wäre die Ausfüllung des Semesters einer Sprachschule, die mir immer vorschwebt und in der ich mich verpflichten würde, in einer Stunde den Hörern mehr von dem Gegenstand beizubringen, als ihnen eine Leihbibliothek der deutschen Literatur vermittelt, und so viel gutzumachen, als zehn Jahrgänge deutscher Zeitungslektüre an ihnen gesündigt haben." (It would fill one semester of a language school, which I always have in mind, and in which I would undertake to teach the listeners more of the subject in one hour than a lending library of German literature could convey to them, and to compensate for as much as ten years of German newspaper reading have sinned against them.)[55] In 1933, Kraus took an even more radical stance against the press as the origin of linguistic decay: "Denn der Nationalsozialismus hat die Presse nicht vernichtet, sondern die Presse hat den Nationalsozialismus erschaffen." (For National Socialism did not destroy the press, but the press created National Socialism.)[56] In World War I already, Kraus accused the press of *creating* events instead of *reporting* on them. Language is deliberately used to generate sales: Instead of fulfilling its task of informing its readers about real events, it abuses the medium for profit-oriented purposes. For example, by sugarcoating the consequences of the war or by portraying the war as an adventurous event. This falsifying, whitewashing use of language was perfidiously intensified under National Socialism: while the goals of the press were geared towards material profit, under National Socialism it was a matter of concealing human extermination and its authoritarian control.

*

In *Dritte Walpurgisnacht*, Kraus also engages in 'Sprachlehre' by quoting passages from the "nationalsozialistische[] Presse Deutschlands" (National Socialist press of Germany)[57] that most obviously demonstrate the mismatch of expression and statement. The following passages are relevant insofar as they represent the few testimonies to Kraus's 'Sprachlehre' under National Socialism:

> Nicht einmal der Umstand, daß die nationalsozialistische Presse Deutschlands die Mahnung erläßt: Deutscher, lese nur arische Zeitungen! oder die auf der nationalen Postkarte empfiehlt: Vergeß nicht, daß du ein Deutscher bist! Also die Erinnerung an ein Ideal, dem sie schulbeispielhaft und ohne Beispiel der Schule entgegenwirkt. Nicht das Scherflein, mit dem sich das österreichische Bruderblatt anschloß: Liest euch die Weisungen genauer durch! Daß sich wegen solcher Zurückhaltung, die leider nicht weit genug geht, die

---

55 F 640–648, 54.
56 Karl Kraus, *Dritte Walpurgisnacht*, ed. Christian Wagenknecht (Frankfurt am Main 1989), 307.
57 Ibid., 123.

deutschbewußte Journalistik von den prominentesten Analphabeten der andern verhöhnen lassen muß, ist gewiß beschämend; aber derlei wird als zum täglichen Hand- und Mundwerk gehörig nicht gut vermieden werden können, wiewohl einer der Feuersprüche bei der Bücherverbrennung doch gelautet hat: Gegen Verhunzung der deutschen Sprache! Für Pflege des kostbarsten Gutes unseres Volkes! Leicht gesagt, schwerer geschrieben.

(Not even the fact that the National Socialist press of Germany issues the admonition: <u>German, read</u> only Aryan newspapers! or that recommends on the national postcard: Don't <u>forget</u> that you are a <u>German</u>! In other words, the reminder of an ideal, which it counteracts in a school-like manner and without example. Not the mite with which the Austrian brotherly newspaper joined in: <u>Read</u> the instructions more carefully! It is certainly shameful that because of such restraint, which unfortunately does not go far enough, German-conscious journalism must allow itself to be ridiculed by the most prominent illiterates of the others; but such things cannot well be avoided as part of daily hand and mouth work, even though one of the slogans in front of the fire at the book burning was: Against the corruption of the German language! For the protection of the most precious asset of our people! Easy to say, harder to write.)[58]

Kraus exposes the relationship between what is said and how it is said: on the one hand, the supposed imperative does not fulfil its task in the sentence structure due to the wrong verb form; on the other hand, the person speaking deprives himself of his authority when he fails to use the national language under the pretence of representing national interests. The request turns out to be a phrase that apparently only pursues the goal of control – for example, by not reading foreign newspapers whose reports differ from the domestic ones – and uses the attribution 'German' for its own purposes.

The fact that Kraus sees the relationship between language and morality assumed in "Language" confirmed precisely by National Socialism can be seen, among other places, in the introduction of the term "Braunwelsch."[59] Irina Djassemy points out that Kraus is thus gauging a linguistic area in which "technisierte Sprache, depravierte philosophische Begriffe und spezifische nationalistische Neubildungen ihre inhumanen Gehalte entfalten" (technicised language, depraved philosophical concepts and specific nationalist neologisms unfold their inhumane contents).[60] It is not only to Kraus's example of the press – which is apparently less interested in language problems than through its "schlechte[s] Deutsch" (bad German) in a "Fememord" (Vehmic murder)[61] – that the term "Braunwelsch" applies;

---
58 Ibid., 123–124. Translator's note: the underlined words are faulty German and impossible to translate.
59 Ibid., 191.
60 Irina Djassemy, *Der "Productivgehalt kritischer Zerstörerarbeit"*. Kulturkritik bei Karl Kraus und Theodor W. Adorno (Würzburg 2002), 371.
61 Karl Kraus, *Dritte Walpurgisnacht*, 191.

it is also the National Socialist propagation of the 'German' that Kraus criticizes: "Und immer neue Begriffsbestimmungen für den Deutschen, für die Deutsche und für das Deutsche, als wäre das alles eben erst von einer deutschen Expedition entdeckt worden. Mammutknochen aus der Scholle geholt. 'Der deutsche Mensch', 'der deutsche Arbeitsmensch', das Staatsvolk, der Reichsbürger, der dem Reichsvolk zugehört, und dergleichen mehr" (And always new definitions for the German man, for the German woman and for the German itself, as if it had all just been discovered by a German expedition. Mammoth bones fetched from the clod.[62] 'The German man', 'the German working man', the people of the state, the citizen of the empire who belongs to the people of the empire, and so on.).[63] The new term "Braunwelsch" can then be understood by means of this criticism of the misuse of the concept of German by the National Socialists: 'Welsch', meaning „[f]remd, ausländisch" (foreign, outlandish),[64] refers to the 'Undeutsch' (Un-German) of the National Socialist use of language, "die Sprache ariogermanischen Wesens" (the language of ariogermanic nature), which Kraus does not comprehend.[65] Moreover, by colouring the language of the National Socialists, he not only gives it a political connotation, but at the same time relates it to the "Gaunersprache" (language of bandits)[66] 'Rotwelsch'. To praise the burning of books as a saving act against the "corruption of German language" is the culmination of a linguistically and physically destructive cultural policy. The act as well as the reason stated for the burning signify a new dimension of the instrumentalisation of language, which Kraus attempts to counter from 1933 onwards with *Dritte Walpurgisnacht* – which he then does not publish for well-known reasons.

Instead, in July 1934, Kraus published the longest-ever *Fackel* (over 300 pages) in which he repeatedly – and this time explicitly – called for the introduction of a so-called language seminar. By attributing National Socialist rule and its consequences

---

62 Cf. Linden in this volume, 102: "The Nazis created a mythology and therefore supplied the element decidedly missing from other political parties and movements . . . ."
63 Ibid., 200.
64 Johann Christoph Adelung, *Grammatisch-kritisches Wörterbuch der Hochdeutschen Mundart*, vol. 4 (Leipzig 1801), col. 1370.
65 Kraus, *Dritte Walpurgisnacht*, 321. Victor Klemperer emphasizes the re-shaping of terms by the National Socialists, analyzing, among other things, the use of the term 'fanaticism'. This was used pejoratively, especially in the French Revolution; in National Socialism, this meaning was replaced by a positive one: "Wenn einer lange genug für heldisch und tugendhaft: fanatisch sagt, glaubt er schließlich wirklich, ein Fanatiker sei ein tugendhafter Held" (If one says long enough for heroic and virtuous: fanatic, he finally really believes that a fanatic is a virtuous hero). Victor Klemperer, *LTI. Notizbuch eines Philologen* (Leipzig 1996), 21; cf. ibid., 29.
66 *Meyers Großes Konversations-Lexikon*, Bd. 17. (Leipzig 1909), 190.

to linguistic problems in "Warum die Fackel nicht erscheint" (Why the *Fackel* does not appear), Kraus once again assigns a central role to the pedagogical task:

> Vor allem hier gilt es, sich zu bewähren: man hat mutig zu sein und Sprachlehre zu treiben! Die Rettung der durch nationale Selbstbesinnung bedrohten Werte, als die wahre polemische Tat, nicht nur so zu vollziehen, daß man deutsche Sprache durch den Vortrag ehrt, sondern auch – denn das unterbrochene Werk zur Sprachlehre wäre nur ein Anfang – wenn möglich durch Errichtung eines Sprachseminars, das zum Zweck diente, durch Vorführung von Greueln der Satzbildung den Möglichkeiten und damit den Geheimnissen der abgründigsten und tiefsten Sprache näher zu kommen, deren unzüchtiger Gebrauch, zu den Greueln des Bluts geführt hat.
>
> (Above all, it is here that one has to prove oneself: one has to be courageous and do language teaching! The salvation of the values threatened by national self-reflection, as the true polemical deed, is to be accomplished not only by honouring the German language through lecture, but also – for the interrupted work on language teaching would only be a beginning – if possible by setting up a language seminar featuring the demonstration of the horrors of sentence building, the purpose of which would be to come closer to the possibilities and thus the secrets of the most abysmal and profound language, the lewd use of which has led to the atrocities of blood.)[67]

The idea underlying the quote above should not be surprising with reference to the essay "Language": the "horrors of blood", physical acts, are directly being traced back to the "horrors of sentence building" and the "lewd use" of language.

If these connections between language and the press, preached by Kraus for decades, should appear as a belief in language that superficially short-circuits socio-political contexts, a draft letter by Bertolt Brecht from the summer of 1933 – during the period when no *Fackel* was published – nevertheless attests to the fact that Kraus's conception of language was not only understood by contemporaries, but even received affirmatively:

> Ich möchte sie noch einmal um die Sprachlehre bedrängen, von der wir einmal sprachen. [. . .] niemand, der ohne besonderen ehrgeiz darin zu zeigen, sprach, brauchte es sich gefallen zu lassen, dass man seine art zu sprechen unter die lupe nahm. und doch wurden vermittels der sprache die schrecklichsten verwüstungen angerichtet. Sie haben dann die greultaten der tonfälle enthüllt und eine sittenlehre der sprache geschaffen; die grammatik wurde zu einem teil der ethik und sie entlarvten die verbrecher, indem Sie ihre sprache als indizium vorwiesen. Ich möchte nicht zu eingehend schreiben, da ich nicht weiss, wo dieser brief Sie trifft; ich meine nur, dass für die fortführung ihrer Sprachlehre die in vielen unglückliche zeit eine glückliche wäre [. . .].
>
> (I would like to press you once again about the teaching of language that we once spoke of. [. . .] no one who spoke without showing particular ambition in it had to put up with having

---

67 F 890–905, 168.

his way of speaking scrutinized. And yet the most terrible havoc was wrought by means of language. They then exposed the atrocities of tone and created a moral theory of language; grammar became a part of ethics and they exposed the criminals by pointing to their language as an indication. I do not want to write in too much detail, as I do not know where this letter meets you; I only mean that for the continuation of your linguistic teaching, this in many aspects unfortunate time would be a happy one [. . .]).[68]

In his letter, Brecht uses comparisons similar to Kraus's vocabulary, when he writes of "criminals", who have wrought "the most terrible havoc [. . .] by means of language". The term "criminals" also implies that Brecht locates the "Sprachlehre" within the sphere of law, in which Kraus exposes and judges criminals.[69] Brecht's analysis of a Göring speech from 1934 ("On the Restoration of Truth"), in which Brecht quotes parts of the speech and juxtaposes them with his translation, makes clear that Kraus' linguistic criticism was appreciated by Brecht. This method can already be found in Kraus' "Harden-Lexikon" (1908), in which Kraus translated Maximilian Harden's ornamental use of language. Brecht's translation, on the other hand, goes so far as to reveal the disguises of National Socialist propaganda and emphasize the actual function of speech. The abuse of language that Kraus accuses is presented by Brecht as an instrument of political power. Brecht's request to Kraus at the beginning of the National Socialist dictatorship to continue with the column "Zur Sprachlehre", which had not been published since 1931, is remarkable. Kraus takes up the same context again almost three quarters of a year later in "Warum die Fackel nicht erscheint" with the passage quoted above. The mention there of the "Sprachlehre", which was "only the beginning" of his further plans, appears almost as an explicit answer to Brecht's request. Kraus apparently understood the announced "Sprachseminar" as a continuation of the "Sprachlehre", which he describes as an "unterbrochenes Werk" (interrupted work). Supposedly, Kraus deliberately stopped its publication in the *Fackel*, instead reacting to the political and linguistic conditions by announcing the seminar.

This "Sprachseminar" would have differed formally from the "Sprachlehre" in that it was not to be held in writing but actually as a seminar. In December 1934, half a year after the announcement in the *Fackel*, Kraus invited people to this seminar on a lecture program:

---

68 Quote from: Eva Dambacher & Friedrich Päfflin, *Karl Kraus*, 457–459.
69 In general, citation plays an important role in *Die Fackel*, especially in the 'Sprachlehre'. The Latin 'citare' means 'to summon' and originally comes from the legal context, where the relevant parties were summoned to court. Cf. Johann Christoph Adelung, *Grammatisch-kritisches Wörterbuch der Hochdeutschen Mundart*, vol. 1 (Leipzig 1801), col. 1336.

Ebenda [in Richard Lányis Buchhandlung] werden Anmeldungen zu einem / Sprachseminar / (Kurs für Sprachlehre) / angenommen, dessen Entstehen von hinreichender Beteiligung und sonstigen Umständen abhängt.

There [in Richard Lányi's bookshop] registrations are being accepted for a / language seminar / (course in language teaching) /, the creation of which depends on sufficient participation and other circumstances.[70]

Kraus thus continued to grapple with his linguistic theoretical considerations in 1934 and was interested in communicating his findings. He did not resign himself to the socio-political circumstances at this time, but on the contrary sought new 'methods'. This intensive continuation of his preoccupation with language testifies to the hope of being able to engage meaningfully with (and against) National Socialism. Moreover, the designation 'seminar' refers to the educational character of the event,[71] which would have qualified the participants equally to engage in "Sprachlehre" and thus pass on Kraus's reflections.

As is well known, Kraus isolated himself on account of his commitment to Dollfuß and his conflicts with the Social Democrats. Therefore, the question of whether doubts about the practical feasibility of such a project or the lack of supporters might have led to the seminar not being held can only be answered hypothetically.[72] It should be pointed out with regard to the further editions of the *Fackel*, in which Kraus dealt mainly with literary themes, that he was aware of the superiority of the National Socialist opponent, against whom the previous means of satire or "Sprachlehre" were bound to fail. Thus, in one of the late *Fackel* issues, Kraus explicitly comments on "Sprachlehre", which is "mit Recht gemieden[]" (rightfully avoided).[73] However, his view of language had not changed even in 1934, as is shown above all by his resumed work on the volume *Language*, which Kraus wanted to prepare for publication again shortly before his death.[74] The compilation and correction

---

[70] 674. Vorlesung am 1.12.1934, Karl Kraus-Archiv, Handschriftensammlung, Wienbibliothek im Rathaus. Quote from: Katharina Prager (unter Mitarbeit von Brigitte Stocker): *Karl Kraus Online (online)*. Wienbibliothek im Rathaus / Ludwig Boltzmann Institut für Geschichte und Theorie der Biographie 2015. https://www.kraus.wienbibliothek.at/content/674-vorlesung-am-01121934 [16. Oktober 2019].
[71] The term 'Seminar' was originally used to describe an institution or the place of education – in the beginning specifically that of theologians – later, teachers were also trained in a seminary. Cf. *Pierer's Universal-Lexikon*, vol. 15 (Altenburg 1862), 825.
[72] Gerald Krieghofer supposes that maybe "zu wenige junge Leute [sich] angemeldet [haben]" (too few young people had signed up). Gerald Krieghofer, „*Die Menschheit weiß noch immer nicht, was geschehen ist und jeden Augenblick geschieht": Karl Kraus nach 1933* in: Geist versus Zeitgeist: Karl Kraus in der ersten Republik, ed. Katharina Prager (Wien 2018), 206–219, here: 214.
[73] F 917–922, 108.
[74] Cf. Philipp Berger's afterword of the first edition: Karl Kraus, *Die Sprache* ed. Philipp Berger (Wien 1937), 398.

of the texts for the collection spanned more than 13 years, from 1923 to 1936. The postponement of this volume for decades as well as the statements on the planned "Sprachseminar" – Kraus describes the project as a "Mutprobe" (test of courage)[75]– testify to certain scruples to which even the convinced Kraus was apparently subject.

## References

*Die Fackel.* Reprint aller Bände von 1899–1936, 12 vol. Frankfurt am Main, 1968–1976.
Kraus, Karl. Proofs of "Language" *Literaturhaus Wien*, N1.23 / 1.2.2-1–1.2.2-3.
Kraus, Karl. *Die Sprache.* Ed. Philipp Berger. Wien, 1937.
Kraus, Karl. *Die Sprache.* Ed. Christian Wagenknecht. Frankfurt am Main, 1987.
Kraus, Karl. *Dritte Walpurgisnacht.* Ed. Christian Wagenknecht. Frankfurt am Main, 1989.
Kraus, Karl. *Briefe an Sidonie Nádherný von Borutin*, auf der Grundlage der Ausgabe von Heinrich Fischer und Michael Lazarus, new ed. and compl. by Friedrich Pfäfflin, 2 vol. Göttingen, 2005.
Kraus, Karl. *Heine und die Folgen.* Ed. Christian Wagenknecht. Göttingen, 2014.
Adelung, Johann Christoph. *Grammatisch-kritisches Wörterbuch der Hochdeutschen Mundart*, 4 Bde. Leipzig, 1801.
Dambacher, Eva & Friedrich Päfflin. *Karl Kraus.* Eine Ausstellung des Deutschen Literaturarchivs im Schiller-Nationalmuseum Marbach. Marbach am Neckar, 1999.
Djassemy, Irina, *Der "Productivgehalt kritischer Zerstörerarbeit".* Kulturkritik bei Karl Kraus und Theodor W. Adorno. Würzburg, 2002.
Groddeck, Wolfram, "Überlegungen zu einigen Aporien der textgenetischen Editionsmethode am Modell von Georg Trakls Gedicht, Untergang'" *TEXT 5* (1999): 27–41.
*Herders Konversationslexikon*, 5 Bde. Freiburg im Breisgau, 1856.
Kirchner, Friedrich / Carl Michaëlis, *Wörterbuch der Philosophischen Grundbegriffe.* Leipzig[5], 1907.
Klemperer, Victor, *LTI.* Notizbuch eines Philologen. Leipzig, 1996.
Krieghofer, Gerald. "Die Menschheit weiß noch immer nicht, was geschehen ist und jeden Augenblick geschieht": Karl Kraus nach 1933. *Geist versus Zeit: Karl Kraus in der ersten Republik.* Ed. Katharina Prager. Wien, 2018. 206–219.
Krolop, Kurt. *Die Hörerin als Sprecherin: Sidonie Nádherný und "ihre Sprachlehre".* Warmbronn, 2005.
Ley, Klaus. "Karl Vossler," *Killy Literaturlexikon. Autoren und Werke deutscher Sprache*, vol. 12. München, 1992. 67.
*Meyers Großes Konversations-Lexikon*, 20 vol. Leipzig, 1905.
*Pierer's Universal-Lexikon*, 19 vol. Altenburg, 1862.
Prager, Katharina (with Brigitte Stocker): *Karl Kraus Online (online).* Wienbibliothek im Rathaus / Ludwig Boltzmann Institut für Geschichte und Theorie der Biographie 2015. https://www.kraus.wienbibliothek.at/content/674-vorlesung-am-01121934 [last access: 16. October 2019]
Scheichl, Sigurd Paul. "Eine Czernowitzer Literaturaffäre in der 'Fackel'." *Deutschsprachige Literatur der Bukowina.* Ed. Dietmar Goltschnigg u.a. Tübingen, 1990.

---

75 F 890–905, 168.

Scheichl, Sigurd Paul. "Aus Redaktion und Irrenhaus – Literaturtheoretische und literaturkritische Aspekte einer Krausschen Polemik." *Karl Kraus – Ästhetik und Kritik*. Ed. Sigurd Paul Scheichl. München, 1989. 83–102.
Schlawe, Fritz. *Neudeutsche Metrik*. Stuttgart, 1972.
Thalken, Michael. *Ein bewegliches Heer von Metaphern: Sprachkritisches Sprechen bei Friedrich Nietzsche, Gustav Gerber, Fritz Mauthner und Karl Kraus*. Frankfurt am Main, 1999.
Vossler, Karl. "Ueber grammatische und psychologische Sprachformen." *Logos* 8 (1919): 1–29.
Vossler, Karl. "Die Grenzen der Sprachsoziologie." *Hauptprobleme der Soziologie. Erinnerungsgabe für Max Weber*. München und Leipzig, 1923. 363–389.
Wagenknecht, Christian. *Das Wortspiel bei Karl Kraus*. Göttingen, 1965.

Ron Mieczkowski
# Die Sprache „der Richter und Henker" und der Genitiv bei Karl Kraus. Vom Paradigma der „grammatischen Methode"

## Vorbemerkung zum Sprachbegriff bei Karl Kraus

Von den frühen Schriften, die Karl Kraus' Schreiben zu einer „Sprachmystik"[1] verklärten, über die Versuche, strukturalistische Modelle auf seine Satiren anzuwenden,[2] bis zu den theoretischen Kurskorrekturen der letzten Jahre, die endlich den performativen Aspekt seiner Texte und Vorträge beleuchten,[3] weisen die meisten Arbeiten ein Defizit auf: Sie setzen sich stärker mit dem auseinander, was sie für den semantischen Inhalt der Kraus'schen Rede halten, als mit der Spezifik seines Sprechens und Schreibens; oder prägnanter formuliert: Sie arbeiten sich, trotz aller anderslautender Erklärungen, immer noch eher an dem ab, *was* Kraus sagt, als an dem, *wie* er es sagt.

Dieser Schiefstand ist nicht unbemerkt geblieben. Michael Thalken etwa, in dessen Arbeit Kraus zwar eine nur nachgeordnete Stellung einnimmt, konstatiert: „[...] gerade der Versuch, Kraus' Sprachverständnis aus seinen Texten zu (re)konstruieren, unterliegt der Gefahr, die Identität von Gedanke und Form, wie Kraus sie in jedem Satz zu verwirklichen sucht, zu übersehen."[4] Für jene Forschungsarbeiten, die dieses „konventionelle[] Vorverständnis von Gedanke und Form"[5] nicht recht überwunden haben, findet Gal Hertz gar einen Sammelbegriff und ordnet sie

---
[1] Josef Quack: Bemerkungen zum Sprachverständnis von Karl Kraus, Bonn 1976, S. 3. Vgl. ebenfalls Gal Hertz: „Words not as Words". Critique of Language, Ideology and Identity in the Work of Karl Kraus (unveröffentlichte Promotionsschrift, Tel Aviv 2013), S. 42, der u. a. auch Leopold Liegler jener Gruppe zuschlägt, die an der Mystifizierung von Karls Kraus' Sprachpraxis mitgewirkt hat.
[2] Vgl. Jay F. Bodine: Karl Kraus. Sprache, Literatur und Wirklichkeit, Michigan 1974.
[3] Luis Miguel Isava (Wittgenstein, Kraus, and Valéry. A Paradigm for Poetic Rhyme and Reason, New York 2002), Michael Thalken (vgl. Anm. 5) und Gal Hertz (vgl. Anm. 2) seien hier als Vertreter der jüngsten Forschergeneration präsentiert.
[4] Michael Thalken: Ein bewegliches Heer von Metaphern. Sprachkritisches Sprechen bei Friedrich Nietzsche, Gustav Gerber, Fritz Mauthner und Karl Kraus. Frankfurt a. M. u. a. 1999, S. 289. Diese Kritik richtet er explizit gegen Jens Malte Fischer (Karl Kraus. Studien zum „Theater der Dichtung" und Kulturkonservativismus. Kronberg/Taunus 1973).
[5] Ebd. S. 290.

allesamt dem „representative paradigm in the understanding of Kraus"[6] zu. Thalken spricht in diesem Zusammenhang vom

> Dilemma mit der Beschäftigung mit Kraus, das immer dann entstehen muß, wenn der Rezipient von der bloßen Medialität der Sprache ausgeht und auch das Kraussche Sprechen nur als die mediale Informsetzung des mitzuteilenden Stoffs begreift.[7]

Denn auch wenn jene Autoren, die ein instrumentelles Sprachmodell an Kraus herantragen, hinreichend Belege für ihr Vorgehen in seinen Selbstaussagen finden können,[8] ist es doch bemerkenswert, wie wenig die exemplarisch von Thalken und Hertz formulierte Erkenntnis in wissenschaftliche Praxis umgesetzt worden ist.

Gegen das Konzept einer im semiotischen Sinne zweistufigen Funktion der Sprache, gegen den Repräsentationsanspruch des Wortes bei Karl Kraus, richtet sich, so möchte ich nun darzulegen versuchen, nicht so sehr der *Sprachbegriff*, der sich aus seinen Texten ableiten lässt, als vielmehr sein *Sprachvollzug*. Von einem systematischen Sprachverständnis kann nämlich keine Rede sein: „Bei Kraus liegt weder eine wissenschaftliche Theorie der Sprache noch eine Sprachphilosophie vor",[9] er ist „Kasuist",[10] der aus dem situativen Einzelfall ebenso in seiner Auseinandersetzung mit der Presse schöpft wie in der Erteilung seiner „Sprachlehre".

Christian Wagenknecht hat in seiner Monographie über das Kraus'sche Wortspiel diesem Beitrag das Vorbild einer präzisen und philologisch fundierten Textanalyse gegeben; wo jene aber streng rhetorisch argumentierte, möchte ich zeigen, wie sehr auch eine Lektüre seiner Sätze anhand der Strukturen von Grammatik und Syntax erkenntnisfördernd sein kann. Schließlich ist die These dieses Beitrags am Zusammenhang zweier Bereiche orientiert: Es soll vorgeführt werden, dass eine Verbindung des Kasuisten Karl Kraus mit dem grammatischen Kasus möglich ist: zentrale Teile des Werks von Karl Kraus lassen sich als Konfrontation von Rhe-

---

6 Hertz, ebd. S. 11.
7 Thalken, ebd., S. 292.
8 Beispielhaft sei hier Christian Wagenknecht angeführt, der eine mögliche Argumentation für die Referenzialität des Kraus'schen Sprachbegriffs anhand einer Passage aus einem später seiner Sammlung zur *Sprache* hinzugefügten Text vorführt: Wenn Kraus vom Wort „Smaragd" spricht, dem „das erste Auge", das den Edelstein sah, „gar nicht anders konnte als ihm diese Konsonanten abzusehen", sei die antike Vorstellung nicht fern, „daß die Wörter ‚von Natur aus' richtige Bilder der Dinge sind." Vgl. Christian Wagenknecht: Das Wortspiel bei Karl Kraus, Göttingen 1964, S. 126 f.; Kraus-Zitat aus: F 572, 40.
9 Quack, ebd.
10 Walter Weiss: Dichtung und Grammatik. Zur Frage der grammatischen Interpretation, München 1967, S. 2.

torik mit dem Potential der Grammatik, oder als Demonstration der Möglichkeit zu verstehen, Wirkung nicht bloß durch rhetorische Stilmittel, sondern auch mithilfe einer dichten Vernetzung grammatischer Bezüglichkeiten und ihrer Bewusstmachung zu erzielen.

## „Vom Besitzfall zum Zeugefall zu erhöhen ..."

Von einem der rätselhaftesten Sätze aus der Zeit, in der sich Karl Kraus' Beschäftigung mit der „Sprachlehre" auf ihrem Höhepunkt befand, scheint die Forschung bisher keine rechte Notiz genommen zu haben. Er steht an prominenter Stelle, im ersten Text der letzten *Fackel* vor Kraus' „Schweigen" angesichts der Machtergreifung der Nationalsozialisten. Sein Titel *Die Sprache*[11] lässt vermuten, dass hier Wesentliches gesagt wird:

> »Volk der Dichter und Denker«: seine Sprache vermag es, den Besitzfall zum Zeugefall zu erhöhen, das Haben zum Sein. (F 885,4)

Wurde der Satz von den wichtigen Werken über Kraus' Sprachbegriff noch übergangen,[12] haben neuere Arbeiten seinen in der Tat schwer zu fassenden Sinn eher noch verdunkelt. Bei der sonst verdienstreichen Arbeit von Luis Miguel Isava taucht er, eingebettet in dessen Auslegung von Kraus' Aphorismen über die Sprache,[13] in einer bemüht sinngemäßen Übersetzung auf:

> 'people of writers and thinkers:' its language is capable of elevating the case of property *(Besitzfall)* to that of witness *(Zeugefall)*, Having to Being [..]. In other words, when we enter the creative attitude I mentioned before, language deprives us, its handlers, of our mastery and turns us into witnesses of its own "generations."[14]

Noch freier und – gleichwohl in den Dienst des eigenen Forschungsanliegens gestellt – übersetzt Hertz den zweiten Teilsatz: „To raise possession to tool, having to being".[15] Angesichts dieser semantischen Freizügigkeit gilt es also – noch vor Bean-

---

[11] Dieser Text schließt – gleichfalls prominent – die gleichlautende Sammlung von Kraus' Aufsätzen über „Die Sprache" ab: vgl. Karl Kraus: Die Sprache, Wien 1937, S. 393–396.
[12] Prominent ignoriert wird er etwa von Josef Quack, der freilich nicht umhinkommt, die Eingangspassage desselben Aufsatzes im Rahmen seiner Behandlung von Kraus' Distinktion zwischen „Sprache als Gestaltung" und als „Mitteilung" zu betrachten, vgl. Quack, S. 141 f.
[13] Vgl. Isava, S. 73–81. Isava dient *Die Sprache* als Beleg, um Kraus zu dessen Konzept der sich der Eigengesetzlichkeit poetischer Sprache verdankenden „passiven Kreativität" zuzuschlagen.
[14] Isava, S. 75.
[15] Hertz, S. 65. Hertz liest den Satz ebenfalls als Hinweis auf jene bereits bei Isava formulierte „passive creativity", erkennt jedoch eine Verbindung zu einer durch Walter Benjamin geprägten

spruchung für die eigene Argumentation –, den eigentlichen Sinn des Satzes festzuhalten. Denn anders als Isava mit seiner Übertragung in „case of property and witness" beabsichtigt, ist mit dem Besitz- und Zeugefall zuallererst der grammatische *casus genitivus* oder *genetivus* gemeint. Der Kasus also, dessen lateinische Bezeichnung seit dem 17. Jahrhundert in Werken zur Grammatik der deutschen Sprache auch in deutschen Entlehnungen auftaucht[16] und bis zu seiner bis heute gültigen Bezeichnung Germanisten zu einer Vielzahl von Wortschöpfungen angeregt hat – „Zeugefall" und „Besitzfall" sind nur zwei Versuche, um den bereits seit der griechischen Antike auf den Begriff gebrachten „genikós (γενικός)" zu übersetzen. 1932, als Karl Kraus seinem Publikum seine eigene „Sprachlehre" erteilt, sind diese Lehnwörter durchaus üblich,[17] während sie heute völlig aus dem Jargon der Linguistik verschwunden sind. Die gegenwärtigen Lesarten von Isava und Hertz dürfen also auch auf die historische Distanz zum Sprachgebrauch der 1930er-Jahre zurückgeführt werden, der noch ganz unter dem Eindruck der Grammatiker des 19. Jahrhunderts stand. Die Sinnverkürzung beider Übersetzungen fällt umso weniger ins Gewicht, als Isava und Hertz mit der Aufmerksamkeit, die sie dem in Rede stehenden Satz widmen, intuitiv seine herausgehobene Bedeutung erfassen. Anders jedoch, als sich in ihren Übertragungen erahnen lässt, ist an diesem Satz nicht so sehr die semantische Ebene interessant,[18] als das Verhältnis seiner einzelnen Bestandteile zueinander. Er steht beispielhaft für ein Vorgehen, das für Kraus' satirisch-kritische Auseinandersetzung mit Welt und Sprache grundlegend ist. In seiner Struktur ist nichts weniger angelegt als eine Methode.

---

Verbindung von Sprach- und Kapitalismuskritik: „The negative notion of "possession" *(Besitzfall)* in this quote, as well as the transition it necessitates from "having" to "being," demonstrates Benjamin's claim quoted in the first part of the chapter, regarding Kraus's critique of the language of capitalism and the reification it brings with it. Kraus's point is not about the class struggle involving private property, but an epistemic change that alters language's social function. The concept of language as shaping and creating opposes mastery and possession."
16 Das Etymologische Wörterbuch datiert die ersten „Verdeutschungsversuche" des Genitivs in deutschen „grammatischen Schriften" ins 17. Jahrhundert, bspw. „Besitzer (1604), Besitzfall, Zwäitfall (1619), Zeugefall, (17. Jh.)", vgl.: Etymologisches Wörterbuch, hg. von Wolfgang Pfeifer, 2. Auflage, Berlin 1993.
17 Der von Kraus häufig mit Polemiken bedachte „Professor Engel" (F 572,2) etwa, dessen „Aversion gegen Fremdwörter" (F 554,13) ihm mehrfach Anlass zur Kritik (etwa: „An die Anschrift der Sprachreiniger") war, vermied den Ausdruck „Genitiv" und sprach konsequent vom „Zeugefall", vgl. Eduard Engel: Deutsche Stilkunst, Neuauflage in zwei Bänden, Berlin 2016.
18 Freilich ließe sich der Satz umstandslos in eine kohärente Lektüre des Aufsatzes *Die Sprache* einfügen und hinsichtlich seiner Aussagekraft im Schema „Sprache als Mitteilung"/„– als Gestaltung" befragen. Eine orthodoxe Auslegung müsste zum Ergebnis kommen, dass der instrumentelle, „mitteilende" Gebrauch der Sprache im „Besitzfall", das gestaltende Dichten dagegen im „Zeugefall" angesprochen ist.

Eine Betrachtung des Satzes im größeren Zusammenhang des Texts, dem er entnommen ist, macht seine besondere Beschaffenheit augenfällig. Kraus geht es in der *Sprache* zunächst um das Vermögen der deutschen Sprache, oder besser: der Sprache des „deutschen Sprachgebiets":[19]

> Den Rätseln ihrer Regeln, den Plänen ihrer Gefahren nahezukommen, ist ein besserer Wahn als der, sie beherrschen zu können. Abgründe dort sehen zu lehren, wo Gemeinplätze sind – das wäre die pädagogische Aufgabe an einer in Sünden erwachsenen Nation; wäre Erlösung der Lebensgüter aus den Banden des Journalismus und aus den Fängen der Politik. Geistig beschäftigt sein – mehr durch die Sprache gewährt als von allen Wissenschaften, die sich ihrer bedienen – ist jene Erschwerung des Lebens, die andere Lasten erleichtert. Lohnend durch das Nichtzuendekommen an einer Unendlichkeit, die jeder hat und zu der keinem der Zugang verwehrt ist. *»Volk der Dichter und Denker«: seine Sprache vermag es, den Besitzfall zum Zeugefall zu erhöhen, das Haben zum Sein.* Denn größer als die Möglichkeit, in ihr zu denken, wäre keine Phantasie. Was dieser sonst erschlossen bleibt, ist die Vorstellung eines Außerhalb, das die Fülle entbehrten Glückes umfaßt: Entschädigung an Seele und Sinnen, die sie doch verkürzt. (F 885,3 f.) [Hervorhebung R.M.]

Innerhalb dieses emphatischen Textes ragt unser Satz eigentümlich heraus. Er tut es zunächst durch die Wendung „Volk der Dichter und Denker", die die einzigen Anführungszeichen des gesamten Texts als Zitat auszeichnen. Auch wenn ihre konkrete Herkunft und der Anlass ihrer Verwendung nicht mehr zweifelsfrei rekonstruierbar ist[20] – Karl Kraus bedient sich ihrer hier nicht zum ersten Mal. „Volk der Dichter und Denker" gehört zu jenen Phrasen, die von ihm häufig in satirischer Absicht umgeformt worden sind, so etwa lyrisch im Oktober 1917 in der „Kriegsfackel":

---

**19** Eine von Kraus häufig gebrauchte Bezeichnung für den deutschen Sprachraum, bspw. in F 795,97: „Wenn ich einmal dazugelangte, wollte ich eine Untersuchung anstellen, gleichermaßen aus der Sprachlehre heraus wie aus der Zeiterkenntnis, auf welcher Grundlage tiefster Humorlosigkeit die Auffassung zustandegekommen ist, die man im deutschen Sprachgebiet von Polemik hat, eine Auffassung, so trostlos wie die Polemik selbst, die man da übt und goutiert."
**20** Die phraseologischen Schlagwörterbücher neuerer Zeit (etwa: Duden. Redewendungen – Wörterbuch der deutschen Idiomatik, hg. von Scholze-Stubenrecht u. a., Mannheim 2008 (3. Aufl.), S. 803) datieren den Beginn der Karriere der Wendung ins 19. Jahrhundert – nicht anders als schon die Zitatensammlung „Geflügelte Worte" von Georg Büchmann. Auf „den Büchmann", der in dutzenden Auflagen bis in das späte 20. Jahrhundert tatsächlich immense Verbreitung in bildungsbürgerlichen Kreisen fand, verweist Kraus oft, wenn es um die Herkunft gezwungen bildungssprachlicher Zitate in den Feuilleton-Artikeln der „Neuen Freien Presse" geht (etwa F 376, 29: „Geheime Verhandlungen mit Zulassung der Presse": „Den Bock zum Gärtner machen ist kein sprichwörtliches Absurdum mehr; es ist eine Möglichkeit geworden neben jenem Unternehmen, das längst die Beachtung des Büchmann verdient: den Schmock zum Gärtner machen.") Auf eine ähnlich mokierende Absicht kann die Anführung des Zitats im vorliegenden Fall zumindest anspielen; ob Kraus jedoch auf „den Büchmann" abhebt, ist für unser Interesse unerheblich.

**In eigener Regie**

Die Deutschen sind das Volk der Dichter und
Denker.
Drum eben nannt' ich sie das Volk der Richter und
Henker.
Stante pede aber köpfte mir ab dies Wort
ein deutscher Denker.
Und gnädig machte dann den Russen sofort
es zum Geschenk er.
Wahr wahr, die Barbaren waren ohne Recht,
da Zaren die Lenker.
Der Deutsche aber ist sein eigener Knecht,
sein eigener Henker.           (F 472,14)

Die hier eigentümlich performativ vollzogene Benennung der Deutschen („drum eben nannt' ich sie Volk der Richter und Henker") ist ihm auch in den *Letzten Tagen der Menschheit* die Chiffre einer Kritik an der Verbindung von Kulturpatriotismus und Kriegseuphorie, die er der Figur des Nörglers in den Mund legt.[21] Für den Kontext der *Dritten Walpurgisnacht* wird dieser satirische Taufakt jedoch abgewandelt: Im Lichte des Nationalsozialismus sind ihm die „Richter und Henker" nunmehr bloß das im Gedicht von 1917 bereits präludierte „Volk der Knechte".[22]

Was in diesen Fällen, die ich zusammenfassend als einen Fall betrachten will, zur Anwendung kommt, ist ein oft und erschöpfend beschriebenes Verfahren der Kraus'schen Sprachsatire. Im Fortschreiten von der vorgefundenen Phrase der „Dichter und Denker" über „Richter und Henker" bis zur Verkürzung auf „Knechte" – in der Sicherheit, auch in dieser Formel noch eine klare Reminiszenz auf die Ursprungsphrase zu finden – gehorcht der Prozess ganz der *lex minimi*, wie sie von Christian Wagenknecht für das Wortspiel im Werk von Karl Kraus formuliert wor-

---

[21] Karl Kraus: Die letzten Tage der Menschheit, Frankfurt a. M. 1986 [Text nach: K. K.: Die letzten Tage der Menschheit. Tragödie in fünf Akten mit Vorspiel und Epilog, Wien/Leipzig 1926], S. 200: „DER NÖRGLER: Die deutsche Bildung ist kein Inhalt, sondern ein Schmückedeinheim, mit dem sich das Volk der Richter und Henker seine Leere ornamentiert."
[22] K. K.: Dritte Walpurgisnacht, Frankfurt a. M. 1989, S. 150. Irina Djassemy legt in ihrer fundamentalen Arbeit die ideellen Verbindungen und Kontinuitäten von Kraus' Schaffen aus der Zeit vor der Machtergreifung der Nazis mit den Inhalten der *Dritten Walpurgisnacht* frei und entdeckt im „Gebrauch der Wörter *Knecht/knechtisch*" eine „versteckte Selbstreferenz" auf die „Kriegsfackel" und *Die letzten Tage der Menschheit*: Damit wäre der Wendung „Volk der Knechte" auch ein dezidiert semantischer Bezug zu seinen früheren Varianten nachgewiesen. Vgl. Irina Djassemy: Die verfolgende Unschuld. Zur Geschichte des autoritären Charakters in der Darstellung von Karl Kraus, Wien 2011, S. 238 f.

den ist.[23] Mit dem Wortspiel auch begegnet Kraus dem aus dem bildungsbürgerlichen Zitatenfundus hervorgegangenen Gemeinplatz vom „Volk der Dichter und Denker"; eine Methode also, die, gleich ihrem Anlass, den Instrumenten einer rhetorischen Analyse offen steht. Der Zwillingsformel „Volk der Dichter und Denker", die ihre rhetorische Schärfe durch Alliteration und Assonanz gewinnt, wird das lautlich verwandte Paragramm des „Volks der Richter und Henker" gebildet, das zwar auf die Alliteration der Ausgangsformel verzichtet, aber durch den bloßen Austausch zweier Buchstaben ihren Bezug eindeutig lässt. In Wagenknechts Klassifikation der Wortspiele bei Kraus gesprochen, handelt es sich also um eine „Interferenz", die durch den Gebrauch „submorphemisch gleichförmige[r] Sprachzeichen" entsteht. Die Reduktion auf das „Volk der Knechte" muss jedoch auf Kraus' Wortbildungsleistung der Weltkriegsjahre bauen. Hier haben wir es nunmehr mit einer „Kontamination" zu tun – ein auch in der Linguistik gebräuchlicher Begriff, dessen weite Definition es immer noch erlaubt, von einem Wortspiel zu sprechen.[24]

Ganz anders jedoch verhält es sich mit der „Mechanik" des Satzes aus der *Sprache*, dem wir uns nun wieder zuwenden wollen. Hat Kraus der Rhetorik der Phrase in der oben skizzierten Weise noch eindeutig rhetorische Stilmittel entgegengesetzt, kann nun nicht mehr von einer rhetorischen Auseinandersetzung gesprochen werden. Freilich hat sich an der alliterativen Assonanz der Wendung „Volk der Dichter und Denker" nichts geändert. Allein: Die Phrase wird nun zunächst durch die Anführung aus der übrigen Textgestalt herausgehoben und so für den folgenden Hauptsatz gewissermaßen fixiert: „seine Sprache vermag es, den Besitzfall zum Zeugefall zu erhöhen." So sicher, wie bereits festgehalten worden ist, dass es sich sowohl bei Besitz- wie auch Zeugefall um Synonyme des grammatischen Genitiv-Falls handelt, so sehr muss die Verbindung mit dem vorhergehenden Zitat erstaunen. Kraus richtet durch ihren Gebrauch die Aufmerksamkeit auf die grammatische Relation der Worte innerhalb der Wendung. „Volk" und „Dichter und Denker" stehen in einer Genitivbeziehung zueinander. Sein Hinweis auf die möglichen Varianten im Verständnis dieser Phrase – nämlich entweder als „Volk" aus „Dichtern und Denkern" („Besitzfall") oder „Volk", dessen Sprache „Dichtern und Denkern" das Leben zu geben vermag, es „zeugt" („Zeugefall") – postuliert einen Unterschied innerhalb derselben grammatischen Kategorie. Als einziger Kasus des Deutschen,

---

23 Die „auf die Verkürzung des Ausdrucks gerichtete[] Absicht", die „lex minimi" entleiht Wagenknecht Jean Paul (Wagenknecht, ebd., S. 35). Anhand Kraus' *Prinzipieller Erklärung* anlässlich des Plans, „Soldatenfriedhöfe dem Fremdenverkehr nutzbar zu machen", macht Wagenknecht nachvollziehbar, wie Kraus' auf Knappheit ausgerichtete Stiltendenz sich auch in seiner Arbeit an einzelnen Formulierungen äußert. Hier strich er ein zweigliedriges Variations-Wortspiel zu einer Amphibolie zusammen, vgl. ebd., S.32 f.
24 Ebd., S. 20 f.

der nicht in erster Linie von Verben oder Präpositionen regiert wird, sondern die Konfrontation zweier Substantive (oder Substantivgruppen) zulässt, erscheint der Genitiv als Anwendungsbeispiel des Kraus'schen *Sprachzweifels*.[25]

Und doch erteilt Kraus in diesem Satz nicht hauptsächlich Sprachlehre. Er demonstriert mit ihm ein Verfahren, dass eine profunde Beschäftigung mit dem Gebiet der Sprachlehre erst zur Voraussetzung hat. Es darf deshalb nicht wundern, dass das konzentrierteste Beispiel dieser Methode erst in der *Fackel* von Dezember 1932 gefunden werden kann, nachdem die maßgeblichen Texte, die später in den Band *Die Sprache* eingehen sollten, bereits verfasst worden sind.[26] Da dieses Verfahren erlaubt, der Phrase oder dem Sprechen schlechthin auf eine von der rhetorischen Umformung des Wortspiels so verschiedene Weise zu begegnen, will ich es provisorisch die *grammatische Methode* nennen.

Wenngleich ihr Gebrauch vermehrt ab jenen Jahren festzustellen ist, denen unser Hauptinteresse gilt, nämlich der Zeit, in der Kraus' Beschäftigung mit Sprachproblemen mit der Machtergreifung Hitlers zusammenfällt, so ist sie doch nicht ohne Vorbild. Andere Spielarten dieser grammatischen Auseinandersetzung finden sich schon in den *Letzten Tagen der Menschheit* – freilich unter anderen Vorzeichen:

> DAS GESCHREI: – Mir gesagt! – Ihm gesagt! – Unter uns gesagt! – Sag i c h Ihnen! – Sagen S i e ! – No wenn ich Ihnen sag! – Also ich sag Ihnen – ! – Was s a g e n Sie! – Sagt e r ! – Auf ihm soll ich sagen! – Ich wer' Ihnen etwas sagen – No was soll ich Ihnen sagen? – Ihnen gesagt![27]

Hier ist es das Verb *sagen*, an dem Kraus gleich mehrere Fälle vorführt: Den Dativ („*Mir*" und „*Ihm* gesagt"), den Akkusativ („Ich wer' Ihnen *etwas* sagen") und natürlich den Nominativ des Subjekts. So wenig diese Fälle als unvermeidliche Bestandteile der deutschen Sprache zur Kennzeichnung der Spezifik eines bestimmten Sprachgebrauchs taugen und sich einzeln für eine sprachkritische Analyse eignen, so sehr führt Kraus in der Aneinanderreihung von Varianten der gleichen syntaktischen Einheit die Redundanz unterschiedlicher, sich strenggenommen nie wiederholender Sätze vor. Vom „Geschrei" bleibt der Eindruck eines Stimmengewirrs, das zur Deklination gerät. Die Sprache wird also – nicht unähnlich der grammatischen

---

25 Kraus' Sprachverständnis kommt einem solchen Auslegung entgegen, sieht er doch im Verhältnis einzelner Wörter zueinander die elementare sprachliche Spannung: „Aber die Sprache gewährt nur solche [Zweifel] und sie läßt nicht zu, daß zwei Worte zusammenkommen, ohne aneinander zu geraten [...]." (K.K.: Es (Abdeckung des Subjekts), in: Die Sprache, ebd., S. 74–81, hier: S. 75.)
26 Tatsächlich datieren die Erstveröffentlichungen der Texte zu Sprachproblemen in der *Fackel* allesamt vor Dezember 1932 und der *Fackel* Nr. 885, der Text *Die Sprache* und der ihr entnommene Satz sind somit zumindest konzeptionell Kraus' letztes Wort zu Fragen der Sprache.
27 *Die Letzten Tage der Menschheit*, V. Akt, 25. Szene (ebd., S. 605).

Vermittlung im Sprachunterricht – *gebeugt,* die Vergeblichkeit des Sprechens bezeichnenderweise am *Sagen* vorgeführt – die vorangestellte Regieanweisung macht den satirischen Charakter der Passage klar: *"Dem Eintretenden tönt ein großes Geschrei entgegen [...]. Näher hinhorchend, vermag man erst genauer zu unterscheiden."* – Unterscheiden lassen sich hier freilich allein die Redeakte, ein semantischer Gehalt ist nicht auszumachen.[28]

Inhaltsleer muss auch der Dialog einer früheren Szene der *Letzten Tage der Menschheit* erscheinen. Wieder ist es die Grammatik, die für die Wirkung der Sprechweise entscheidend ist:

12. S<small>ZENE</small>
*Bad Gastein. Der Abonnent und der Patriot im Gespräch.*

D<small>ER</small> A<small>BONNENT</small>: Ich bin überzeugt, daß durch den Ausbau des Bündnisses –

D<small>ER</small> P<small>ATRIOT</small>: Ich zweifle nicht, daß dann der Abbau des Hasses –

D<small>ER</small> A<small>BONNENT</small>: Vermutlich würde durch die Vertiefung des Bündnisses –

D<small>ER</small> P<small>ATRIOT</small>: Ich glaube, daß dadurch eine Erhöhung der Preise –

D<small>ER</small> A<small>BONNENT</small>: Ohne Zweifel könnte der Abbau der Preise –

D<small>ER</small> P<small>ATRIOT</small>: Mir scheint, daß dafür eine Erhöhung des Hasses –

D<small>ER</small> A<small>BONNENT</small>: Ich glaube aber, daß ein Ausbau der Preise –

D<small>ER</small> P<small>ATRIOT</small>: Ich meine, daß dadurch eine Vertiefung des Hasses –

D<small>ER</small> A<small>BONNENT</small>: Vermutlich würde durch eine Erhöhung des Bündnisses –

D<small>ER</small> P<small>ATRIOT</small>: Mir scheint, daß dadurch ein Ausbau des Hasses –

D<small>ER</small> A<small>BONNENT</small>: Andererseits bin ich überzeugt, daß sich durch einen Abbau des Bündnisses –

D<small>ER</small> P<small>ATRIOT</small>: – unschwer eine Vertiefung der Preise herbeiführen ließe.[29]

---

[28] Gal Hertz' Lektüre dieser Passage deckt sich in diesem Fall mit meiner Beobachtung, für ihn ist diese Passage eine Demonstration des „zero degree" der Tragödie: „The characters repeat pronouncing the verb Sagen (to say) in different conjugations. The logic of what they saying is thus something like "I am telling you that I am telling you". There is no actual content to the conversation." (Hertz, S. 117 f.)
[29] Ebd., V. Akt, 12. Szene (S. 578).

Während der wiederkehrenden Konjunktion „daß" hier ebenso wenig wie der Präposition „durch" eine stilbildende Funktion zukommt, dominiert die Genitivbeziehung zweier Substantive jeden einzelnen der abgebrochenen Sätze. Am Genitiv demonstriert Kraus etwas, das er andernorts als das „Problematische der Fügung"[30] bezeichnet. Indem er vier Substantive (Ausbau, Abbau, Vertiefung, Erhöhung) mit drei Genitivattributen (Bündnis, Hass, Preise) in allen möglichen Konstellationen miteinander kombiniert, bleibt die Fügung, also die Genitivbeziehung, die einzige Konstante. Die semantische Austauschbarkeit der Substantive wird augenfällig, weil sie tatsächlich gegeneinander ausgetauscht werden. Im Permutationsspiel mit der Sprache werden ihre „combinatorial possibilities" vorgeführt, die Isava schon für Kraus' Sprachverständnis in Anspruch nimmt.[31] Das Ergebnis unterscheidet sich nicht sehr vom „Geschrei", das in der Deklination des Sagens seine eigene Sprachlosigkeit fassbar macht. Nur die Autorintention tritt hier deutlicher hervor: in den Figuren des Patrioten und des Abonnenten werden die Kriegsrhetorik der Presse, gefiltert durch diese beiden Typen, konkret vorgeführt.

Auf der formalen Ebene montiert Kraus einen zweistimmigen Monolog, dessen Inhalt zwar kein semantischer ist, aber durch seine Beschaffenheit doch absichtsvoll auf eine semantische Ebene abhebt: Die Wirkung, die die Sprache der Presseberichte nicht nur auf das Sprechen, sondern auf die Wirklichkeitswahrnehmung hat, wird hier greifbar; der monologische Dialog verzichtet – obwohl davon ausgegangen werden muss, dass seine einzelnen Elemente von Kraus auch hier als Zitate aus der Presse übernommen worden sind – darauf, auf Inhalte außerhalb seiner selbst Bezug zu nehmen; das Medium (als Sprache) wird selbst zum Thema. Entlarvt wird seine Selbstbezüglichkeit durch das bloße Bewusstmachen und Vorführen der grammatischen Beschaffenheit seiner Rede. Um dieser Wirkung zu erliegen, bedarf es strenggenommen keiner Sprachlehre und keiner Kenntnis der Grundbegriffe von Grammatik und Syntax. Beide können sie jedoch das Verständnis begünstigen, wie eine andere Szene aus den *Letzten Tagen der Menschheit* zeigt. In ihr macht „der Nörgler" in einmaliger Klarheit anschaulich, wie nach der *grammatischen Methode* zu verfahren ist:

---

30 Kraus: Die Sprache, S. 75.
31 Isava, ebd., S. 67.

*(Ein Zug von Rekruten, die graue Bärte haben, geht vorbei.)*

DER OPTIMIST: Sehn Sie, die rücken ein.

DER NÖRGLER: Und dennoch sind sie nicht Einrückende.

DER OPTIMIST: Sondern?

DER NÖRGLER: Einrückend gemachte, wie sie mit Recht heißen. Das Partizipium der Gegenwart allein würde noch eine Willenstätigkeit bekunden und darum muß schon ein Partizip der Vergangenheit dabei sein. Es sind also einrückend Gemachte. Bald werden sie einrückend gemacht sein.

DER OPTIMIST: Nun ja, sie müssen in den Krieg ziehen.

DER NÖRGLER: Ganz richtig, sie müssen, die allgemeine Wehrpflicht hat aus der Menschheit ein Passivum gemacht. Einst zog man in den Krieg, jetzt wird man in den Krieg gezogen. Nur in Deutschland ist man schon darüber hinaus.
[...]

DER OPTIMIST: Sie waren schon im Frieden ein Nörgler und jetzt –

DER NÖRGLER: Jetzt geb' ich sogar der Phrase die Blutschuld.

DER OPTIMIST: Ja, warum sollte der Krieg Sie von Ihrer fixen Idee befreit haben?

DER NÖRGLER: Ganz richtig, er hat mich sogar darin bestärkt. Ich bin mit dem höheren Zweck kleinlicher geworden. Ich sehe einrückend Gemachte und spüre, daß es gegen die Sprache geht. An Drahtverhauen hängen die blutigen Reste der Natur.

DER OPTIMIST: Wirklich also, mit Grammatik wollen Sie den Krieg führen?

DER NÖRGLER: Das ist ein Irrtum, mich interessiert kein Reglement, nur der lebendige Sinn des Ganzen. Im Krieg gehts um Leben und Tod der Sprache.[32]

Mit der Grammatik will der Nörgler hier tatsächlich keinen Krieg führen – wohl aber mit ihrer Hilfe das Sprechen über ihn bloßstellen: Am Anfang dieses Ausschnitts steht ein Ausdruck aus der Militärterminologie und der Mobilmachung („einrücken" als Prädikat, die „Einrückenden" als Partizip) und die Reflexion über seinen Gebrauch – der Nörgler erteilt Sprachlehre. Sein Vorgehen ähnelt ganz dem des späteren Kraus in seinen Texten über Präpositionen, Konjunktionen, Pronomen oder Satzzeichen, der auf den *Wortgehalt* einer bestimmten *Wortgestalt* hinweist und somit aus Form auf ihren Inhalt, aus der grammatischen

---

[32] Die letzten Tage der Menschheit, II. Akt, 10. Szene (ebd., S. 253 u. 255)

Beschaffenheit einer Wendung auf ihre Intention schließt. Auch hier ist es ein Sprachgebrauch – der von den „einrückend gemachten, wie sie mit Recht heißen" –, dessen Gehalt erst durch die Bewusstmachung seiner Struktur, hier allein der grammatischen, offenbar wird. Dem Nörgler genügt es freilich nicht, diese bloß zu beschreiben; er legt frei, wie sich mit dem Sprechen über die Rekruten, die synekdochisch auf ihre Tätigkeit (das Einrücken) beschränkt werden, eine regelrecht letale Entmenschlichung vollzieht. Die rhetorische Synekdoche zerlegt er in ihre grammatische Struktur: Aus dem „Partizip der Vergangenheit", das gleichermaßen ein Passiv ist, bildet er das Partizip Perfekt: „Bald werden sie einrückend gemacht sein." – Hier ist nicht nur der Zustand gemeint, in dem aus Rekruten Soldaten geworden sein werden; in diesem Perfekt ist ihr Tod bereits grammatisch vorweggenommen. Auf eine weitere Erklärung kann der Nörgler verzichten.

Doch trotz seiner hier demonstrierten Annäherung an die Wortbedeutung durch die Mittel grammatischer Beschreibung ist Kraus der mustergültigen „Sprachbeherrschung" unverdächtig. Auch dort, wo Kraus sein Sprachvermögen gegen seine Antipoden nutzt, sind seine Hinweise auf deren Sprachfehler mehr als nur „grammatische[s] Bescheidwissen". Sie geben einen Eindruck davon, was unter „Sprachfühlen" zu verstehen ist.[33] Heine etwa, der „mit Dativ und Akkusativ gekämpft" habe (F 406, 59), werden nicht einfach Fehler nachgewiesen. Seine Fehler sind im „abgründigen" Sinn keine, sondern im Gegenteil nur allzu richtig, gibt seine sprachliche Leichtfertigkeit doch Aufschluss über seinen Charakter, ist jeder grammatische Lapsus Heines also Zeugnis einer hinter dem Wort verborgenen Wahrheit. Hier gilt wieder, was Michael Thalken festgehalten hat: „Die Verfügungsgewalt über die Sprache, die sich das Individuum anmaßt, die Instrumentalisierung der Sprache [...] wird für Kraus Gradmesser der jeweiligen Zustandsbeschaffenheit des Sprecherethos",[34] oder um mit Kraus zu sprechen: „Im Druck- oder Schreibfehler" – man möchte hinzufügen: im Sprachfehler – „[...] liegt der Wert."[35]

Was die Haltung, die einen Fehler um seines Wahrheitswertes willen schätzt und ihn seines Verweischarakters wegen bewahren will, für die These bedeutet, Kraus' Werk sei das Projekt der Konfrontation der Rhetorik mit den Mitteln der Grammatik, wird nirgendwo so deutlich wie im Umfeld der *Dritten Walpurgisnacht*. Hier wird das Anliegen um die Sprache zur pro-grammatischen Erklärung.

---

33 Mit dem Gegensatzpaar von „grammatischem Bescheidwissen und Sprachfühlen" operiert Kraus etwa, wenn er auf ungerechtfertigte Briefe grammatisch geschulter Leser auf vermeintliche Fehler in der *Fackel* reagiert, vgl. F 572, 46 ff., später abgewandelt veröffentlicht als „Es (Abdeckung des Subjekts)" in: K.K.: Die Sprache, ebd., S. 74–81.
34 Ebd. S. 296.
35 K.K.: Eine Richtigstellung, in: ders.: Die Sprache, S. 82–90, hier: S. 87.

In *Warum die Fackel nicht erscheint* formuliert er seinen Verzicht auf die Veröffentlichung der vollständigen *Fackel* zur Machtergreifung Hitlers – nicht ohne jedoch aus eben dieser erst posthum erscheinenden *Dritten Walpurgisnacht* zu zitieren:

> Wir glauben, Ihnen klar gemacht zu haben, daß ein Übel, vor dem der Polemiker genötigt wäre, davonzulaufen, kein polemisches Objekt ist, wenn seine Intervention nicht das Mittel bedeutet, Ihre Sicherheit zu verbürgen, wofür Sie offenbar sein Opfer verlangen. Gleichwohl will er sich zusammennehmen, Ihnen eine Lektüre zu erhalten. Denn während es gegenüber dem Phänomen der Gewalt keine Polemik geben kann und vor dem des Irrsinns keine Satire, bleiben ihm die Frechheit und namentlich die Dummheit (die weit stärker als Hunger und Liebe die Welt betreibt) als Objekte erhalten, und die alte Schwierigkeit, satiram non scribere, trete wieder in ihre Rechte. (F 890,167)

Hier wie dort – in der *Dritten Walpurgisnacht* – sind es also nicht die Mittel der Polemik und der Satire, mit denen Kraus dem Nationalsozialismus beizukommen gedenkt. Objekt jedoch, wenn auch kein polemisches, bleibt „das Ereignis Hitlers" und alle es begleitenden Symptome – in seiner „Frechheit und namentlich [...] Dummheit". Der „Entschluß, sich jenen ,bessern Gegenständen' zuzuwenden, die das Theater der Dichtung und die Sprache betreffen" (ebd.) ist ein Rückzug, der in seiner Paradoxie unmittelbar nachvollziehbar wird:[36]

> Es handelt sich um die Teilnahme an dem eigentlichen und einzigen Protest, der der Verwüstung kultureller Werte durch die Zeit entgegenzusetzen ist [...] [U]m den Nachweis, daß die Deutschen, hörig ihrer Nation, abtrünnig ihrer Sprache, alles können, nur nicht Deutsch. Vor allem hier gilt es, sich zu bewähren: man hat mutig zu sein und Sprachlehre zu treiben! (F 890, 168)

Das Unvermögen der Deutschen im Deutschen vorzuführen wird tatsächlich zur Hauptaufgabe der *Dritten Walpurgisnacht*. „Sprachlehre" jedoch – so viel sollte nun hinreichend bewiesen worden sein – darf nicht verstanden werden als gram-

---

[36] Einem Exkurs müsste es überantwortet sein, zu zeigen, inwiefern sich die der grammatischen Behandlung von Worten, Ausdrücken und Phrasen innewohnende Paradoxie auch in Kraus' Stil niederschlägt. In F 400, 53 f. demonstriert Kraus an einem Epigonen, dem er vorwirft, eine „Parodie [s]einer Tonart" zu schreiben, inwiefern sich ein im apokalyptischen Duktus gehaltener Text voller auf mehrere syntaktische Einheiten verweisender Pronomen trotz stilistischer Ähnlichkeit fundamental von Kraus eigenem Stil unterscheidet. Mit der Quittierung: „Er ist für diesen Posten prädestiniert, aber bei weitem nicht geeignet." führt Kraus eine Fähigkeit vor, die seinen Nachahmern abgeht: Im Gebrauch von üblichen Synonymen (Prädestination, Eignung) ihre Unverträglichkeit zu erkennen und also auf eine grammatische Paradoxie hinzuweisen.
Auch Jan Philipp Reemtsma (Ders.: Der Bote. Walter Benjamin über Karl Kraus, in: Sinn und Form 1/1991, S. 104–115, hier: S. 107) bemerkt Kraus' „Praxis, die nicht im oberflächlichen Sinn widersprüchlich, sondern zutiefst paradox ist".

matische Besserwisserei, denn als Demonstration sprachlicher Potentiale, die, vom teutonischen Furor der Sprecher nicht begriffen, zur Bloßstellung, Demaskierung und folglich auch sprachlichen Bändigung der Ereignisse ab 1933 dienen. Die Grammatik ist bei diesem Ansinnen Mittel und Gehilfin zugleich, wie ein Beispiel aus der *Dritten Walpurgisnacht* zeigt:

> und wenn sich die Sprache findet, vergeht sie sich wieder im Irrgarten tausendfacher Antithetik, wo sich die Motive stoßen und ein Wort das andere gibt: sie erlebt die Schmach, sich zu verlieren, und das Glück, zu sich zu kommen, immer hinter einer Wirklichkeit her, von der sie nichts trennt als das Chaos. Wer sich da einem Führer anvertrauen könnte! Wer sich da alles ersparen könnte, um schlicht zu sein wie jene! Denn
>
> das eben ist ja das große Wunder, daß der Schöpfer des neuen D e u t s c h l a n d s
>
> (welches immerhin im Genitiv biegbar erscheint)
>
> die bezwingende Gewalt besitzt, s e l b s t  d i e  k o m p l i z i e r t e s t e n  M i t m e n s c h e n  w i e d e r  z u r  v o l k h a f t e n  S c h l i c h t h e i t  z u  f o r m e n.
>
> Und ich soll mich in das Problem vertiefen, ob sich die ungeheure Erfüllung des Gebots »Deutschland erwache!« so reibungslos vollzogen hätte, wenn ihm nicht die einfachere Weisung »Juda verrecke!« angeschlossen und unmittelbar befolgt worden wäre![37]

Abgesehen vom Inhalt dieser Passage, in der sich das Grundthema der *Dritten Walpurgisnacht* und Kraus' These von der Verquickung der Phrasen „Deutschland erwache!" und „Juda verrecke!" herausschält, ist das hier angewandte Verfahren bemerkenswert. Seine Montage- und Zitattechnik trifft auf eben jene *grammatische Methode,* die hier sich als Methode nochmals vorstellt. Das falsche Genitiv-S in einem Zitat aus der völkischen Presse wird für Kraus zur Gelegenheit, die „tausendfache Antithetik" der Sprache zu entdecken und ihre Sprecher zu überführen: Das „neue Deutschland" des beginnenden Faschismus wird nicht nur grammatisch *beugbar,* also: deklinierbar; die „Richter und Henker" gleichwohl wie ihre Knechte werden gar *„biegbar",* also: überwindbar. Der Genitiv wird hier zum Mittel der performativen Errettung vor dem Nationalsozialismus.

Was so vieldeutig in unserem Ausgangssatz vom „Volk der Dichter und Denker" angeklungen ist, scheint hier tatsächlich eingelöst: seine Sprache vermöchte es, die Wandlung zu den „Richtern und Henkern" und schließlich zu den Knechten des Nationalsozialismus erst zu verhüten. In diesem Sinne formuliert Kraus auch das Ansinnen, wie er die Zeit der Machtergreifung Hitlers von der *Fackel* begleiten sehen möchte:

---

37  K.K.: Dritte Walpurgisnacht, ebd., S.24 f., ebenfalls: F 890, 159.

> Die Rettung der durch nationale Selbstbesinnung bedrohten Werte, als die wahre polemische Tat, nicht nur so zu vollziehen, daß man deutsche Sprache durch den Vortrag ehrt, sondern auch – denn das unterbrochene Werk zur Sprachlehre wäre nur ein Anfang – wenn möglich durch Errichtung eines Sprachseminars, das dem Zweck diente, durch Vorführung von Greueln der Satzbildung den Möglichkeiten und damit den Geheimnissen der abgründigsten und tiefsten Sprache näher zu kommen, deren unzüchtiger Gebrauch zu den Greueln des Bluts geführt hat. (F 890, 168)

„Sprachlehre" und das „Theater der Dichtung" sind die Schlüssel zu jener Haltung, die Karl Kraus die einzig angemessene scheint. Für sein Schreiben heißt das konkret: konsequenten Vollzug eines Sprachbewusstseins und Einsatz des *Sprachzweifels* gegen die „Greuel der Satzbildung", die Stellvertreter sind für die „Greuel des Bluts". Entgegen der Vorwürfe der „Hübener und Drübener jeglicher Couleur" (F 890, 166), also jener europäischer Linksintellektueller, die die *Fackel* als polemische Instanz gegen das Hitlerregime berufen sahen, und der Rechten, die über Kraus' „Schweigen" im Jahre 1933 spotteten, sucht Kraus tatsächlich die Konfrontation mit dem Nationalsozialismus: Konfrontativ nämlich ist Kraus' Sprache in eigentümlicher Weise bis in die Struktur seiner Sätze hinein. Beobachtet Christian Wagenknecht etwa besonders für die letzten Jahrgänge der *Fackel* eine beispiellose Zunahme der Dichte von Wortspielen,[38] sollte die Frage erlaubt sein, ob gleiches womöglich auch für die Betonung genuin grammatischer Bezüglichkeiten in seinen Sätzen gilt. Die „wachsende Hermetik des Stils", die Wagenknecht zufolge im letzten Text der *Fackel* unter dem Titel „Wichtiges von Wichten – (In verständlicher Sprache)" kulminiert,[39] gilt zweifelsohne nicht nur für die kaum noch durchschaubare Komplexität seiner Wortspiele. In *Warum die Fackel nicht erscheint* jedenfalls gibt es unzählige Sätze, die nicht weniger rätselhaft erscheinen als jene Passage, von der diese Überlegungen ihren Ausgang genommen haben. Auf die „Wichte" weist auch der dem vorstehenden Zitat unmittelbar folgende Satz voraus, mit dem die Beispiele der *grammatischen Methode* bei Karl Kraus abschließen sollen:

> Solche Mutprobe könnte mit dem Beispiel einsetzen, daß, wenn von einem toten Löwen und einem Eselsfußtritt die Rede ginge, in diesem Genitiv der seltene Fall einer Objektivbeziehung nachzuweisen wäre. (Abgesehen davon, daß der Esel auch seltener den lebenden Löwen erkannt hat, als dieser den Esel.) (F 890, 168)

Mit der Rede vom „toten Löwen" greift Kraus nicht nur eine Bezeichnung auf, die in der Presseresonanz auf die *Fackel* Nr. 888 mit der Grabrede auf Adolf Loos und

---
**38** Wagenknecht, ebd., S. 23–31. Die Zahlen der strichprobenartigen erfassten Wortspiele sprechen für sich: besonders die letzten beiden *Fackel*-Jahrgänge verzeichnen eine quantitative Verdopplung von Wortspielen gegenüber etwa der Jahre der „Kriegsfackel".
**39** Ebd., S. 48.

dem Gedicht „Man frage nicht" mutmaßlich gegen Kraus und seinen vermeintlichen „Abschied" gebraucht worden ist. Der „tote Löwe" ist eine Chiffre, die bis auf alttestamentarische Überlieferung verweist[40] und in Verbindung mit dem „Eselsfußtritt" zur Phrase wird. Eben diese Tritte, die Kraus als „Nachrufe auf Karl Kraus" (F 889, Juli 1934) zusammengefasst präsentiert, entlarven sich in ihrer Unerheblichkeit – wieder ist es der Genitiv, den Kraus hier nun schon polemisch gegen seine Kritiker wendet, wenn er im ‚Fußtritt der Esel' eine „Objektivbeziehung" ausmacht. Die Esel haben sich also selbst getreten, es bleibt Kraus' zuvor ausgesprochene Warnung in Kraft:

> Vorsicht vor »toten Löwen«! Was so einer noch vermag, wird Passe-temps sein, Vertrieb einer miesen Zeit in Form kürzerer Verlagsbriefe. [...] (F 890, 166)

## Literaturverzeichnis

Kraus, Karl. *Die Fackel*, 992 Nummern in 37 Jahrgängen. Wien, 1899–1936.
Kraus, Karl. „Die letzten Tage der Menschheit." *Karl Kraus: Schriften*. Hrsg. v. Christian Wagenknecht, Bd. 10. Frankfurt a. M., 1986 [1926].
Kraus, Karl. *Die Sprache*. München, 1956 [1937].
Kraus, Karl. „Dritte Walpurgisnacht." *Karl Kraus: Schriften*. Hrsg. v. Christian Wagenknecht, Bd. 12. Frankfurt a. M., 1989.
Bodine, Jay F. *Karl Kraus. Sprache, Literatur und Wirklichkeit*. Michigan, 1974.
Djassemy, Irina. *Die verfolgende Unschuld. Zur Geschichte des autoritären Charakters in der Darstellung von Karl Kraus*. Wien, 2011.
Hertz, Gal. *Words not as Words. Critique of Language, Ideology and Identity in the Work of Karl Kraus* (unveröffentlichte Promotionsschrift). Tel Aviv, 2013.
Isava, Luis Miguel. *Wittgenstein, Kraus, and Valéry. A Paradigm for Poetic Rhyme and Reason*. New York, 2002.
Quack, Josef. *Bemerkungen zum Sprachverständnis von Karl Kraus*. Bonn, 1976.
Reemtsma, Jan Philipp. „Der Bote. Walter Benjamin über Karl Kraus." *Sinn und Form* 1 (1991): 104–115.
Thalken, Michael. *Ein bewegliches Heer von Metaphern. Sprachkritisches Sprechen bei Friedrich Nietzsche, Gustav Gerber, Fritz Mauthner und Karl Kraus*. Frankfurt a. M. u. a., 1999.
Wagenknecht, Christian. *Das Wortspiel bei Karl Kraus*. Göttingen, 1964.
Weiss, Walter. *Dichtung und Grammatik. Zur Frage der grammatischen Interpretation*. München, 1967.
Pfeifer, Wolfgang (Hg.), *Etymologisches Wörterbuch*, 2. Auflage. Berlin, 1993.

---

[40] Prediger 9,4: „Ein lebender Hund ist besser als ein toter Löwe." Nicht unbedeutend ist die Wiederaufnahme des Bildes etwa durch Abraham a Santa Clara, bspw. In: Abraham a Sancta Clara: Judas Der Ertz-Schelm/ Für ehrliche Leuth/ Oder: Eigentlicher Entwurff/ vnd Lebens-Beschreibung deß Iscariotischen Bößwicht. Bd. 2. Salzburg, 1689: „Dem Samson hat wolgeschmeckt das Hönig auß deß todten Löwen Rachen."

Gal Hertz
# Poetry and Truth in the Third Reich – Karl Kraus's Ethical Campaign 1933

> ... symptomempfindlich wie ich bin, erschließe ich Krieg und Hunger aus dem Gebrauch, den die Presse von der Sprache macht, aus der Verkehrung von Sinn und Wert, aus der Entleerung und Entehrung alles Begriffs und alles Inhalts. Sicherlich, wenn sie heroischem Erinnern frönt, so ersteht das Projekt als Alpdruck.[1]
>
> [... sensitive as I am to symptoms, I derive war and famine from the use of language made by the press, its inversion of meaning and value, its exhaustion and degradation of any concept and content. Surely, when it indulges with heroic memory, the project becomes a demonic nightmare.]

The extensive literature on Karl Kraus varies in its focus on different aspects of his project: his satirical feuilleton *Die Fackel* [The Torch] which he published between 1899 until his death in 1936, his public appearances at the *Theater der Dichtung* [Theater of Poetry], the manifold polemics he provoked, his political activity as well as his theatrical writings and adaptations. However, these various aspects neither amalgamate into a comprehensive picture of his critique nor do they facilitate a full understanding of his social philosophy. Furthermore, scholars are divided as to what Kraus sought to achieve in his sharp, and often devastating, critique, which was directed at nearly every ideological movement or public institution: Was he a socialist or a liberal? Conservative republican or radical anarchist? Self-hating Jew or messianic revolutionary? Kraus himself often regarded the different ways in which his project was described with scorn, and disputed those who attempted to classify or define him, referring to them as those who cannot understand his meaning beyond his contradictions [Widersprüche]. It seems to correlate to Wittgenstein's famous formulation: "I find it important in philosophizing to keep changing my posture, not to stand for too often on one leg, so as not to get stiff."[2] Indeed, Kraus was a man of contradictions and paradoxes, however what I will strive to show here is that there is nevertheless an inner logic to his work, which culminates into a theory of language around 1933. While a systematic social doctrine or coherent political theory is not the issue here – Kraus was neither a political philosopher nor sociologist – he certainly produced

---

1 Karl Kraus, *Dritte Walpurgisnacht* (Nach der von Heinrich Fischer herausgegebenen Fassung, München: Kösel, 1967) Satz: Wolfgang Hink, Berlin 2010, p. 394.
2 Ludwig Wittgenstein, *Culture and Value*, trans. Peter Winch, Oxford: Blackwell, 1970, § 27.

a methodological-analytical approach and poetic-critical praxis in terms of which he produced a comprehensive critical project.

In what follows, I argue that Kraus was first and foremost a social thinker and activist who dealt predominantly with questions of *justice and morality*. Yet, his ethical critique often evades scholars precisely because it is not founded on any normative standard or already-constituted position, but rather on a linguistic practice whose purpose is to produce the position from which moral critique is feasible. This involves linguistic skepticism as a condition for morality – in Kraus's words: "could we imagine a better guaranty for morality than the linguistic doubt?"[3] This statement means: A. that ethics goes beyond the boundaries of the given language. B. a practical rather than deontological approach to morality. The poetic-critical language Kraus created and mastered was opposed to communicative-normative language. It was not intended to represent the world or to criticize ideas or thoughts, but to destabilize the linguistic act – that which defines and stabilizes meaning – and transform it into an open and diverse poetic space. The word does not express the thoughts of the speaker, but rather the constant tension between experience and reality, individual and collective, memory and legacy, and a concrete historical moment. Like the poetic text – as opposed to the press's catchphrases – reality itself is for Kraus a contentious space of contradicting logics, ambiguous positions, and complexities that highlight the "corporeality" of words. Thus, by way of re-presenting (in a theatrical sense) the gaps, contradictions, wordplay, and the ambivalence of linguistic expressions (like in his readings of Shakespeare or the montage of quotations in his plays), Kraus proposes an alternative idea of language (*Sprachgestaltung*). Kraus's satirical writing, extensive use of quotations, and his theatrical adaptation-translation projects generate defamiliarization and duality within the language, which functions to suspend meaning, and bring to the fore what Kraus refers to as "the unsaid" of the world of experience, memory, and associations. The reader must learn that "language includes not merely what is speakable, but also in it all that is not spoken can be experienced."[4] Poetic language is a form of seeing and hearing, and of adding dimensions to utterance, which can be provoked when "actions speak louder than words," that is, when one listens attentively to the syntax and transforms the quotation into an act of imagination and creation.

The year 1933 was shocking for Kraus, despite never having been much of an optimist, and was one of the early critics to foresee the atrocities that National

---

[3] Karl Kraus, *Die Sprache*, Suhrkamp Verlag, Frankfurt a. M. 1987, p. 8. „Mit dem Zweifel, der der beste Lehrmeister ist, wäre schon viel gewonnen: manches bliebe ungesprochen."
[4] Kraus, F. 483–84, p. 41.

Socialism brought with it. Yet against interpretations that viewed him as falling into desperation succumbing to an endorsement of "lesser evil"[5] – his writings of the time indicate a different approach. His publications in *Die Fackel*, the writing of the *Third Walpurgisnacht* and the translation-adaptation project which he continued during this period. All these activities, I claim, are part of his critical project and provide an insight to his ethical endeavor based on the radical crossing of the boundaries of reality and fiction, poetry and realism, life and language. Morality, from such a perspective, is far more than telling the truth or uncovering corruption: It must address a crisis of meaning, the lack of the possibility to simply promote 'just conduct' through imperatives or demands.

Coming to terms with Kraus's ethics has several dimensions. First, it is important to look at the way in which Kraus used the linguistic medium in his own (anti-)feuilleton. *Die Fackel* was not only a platform for critiquing the press in terms of its content, but no less so in terms of its form – the use of formative and syntactical language, cliché adjectives, distorted language, and wordplay, and even the size of headlines and the juxtaposition of articles – all of which for Kraus were expressions not only of poor taste or economic interests, but of a different effect on the readers. Kraus did not report on or review the press in the regular sense; he quoted and disrupted the articles and reports in order to question processes sof reading and comprehension. He intended to show what the language of the press was covering up and aiming to "immunize the readers." Reading *Die Fackel* is not like reading a newspaper, it constantly confronts the reader with linguistic impasses in multiple voices and layers; it is, indeed, a lesson in linguistics that serves as an *exercise in reading*.[6]

Second, in terms of questions concerning morality and ethics, in his earlier writing Kraus focused on legal sensations, which were not only motivated by voyeurism or as a means to satisfy the public's appetite for excitement, but which facilitated the struggle to maintain the normative boundaries (gender, socioeconomic status, ethnic background) and to enforce and entrench them. Kraus's critique dealt with a liberal crisis, and specifically engaged with questions such as: what is law and in whose name does it speak? How does exercising the law serve the exclusion and discrimination of social groups (female prostitutes, homo-

---

[5] See for example: Lucile Dreidemy, "Ein leuchtend Zwerglein! – Karl Kraus' Bewunderung für Österreichs Diktator Engelbert Dollfuß", in: Katharina Prager (Ed.), *Geist versus Zeitgeist – Karl Kraus in der Ersten Republik*, Metroverlag, 2018.
[6] Ari Linden suggests an insightful reading of Kraus's citations of Goethe's Faust in *Dritte Walpurgisnacht* which highlights the relation between literature and social (dis)order. See: Linden, A. (2017). "Wo Ungesetz gesetzlich überwaltet": Karl Kraus's Reading of National Socialism. *Oxford German Studies*, 46(1), 75–91.

sexuals, Jews, low-class citizens)? How did the Darwinist social discourse render entire groups criminals, based solely on their being, and justify violence against them? To emphasize, Kraus is not simply denunciating the legal system, but instead deconstructs its literary and performative devices (words spoken by the prosecutor alongside quotes from Shakespeare's plays; describing the persecution of female prostitutes as a modern witch hunt; employing "public opinion" as a manipulation in court). He does not embellish his critique with citations but undermines the journalistic genre and legal discourse, while not only demanding that the justice systems function properly, but also by challenging the perception of the law itself: the law cannot be based on a perception of abstract normativity, in which case it would lose its concrete human drama and became an agent of power. On the other hand, Kraus's focus, although always specific, is not only upon a particular defendant or particular trial, but also poses a case study for, or symptom of, the systemic malfunction of the law and its institutions. In place of adhering to the authority of the word of the law, he calls upon judges to become critics of the language of the law. Against the authority of judges and the interests of journalists, Kraus presents the polysemous logic of the literary canon, and the rules of grammar in place of legal norms. The judicial ruling is obligated, like literary interpretation, to set boundaries to meaning and to reexamine the norms and their significance, rather than ratify conventions and enforce principles. The law is required to create the imperative connection between concepts and principles and human experience. We should stress the fact that Kraus is not stating but quoting, not condemning but making use of satirical language – allowing texts of others to speak for themselves. The defamiliarization of the speaker's position is an expression of the notion that the moral issue is not the starting point for deliberations but its outcome, which, most often, is not manifested in court. That is, something emerges which could not have been perceived before – the defendant is usually a victim of social circumstances – and therefore generalized accusations and moralistic denunciations are of no help here. The legal sensations of fin-de-siècle Vienna are distinct cases of moral panic – social crises in which the normative implementation of the law and the use of force cannot provide a suitable response (therefore these cases are so provocative). Thus, coping with them calls for other means associated with empathy, understanding the context, dealing with the inevitable contradictions of the human condition, the ability to appreciate the tragic circumstances of those who end up in court, and the recognition that justice necessitates a creative interpretation of the legal language rather than its literal application.

Such a critique of language is also the focal point of Kraus's critique of violence, mainly developed during World War I. Propaganda, for example, does not amount to the dissemination of disinformation about events. Rather, it constitutes the manipulative usage of information for the purpose of replacing rational thinking with emotional identification, and the urge to observe reality with the obsessive consumption of de-contextualized fragments of information lacking context supplied in newspapers' "special editions" (*Extraausgabe*). The reader does not know what is occurring on the front, but is rather inundated with slogans and clichés that destabilize his ability to think or understand, and which renders them, as Kraus saw it, an undiscerning marionette. Put differently, even before one speaks in favor of or against the war, it is necessary to produce an addressee, a possibility to reflect, judge, thus to provide a moral account for actions. Yet, on the eve of the First World War, the impassioned press caused masses to congregate in the streets yelling: "Serbia must die!"[7] Thus, contrary to the view that language is solely a means of representation, Kraus sees language itself as a conscripting apparatus. It should be emphasized that the uniqueness of Kraus's project does not amount merely to his proposing a critique of the conscripting press and war propaganda. He was not a cantankerous pacifist who reprimanded leaders and condemned violence, because 'war is not a nice thing.' As a social thinker, Kraus could not accept such oppositional positions either, as this, too, is based on a conventional approach to criticism that he rejects (and even satirizes its arguments by way of the cheek-in-tongue character 'The Optimist' in his play *The Last Days of Mankind*). For Kraus, war is a "techno-romantic adventure," (a title of yet another critical piece from 1918) a tragic attempt to restore substance to empty symbols and false ideas (the old order of the Austro-Hungarian empire), while becoming intoxicated with power amidst an apocalypse of destruction. In other words, opposition to the war cannot amount to denunciations or displaying its horrors. Instead, the critique needs to deal with the ways in which words of war and power operate on the senses, how it incites and engorges public opinion, and the ways in which it is not only a means to political ends but a different manifestation of the political order: in the age of manufactured mass culture, ideology is no longer an accumulation of ideas and worldviews, but an economic-consumerist logic that functions as if on its own by way of the social institutions and state mechanisms that serve it. However, it is precisely because there is no single responsible figure at which to point the finger of blame, the ideology becomes present nearly everywhere in the social discourse. In other words, this is not an act of communication per se, but an ideological discourse.

---

7 This expression characterizes the way in which newspaper headlines, by turning them into street slogans, become a process (or: result) of no-thought. In another aphorism Kraus writes: "Weil ich den Gedanken beim Wort nehme, kommt er" (A, 236) [Only because I take the thought literary does it come].

The critique of the war's horrific violence is not articulated as a means to an end (protecting the homeland) but as an expression of the shift in the political order whose objectives are different (protecting real estate, serving the interests of corrupted elites). It is about understanding the mechanisms of the ideological discourse, which does not aspire to convince or influence, but to operate on the collective consciousness and to construct the citizens in its image. Kraus went on to his extensive work, *The Third Walpurgis Night* (hereafter *DW*), which was published posthumously. By means of a nightmarish collage of theatrical quotations, newspaper reports, and speeches by and on behalf of court philosophers and intellectuals, Kraus attempts to criticize the discourse of the Third Reich, and more so, to criticize the logic of the sovereignty upon which it was founded: the manner in which the governing regime can speak to the soul of the masses, exploit the magical power of myth.

For Kraus, the point is not to condemn the new regime, nor to expose the hypocrisy of its leaders. Rather, he stresses the condition of the possibility of the existence of such a government, a result not only of political struggle or contingent situation, but as collapse of collective consciousness. Here is an example from DW:

> Als ob nicht der intelligente Propagandaminister ausdrücklich erklärt hätte, daß alle Versuche, dem Neuen mit dem Intellekt beizukommen, verfehlt seien, da jetzt nur Seele am Platz ist und vorerst mal der Gefühlsraum einzunehmen, bevor man sich Gedanken macht (198).

> [As if the intelligent Propaganda Minister had not made explicitly clear that all attempts to perceive the New intellectually should fail, because only Soul is needed and the realm of feeling must first be absorbed before coming up with ideas.]

The point here is that the new form of government is based not on the linguistic potential to inspire thought, but rather – in a similar fashion to Kraus's critique of the press – the annihilation of thought through the emotional effect of communication. Kraus's point here goes further than a critique of Goebbels's propaganda. He has a statement about language, or better: that such politicization of speech is nothing less than *nihilism*. Such language can be exploited by organized violent forces, determined to eliminate all which is associated with modern culture. In this sense, discharging thinking reduces words to mere sensation, they are attached not to understanding or thinking, but to ressentiment and emotional identification. Under such conditions, resistance requires first and foremost an alternative semiotics, one that could save the meaning-making process and reactivate it against the new common (lack) of sense.

Kraus's critical project vis-à-vis the Third Reich is based on a linguistic practice that he forms and develops, and in terms of which he produces an ethical critique that does not scrutinize the extent to which the norms are implemented but rather scrutinizes the norms themselves. It does not question their meaning but tracks the ways in which they generate meaning, and their usage in discourse. Kraus does not only contest the communicability of the language but replaces it, as an alternative, with poetic language, the polysemic language that deviates from the representational principle. Poetic language is not a different aggregate of signifiers, expression of opinion or social theory, but a 'language-paradigm,' an opportunity to articulate what the ideological discourse silenced, to create a rejuvenated linkage between language and experience, morality, and imagination. In his essay *Die Sprache* [The Language], Kraus formulates this notion, in his usual manner, with striking accuracy: "With doubt, which is the best teacher, much would be gained: some things would remain unsaid."[8]

This is again not far from Wittgenstein, as philosopher Anat Matter explains:

> By examining the logic of language, he [Wittgenstein] draws a clear line between the thinkable, which is also clearly expressible, and that which lies beyond the pale and is thus nonsensical, meaningless. Hence his famous conclusion: 'what can be said at all can be said clearly, and what we cannot talk about we must pass over in silence'. Ethical propositions clearly belong to the second category. They attempt to express something sublime and valuable, but the logic of our language does not allow such transgression.[9]

It is indeed such transgression of language that Kraus is aiming at. As further elaborated in this volume in the essay of Isabel Langkabel, Kraus's critique of language was reaching its most articulate phase in 1933. It focuses on the processes and conditions of its production. This shaping and creating process has a material aspect. The "corporeality" or "embodiment" of the word according to Kraus, which we have already encountered, is constituted through the activation of its own creative power. It is not the dress (*Kleid*) of a thought but its flesh (*Fleisch*). Thus, the word as shape (*Wortgestalt*) has to do with its physical coming to being. Thought is not only shaped; it is embodied, contextualized and expressed through speech or writing. This process, however, is very different than that of the reifying language of the press. The latter is not an expression of an experience but rather a fabricated, superficial speech. Hence, while the phrases of journalists can simply be printed and distributed, a *Wortgestalt*, if it were to remain true to its anti-media essence, demands constant reenactment of its own creation in a recurrent act of speech or writing.

In the essay *Wortgestalt*, Kraus explains this concept through what he considers to be the best example, the word *Turm* (tower) from the last scene of Shake-

---

8 Kraus, the Language, in this volume
9 Anat Matar, *The Poverty of Ethics*, London and New York: Verso (2022), p. 42.

speare's Henry 6<sup>th</sup> Part III.¹⁰ From a conservative point of view, this seems like a strange choice for a number of reasons. First, it is a translated piece and not an original German play. Second, 'tower' is neither the most important word nor motif in the play. Third, it refers to a place, the tower of London, and not to an idea or concept. But the most puzzling aspect is that the word *Turm* in the passage Kraus cites functions as a replacement of speech, as what is used to hide more than to reveal. It marks the border of what cannot be said at that present moment in the play and will only be revealed later.

Here are the lines Kraus quotes followed by Shakespeare's English:

Gloster: Clarence, entschuld'ge mich bei meinem Bruder.
In London gibts ein dringendes Geschäft:
Eh ihr dahin kommt, sollt ihr neues hören.

Clarence: Was? Was?

Gloster: der Turm! der Turm! (ab)

GLOUCESTER: *Clarence, excuse me to the king my brother;*
*I'll hence to London on a serious matter:*
*Ere ye come there, be sure to hear some news.*

CLARENCE: *What? what?*

GLOUCESTER: *The Tower, the Tower.* (Exit)

These lines are a dialogue between Richard of Gloucester and his brother, the Duke of Clarence. Richard says that he needs to hurry for an urgent business (*Geschäft*) in London about which his brother will soon "hear the news". The eager Clarence asks: "What? What?", and Richard vaguely replies "The tower, the tower!" As the audience learns in the following scene of the play, Richard hurries to murder the king which is held prisoner in the tower of London. Instead of telling his brother about his scheme, Richard only says "tower." This might be regarded as a metonymic reference to the king inside the tower. The doubling of the word, however, as well as the fact that both the king and, more importantly, the nature of Richard's "business" (murder) go unsaid, reveal that what is at stake is not a gap between what Richard says and *how* he says it ("tower"/"king") but a tension between what Richard says and *does not* say ("tower"/"murder"). Kraus remarks:

---

10 Kraus, *S* (Frankfurt am Main: Suhrkamp, 1987), p. 284–289.

Wie dieser ungeheuren Fügung ein Monstrum in Menschengestalt entspricht, wird erst – im Unterschied zweier dramatischen Abgänge – die ganze Macht wie Ohnmacht des Wortes sinnfällig (p.285)

Like this tremendous destiny, corresponding to a monster in human-figure, demonstrates, it is only then – through the difference in the two dramatic exits – that the whole power and powerlessness of the words manifests itself

In other words, the drama has to do with the manifestation of words that do not represent or signify, yet still operate in a "monstrous" way. It is a constitutive scene that charges the word *Turm* with different levels of meaning. It is now associated with the deceit, plots and lies, with the murder of the king, the venue where this horror took place, and with the figure of Richard of Gloucester who, through this murderous acts, would eventually become Richard the Third (the hunchback king, who would later serve as one of Kraus's theatrical figurations of the First World War, and was also the demonic alter-persona of Kraus himself). *Turm* holds in it a world of stored associations and possibilities that unwrap themselves out through its utterance. It is not an empty signifier on the one hand, nor linguistic content in the usual sense on the other, but a collection of possibilities that trigger associations of thought and action.

Thus, Kraus finds in Shakespeare's theater a space of creativity through the void that the speech opens, a speech which is a deferral or refrains from representation.[11] It hides what it is supposed to deliver and at the same time seems to express too much (*ungeheuer*). This is exactly the kind of speech act that John Austin considered as parasitic, hollow and ill.[12] It is the illness or feeling of decay that Lord Chandos in Hofmannsthal's story sensed but could not cope with.[13] For Kraus, this illness or void is highly crucial. It has to do with the power of sovereignty and political violence, and is at the same time what defines art and literature.

---

[11] Werner Kraft noted: "Why is the end of 'Iphigenia' so great? Because the deep emotional struggle of King Thomas is not represented here, but rather to the extent sealed in a word of farewell." Werner Kraft, *Das Ja des Neinsagers* (München: edition text u. kritik, 1974), p. 82 (my translation).
[12] In Austin's words: "(. . .) as *utterances* our performances are also heir to certain other kinds of ill, which infect *all* utterances (. . .) language in such circumstances is in special ways – intelligibly – used not seriously, but in many ways parasitic upon its normal use – ways which fall under the doctrine of the etiolations of language. All this we are excluding from consideration. Our performative utterances, felicitous or not, are to be understood as issued in ordinary circumstances." See: *Deconstruction: critical concepts in literary and cultural studies*, Volume 1, edited by Jonathan D. Culler (London: Routledge, 2003), p. 238–239.
[13] It is important to note that Hofmannsthal's Chandos letter is dated to 1603, the year of the death of Queen Elizabeth I and the times when Shakespeare wrote Hamlet. Both he and Kraus turn to this period when they confront the crisis of language.

This example – which, as mentioned, refers to a 'foreign' text (Shakespeare) as paradigm – reveals that every *Wortgestalt* relies on a logic of citation. Alexander Gelley wrote about the concept of citation in Kraus and Walter Benjamin that:

> Citation underscores an activating moment, the emergence of a new affectivity of what is being cited, whether it be a word or a historical moment . . . citing involves not only retrieval of a text or concept, but intervention into the temporal process, the activation of a past in the present: citing as *inciting*.[14]

This explanation can also be applied to Kraus's *Wortgestalt*, and the way he suggests to think about the *Turm* not only as an example for creating and shaping but as a way of introducing the seventeenth century drama of sovereignty into twentieth century Vienna. The many Shakespeare quotations found throughout Kraus's writings reveal that time is, indeed, 'out of joint.' Whereas for Hofmannsthal's *Lord Chandos* quotation represented repetition and return of the same, provoking an over-determinate speech, Kraus turns the quotation itself from content to form, from reference to a static, past context to a dynamic movement between past and present, an utterance that estranges itself. The staging of the utterance, its medium of theatricality, provides the hollow space, the void, the suspension, that, although it appears just for a moment, transforms the logic of time and creates interruption and rupture in it.

For Kraus, the Third Reich brought modernity's impasse to an extreme. It was not new in its quality, but the extent of its disruptive power had a different social impact. This was for Kraus not a moment of paralysis or despair, but the moment when he theorized and formulated his critique of language in the most profound way. Reading the literary works, the theatrical citations and the analogies provides a different mode of moral position, and an alternative way of calling for justice. In the face of what he viewed as the political conscription of the demonic force of myth, and again: not violence as a means to an end but how it itself becomes the political action – Kraus evokes language (in a cultural mediative field) against discourse as a manipulative strategy of control. This is what Kraus calls: 'non-rational socialism.' Coincidingly, Kraus translates, or more precisely, adapts Shakespeare's sonnets with the intention of enabling a different future to develop after the impending catastrophe passes.

To conclude, I proposed several contemporary insights, which Kraus, had he been perhaps a current day critical blogger, could have contributed, and discuss how his approach can provoke thought and provide inspiration for those who wish

---

**14** Alexander Gelley, *"Epigones in the House of Language: Benjamin on Kraus"*, in: *Partial Answers: Journal of Literature and the History of Ideas* (Vl. 5, Nr. 1, January 2007), p. 25.

to engage in social and moral criticism at times of liberal crisis, war, and new forms of nihilism. Kraus does not offer solutions, but he certainly points to the terms and myths of criticism, and to the depository of the good intentions of too-radical or not-daring-enough social philosophers. Again, the issue is not simply that totalitarian regimes do not 'respect' human rights, but that they operate with a different normative premise: one that, even if it does not completely empty notions like liberalism, citizenship, democracy, equality, and so forth, clearly redefines them. What is rejected by such regimes (and by this I do not mean to suggest they are all one and the same: what we are seeing today is not, simply speaking, 'fascism') is not the content of ideas such as 'all humans are born equal,' but the very meaning of what is 'human' – which, as Hitler had it, needs to undergo not a *revolution* but an *evolution*. My suggestion is therefore to read DW as pointing, first, to these conflicting notions of moral grammar. And, second, perhaps more importantly, pointing to the *limits* of the liberal approach in providing a critical position *against* these attacks. As I shall try to explain, this is not exactly to say that liberalism is 'wrong,' but rather that it proves itself *insufficient* when put under such attacks.

Thus, one should not be too quick in drawing a dichotomy between a just, liberal society on the one hand and an unjust, violent totalitarian one on the other. Unlike the way he is often portrayed, this is not what Kraus had in mind. His point is not that national socialism *hijacked* the *Weimar Republic*, but that the contradictions within the liberal order itself and its own failures of coming to terms with them – *Hüben und Drüben* [Here and There] – contributed significantly to the success of such a violent and criminal regime. By not coming to terms with these internal tensions within liberal ideology (and Kraus provides many such examples throughout his *Fackel*), and by leaving notions such as *freedom* and *democracy* as empty slogans without reflection (which is what he accuses the Social Democrats of doing), it is impossible to block and defeat those counter-movements that are built on a *ressentiment* that is bred by and from within the existing order. (And one doesn't have to go too far to see the relevance of these questions for understanding the electoral results of recent years in Europe, the US, and elsewhere, not to mention the ghost of the Weimar Republic appearing in the current failure to build a government in Germany for the first time since 1930). This is the point where I believe we need to read Kraus together with other thinkers like those I mentioned. To read him not as a humanist fighting a liberal cause (which, I stress again, does not equal the simplistic view that 'liberalism is bad'), but as an immanent-critic (as

Adorno defined him[15]) who believes that the critique of national socialism must relate to the story of the enlightenment, to the institutions of the liberal society, to its alleged culture, morals and literary canon.

## References

Culler, Jonathan D. (Ed.). *Deconstruction: critical concepts in literary and cultural studies*, Volume 1. London: Routledge, 2003.

Djassemy, Irina. *Der "Productivgehalt kritischer Zerstörerarbeit": Kulturkritik bei Karl Kraus und Theodor W. Adorno*. Würzburg: Königshausen & Neuman, 2002.

Dreidemy, Lucile. "Ein leuchtend Zwerglein ! – Karl Kraus' Bewunderung für Österreichs Diktator Engelbert Dollfuß." *Geist versus Zeitgeist – Karl Kraus in der Ersten Republik*. Ed. Katharina Prager. Wien: Metroverlag, 2018, 86–99.

Gelley, Alexander. "Epigones in the House of Language: Benjamin on Kraus." *Partial Answers: Journal of Literature and the History of Ideas* Vl. 5, Nr. 1 (January 2007): 17–32.

Kraft, Werner. *Das Ja des Neinsagers*. München: Edition Text u. Kritik, 1974.

Kraus, Karl. *Die Sprache*. Frankfurt a. M.: Suhrkamp Verlag, 1987.

Kraus, Karl. *Dritte Walpurgisnacht*. Nach der von Heinrich Fischer herausgegebenen Fassung, München: Kösel, 1967, Satz: Wolfgang Hink. Berlin, 2010.

Linden, A. "'Wo Ungesetz gesetzlich überwaltet': Karl Kraus's Reading of National Socialism." *Oxford German Studies* 46(1) (2017): 75–91.

Matar, Anat. *The Poverty of Ethics*. London and New York: Verso, 2022.

Wittgenstein, Ludwig. *Culture and Value*, trans. Peter Winch. Oxford: Blackwell, 1970.

---

15 Adorno's views on Kraus are beautifully articulated and analyzed by Irina Djassemy, see: *Productivgehalt kritischer Zerstörerarbeit* Kulturkritik bei Karl Kraus und Theodor W. Adorno: Der „Productivgehalt kritischer Zerstörerarbeit": Kulturkritik bei Karl Kraus und Theodor W. Adorno (Würzburg: Königshausen & Neuman, 2002).

António Sousa Ribeiro
# Kraus's Poetics of Quotation in Times of Despair

*Dritte Walpurgisnacht*, Kraus's almost immediate reaction to the *Machtergreifung*, remains probably the most complex and, at the same time, most controversial and, one can certainly say, most misunderstood text by Karl Kraus. As Michael Scharang once wrote, "there are probably few sentences, that have been so maliciously taken out of context to be used against its author"[1] as the famous initial statement, "Mir fällt zu Hitler nichts ein". Since *Dritte Walpurgisnacht* also is one of the most ignored of all masterpieces in German-language literature I do not think, however, that malicious intent suffices as an explanation. There is more to it: the true question is that an adequate understanding of this most difficult text would not only require reading the over 300 pages that follow that sentence and in the course of which Kraus certainly could think of a lot to say about Hitler, one has also to be knowledgeable about the polemic and satiric strategies governing the whole of Kraus's oeuvre, especially under the perspective of their essential definition as a poetics of quotation.[2] The demand, repeatedly raised by Kraus, that, in order to be properly understood, his texts should not be read in isolation certainly applies in a very concrete way to *Dritte Walpurgisnacht*. In the following, I will approach some central issues in the text, keeping in mind how it does not represent a real departure from Kraus's well-proven satiric and polemical method, but, rather, under the brutal impact of the Nazi seizure of power, simply a paroxystic extension of that method.

It should not be disregarded that the famous, often misquoted sentence "Mir fällt zu Hitler nichts ein" is not the actual beginning of the text – Heinrich Fischer's edition of 1952, which omits the epigraph, is certainly responsible for this misleading assumption. In this sense, we are not dealing here with an initial sentence: the true beginning is, instead, the extensive collage of fragments from Goethe's *Faust*, setting the scene for the extended polemics that follows in ways I will be later commenting upon. Only after three pages do we actually come to hear the author's own voice. The fact that this voice emerges as it were from the Faustian universe powerfully conjured up at the beginning adds decisively to the meaning of the sen-

---
1 Michael Scharang, "Zur Dritten Walpurgisnacht," *Literatur und Kritik* n° 213/214 (1987): 153. Unless otherwise specified, translations are my own.
2 See António Sousa Ribeiro, "Karl Kraus e Shakespeare – Uma poética da citação" [*Karl Kraus and Shakespeare – A Poetics of Quotation*] (PhD diss., University of Coimbra, 1991).

tence. "Mir fällt zu Hitler nichts ein" contains, in itself, a justification for the use and the function of the opening quotation – as if the *Faust* quotation would have occupied the space brought about by the silence of the satirist, while, at the same time, providing and, indeed, fuelling the energy that is necessary for that silence to be overcome. At the same time, as so often in Kraus, the emergence of the authorial voice is framed by a performative gesture that should not go unnoticed. It seems to me quite evident, although, if I am correct, it has not often been duly pointed out, that the anteposition of the personal pronoun is aimed at highlighting the singularity of the author's position, providing a sharp demarcation against other positions in the anti-Nazi public sphere – "*Mir* fällt zu Hitler nichts ein", i.e., contrary to so many others, who seem to have a lot to say about Hitler, I can think of nothing to say. At the same time, the sentence, while rigorously defining the horizon of expectation that the following 300 hundred pages will allow, also points at a genre definition: the reader should not expect satire and the "Einfälle" that are characteristic of satiric discourse; he will, instead, be offered a polemical essay based on a wealth of documentary material.

Now, the gesture of demarcation, characteristic, in Edward Timms's words, of Kraus's stance of "embattled isolation,"[3] is quintessential to the building of the mask of the satirist along the many thousands of pages of *Die Fackel*. Under this light, one could trace the initial gesture of *Dritte Walpurgisnacht* back to the first salient occurrence of Kraus's polemic against his own audience: the text "Apokalypse", published in 1908. In this text, in which, it may be recalled, Kraus announces the imminent end of the publication of *Die Fackel*, one could read passages like the following:

> What can a satirist do, faced with a mechanism to which, anyway, a roar of scornful laughter from hell responds every hour? He can hear, while the others are deaf. But if he himself is not heard? And if he himself becomes scared? (F261–62: 7)[4]

In this important text, the reflection on the precariousness of, and the ultimate impotence of satire casts a long shadow over the very possibility of a satirical enterprise like the publication of *Die Fackel*. Such a reflection on the possibilities and the limits of satire, which is in the end coterminous with the reflection on the possibilities and limits of language itself, is present from very early on in the

---

[3] Timms, Edward, *Karl Kraus Apocalyptic Satirist. Culture and Catastrophe in Habsburg Vienna* (New Haven: Yale University Press, 1986).

[4] "Was vermag nun ein Satirenschreiber vor einem Getriebe, dem ohnedies in jeder Stunde ein Hohngelächter der Hölle antwortet? Er vermag es zu hören, dieweil die anderen taub sind. Aber wenn er nicht gehört wird? Und wenn ihm selbst bange wird?" References to *Die Fackel* are given in the text in abridged form with the initial F followed by mention of the issue number.

pages of Kraus's journal and represents a problem that is central for the self-definition of the position of the satirist. It is well-known how the eruption of the First World War dramatically radicalized that reflection. In the speech "In dieser großen Zeit", from November 1914, silence as a gesture is the rhetorical focal point structuring the whole of the text. Amidst the cacophonic concert of those voices dominating the public sphere with nationalistic and chauvinistic discourses and slogans, the only solution seems to be the one presented by Kraus in the initial part of his text: "Expect no words of my own from me. [. . .] Let him who has something to say come forward and be silent!"[5] In the poem "Man frage nicht," written in 1933, this same attitude is clearly expressed: "Ich bleibe stumm / und sage nicht, warum", "Wordless am I / And won't say why".[6] One could easily transpose the famous statement of *Dritte Walpurgisnacht* into the context of "In These Great Times". It would then read like this, perhaps: "Mir fällt zum Kriegsausbruch nichts ein". The exact correlation may be further highlighted if we recall one of the very few instances of a sympathetic and understanding reaction to the poem "Man frage nicht", Bertolt Brecht's poem, "On the meaning of the ten-line poem in the issue 888 of *Die Fackel*":

> When the loquacious one asked for forgiveness,
> Because his voice was failing
> Silence approached the judge's bench
> Took the scarf off its face
> And identified itself as a witness.[7]

The fact that, in these lines, silence appears as the central character in a drama situation, more specifically, a tribunal scene, highlights the performative understanding of silence as, literally, a meaningful gesture of public intervention. It is significant that, in a conscious or unconscious manner – one cannot be sure, and it is perhaps even unlikely, that while writing his lines Brecht had in mind "In These Great Times" –Brecht's poem actually projects into the context of the year 1933 the rhetorical figure so effectively used by Kraus in the context of the outbreak of the First World War, thus implicitly stressing the inner consistency of

---

5 Karl Kraus, "In These Great Times," in *In These Great Times*, ed. and trans. Harry Zohn (Manchester: Carcanet, 1984), 71. "Erwarten Sie von mir kein eigenes Wort. [. . .] Wer etwas zu sagen hat, trete vor und schweige!"
6 Zohn, *In These Great Times*, 259.
7 Bertolt Brecht, "Über die Bedeutung des zehnzeiligen Gedichtes in der 888. Nummer der Fackel," in *Werke. Große kommentierte Berliner und Frankfurter Ausgabe*, ed. Werner Hecht *et al.* (Berlin und Weimar: Aufbau; Frankfurt am Main: Suhrkamp, 1993), vol. 14, 197. "Als der Beredte sich entschuldigte, / dass seine Stimme versage / trat das Schweigen vor den Richtertisch / nahm das Tuch vom Antlitz und / gab sich zu erkennen als Zeuge."

the satirist's stance in both historical moments. Under this light, the sentence "Mir fällt to Hitler nichts ein" should not actually have come as a surprise; it simply represents the dramatic radicalization of a problem that had been present throughout the whole of Kraus's satirical career. And, in fact, the very last sentence in the last issue of *Die Fackel*, from February 1936, still insists on the same topic, in the context of Kraus's rejection of the criticism of those who are under the illusion "that the satirist finds something to say about a jaguar as promptly as about a fool" (F917–922: 112).[8]

Of course, one cannot and should not disregard the specificity of the given context. To come back once again to the text "Apocalypse" from 1908, one can find a much-quoted statement:

> The real apocalypse is the destruction of the spirit, the other one depends on the indifferent attempt to ascertain if, after the destruction of the spirit, there can still be a world. (F261–62: 7)[9]

In *Dritte Walpurgisnacht* one can find the ironic sentence "While the apocalypse is happening, I want to withdraw into the private sphere" (DW: 34).[10] It is apparent that the meaning of the word "apocalypse" is not exactly the same in both instances. In 1908, it represented a familiar topos in cultural criticism and remains fundamentally abstract; in 1933, it had acquired a very concrete meaning, pointing at the coming to power of the National-Socialists in Germany. Under this light, "Privatisieren" cannot be taken literally; it does not simply mean to withdraw into a private sphere, it means instead, in its ironic ambiguity, to have to find a different platform to be able to cope with the catastrophic events. As a matter of fact, between 1908 and 1933 a vital development had taken place, leading to that which, having in mind particularly *The Last Days of Mankind*, I have called elsewhere a poetics of compassion intent on exposing the concrete suffering of particular individuals.[11] Particularly in the context of the war, the critical method of "draining the large swamp of the commonplaces"[12] put forward in the very first issue of the journal (F1: 2), the method of discourse critique, came unmistakably to be increasingly aimed at the problematization of the uses of language that

---

8 "[. . .] "dass dem Satiriker zu einem Jaguar so schnell etwas einfällt wie zu einem Trottel".
9 "Der wahre Weltuntergang ist die Vernichtung des Geistes, der andere hängt von dem gleichgiltigen Versuch ab, ob nach Vernichtung des Geistes noch eine Welt bestehen kann."
10 Quotations from *Dritte Walpurgisnacht* are given in the text in abridged form. They are taken from Karl Kraus, *Dritte Walpurgisnacht*, ed. Christian Wagenknecht (Frankfurt am Main: Suhrkamp, 1989). "Beim Weltuntergang will ich privatisieren."
11 Ribeiro, António Sousa. "Uma estética da compaixão. A Primeira Guerra Mundial na literatura europeia.", in M. C. Carvalho et al. (eds.), *Concordância e diferença*. Coimbra: Instituto de Estudos Filosóficos, 2024, 277–290.
12 "Trockenlegung des weiten Phrasensumpfes".

make invisible the concrete suffering of individuals. In the documentary detail that provides the basis to the sustained polemic carried out throughout the text, *Dritte Walpurgisnacht* builds the logic conclusion of this method, while, at the same time, highlighting its very precariousness. Drawing on perceptions that had been developed at length e.g. in the essay "Brot und Lüge", "Bread and Lie", of 1919 (F519–520: 1–32), compassion with the innocent victim of violence is a main driving force behind the whole of the 1933 polemics. "[. . .] that the last private existence as a victim of violence is nearer to the spirit than the whole bankrupt commerce of the intellect"[13] (DW: 113–114) is a central assumption in this context. Accordingly, the crucial issue comes to be formulated as follows: "That death, no longer a simple cliché, is the first and last reality offered by political life – how could this experience become creative?"[14] (DWN: 33). The answer to this central question had been provided right at the start: "To express what has happened, language can only repeat it in stammering words"[15] (DW: 16): in the face of the monstrous dimension of the events, language has to resort to a logic of repetition, articulating itself through the use of quotation. This is how in the end it may find the means to address unheard of patterns of violence, thus questioning and finally overcoming the initial reduction to silence – also in the sense that silence does not simply disappear but remains present throughout as an open question and a fundamental interpellation.

In his essay on Karl Kraus, Walter Benjamin defines the practice of quotation of the satirist as a silence in reverse, "ein gewendetes Schweigen", thus pointing to the close intertwining of language and silence in the discourse of *Die Fackel*.[16] In 1929, Kraus vindicated for himself the at first sight oxymoronic title of the "creator of quotation", or even, the inventor of quotation, boasting of being „der Schöpfer des Zitats" (F800–805: 2). "The art of language consists in dropping the quotation marks, in committing plagiarism with the suitable fact, in the gesture that transforms its cutting into a work of art"[17] (F800–805: 2). Elias Canetti once referred to "the strangest of all paradoxes: this man, who hated so much [. . .] let

---

13 "[. . .] dass die letzte Privatexistenz als Gewaltopfer dem Geist näher steht als alles runierte Geistgschäft".
14 "Dass der Tod, dem Schlagwort entbunden, die erste und letzte Wirklichkeit ist, die das politische Leben gewährt – wie würde dies Erlebnis schöpferisch?".
15 "Um zu sagen, was geschah, kann es die Sprache nur stammelnd nachsprechen."
16 Walter Benjamin, "Karl Kraus," in *Gesammelte Schriften*, ed. Rolf Tiedemann and Hermann Schweppenhäuser (Frankfurt am Main: Suhrkamp, 1980), vol. 4, 338.
17 "Die Sprachkunst besteht da in der Weglassung der Anführungszeichen, in dem Plagiat an der tauglichen Tatsache, in dem Griff, der ihren Ausschnitt zum Kunstwerk verwandelt."

*everyone*'s voices be heard".[18] This is why, to my view, the characterization of Kraus's writing as a poetics of quotation is so much to the point. Indeed, Bakhtin's concept of dialogism offers the most suitable framework for an analysis of the interdiscursive dynamics alluded to by Canetti. In the sense of Bakhtin's category, we are dealing with the clashing of ideological, discursive levels that are, at least in part, incompatible. In this sense, 'double coding', following the definition Renate Lachmann in turn draws from Bakhtin,[19] is the fundamental mark of dialogism; it will not be difficult to recognize this 'double coding' as a defining feature of Kraus' s discourse, which recurrently emphasizes the pre-marked and pre-structured nature of its material as a central device. In other words, if it is to be effective, the authority of the satirist has to assert itself not in the terrain of abstract ideas and principles, but through a permanent confrontation on the concrete ground of the multiple utterances that compose the whole universe of public discourse of its time, and it has to prove its effectiveness through the successful appropriation of those utterances, as the true cannibal which, in Benjamin's famous phrase, the satirist is. So it is that Kraus's satire is full of voices, it is intrinsically dialogic. This implies that the recurrent use of documentary quotation does not simply fulfil the function of making available a set of references and naming the exact source for Kraus's polemic and satiric indignation; more than that, it has a profoundly dramatic function, in that it provides his essays with a dynamic contrapuntal structure made of the clash of conflicting voices that has often more to do with the theatre than with the conventions of essayistic discourse. Kraus's approach to the scene of writing thus acquires a distinctly performative character, in that his use of language does not rest on the assumption of a pre-established meaning, but, instead, on the dialogic, polyphonic dynamics of a discursive space where a multitude of conflicting voices keeps reverberating.

This is exactly the method that has a constitutive significance for *Dritte Walpurgisnacht*. In one of his many enlightening essays, the late Kurt Krolop has put forward the suggestion that Kraus's aesthetics should be understood as a kind of "Materialästhetik".[20] In this sense, there is nothing that cannot be said if an existent utterance is incorporated within a discursive context that makes it speak. In an aphorism of 1911 directed against Max Brod, Kraus writes: "Because what is essen-

---

[18] Canetti, Elias, "Karl Kraus. Schule des Widerstands," in *Das Gewissen der Worte* (Frankfurt am Main: Fischer, 1982), 46. "Es war das Sonderbarste aller Paradoxe: dieser Mann, der so viel verachtete [. . .] ließ *alle* zu Worte kommen."
[19] Lachmann, Renate, "Ebenen des Intertextualitätsbegriffs," in *Das Gespräch*, ed. Karlheinz Stierle and Rainer Warning (München: Fink, 1984).
[20] Krolop, Kurt, "Ästhetische Kritik als Kritik der Ästhetik," in *Reflexionen der Fackel. Neue Studien über Karl Kraus* (Wien: Verlag der Österreichischen Akademie der Wissenschaften, 1994).

tial is the atmosphere in which a word breathes, and, in a bad atmosphere, even a word by Shakespeare is bound to die"[21] (F326–27: 35–36). Under this light, the work of quotation is not qualitatively different from the work of language, since the language artist, "the servant of the word", has to deal in any case with existent material, the vital move being to provide the "good atmosphere" that will make it resonate, i.e. the new discursive context governed by the interplay between the authorial voice and the many voices it brings into its verbal universe. In his important book *La seconde main ou le travail de la citation*, Antoine Compagnon makes the fundamental statement that the meaning of a quotation is not the meaning of an utterance, but the meaning of the repetition of an utterance.[22] In Wittgenstein's terms, this is tantamount to defining the act of quotation not as a way of saying, but of showing. In other words: that which cannot be said need not remain silenced; it can be quoted. Under this light, "stammelnd nachsprechen", "to repeat in stammering words", is all that is left for the satirist to do, as one can read in the initial pages of *Dritte Walpurgisnacht*, which stress the precarious nature of the role of quotation as the main principle of composition of the text that is to follow. Yet this gesture also implies the affirmation of the power of the satirist, who once again will be able to demonstrate the potential of his strategy of silence-in-action through a work of language based on intertextual reference.

The political analysis of National-Socialism presented by *Dritte Walpurgisnacht* is in many respects clear-sighted. It is impressive that, although stressing continuity and the connection to the political constellation of the 20s, Kraus is alert to the essentially new quality of the National Socialist movement. In particular, the perception of the modernity of Nazism, as a modern form of political domination, as the "simultaneity of electrotechnics and myth, destruction of the atom and burning stake"[23] (DWN: 34) should be highlighted as a ground-breaking insight. The development of Kraus's argument is grounded in an impressive array of quotations from very different sources, which build a fundamental documentation of the new situation in Nazi Germany. However, a close analysis of the ways in which the documentary material is appropriated as one of the essential layers in the composition of the text provides, to my view, the most incisive demonstration that the commonplace distinction, drawn from Benjamin's Kraus essay, between "strafendes und rettendes Zitat" – a negative-punitive and a positive-utopian use of quotation – is not in a position to address the complexity of the dialogic nature of Kraus's polemic and satiric discourse in an adequate manner. Of course, the documentary quotation

---

21 "Denn es kommt auf die Luft an, in der ein Wort atmet, und in schlechter Luft krepiert selbst eines von Shakespeare."
22 Antoine Compagnon, *La seconde main ou le travail de la citation* (Paris: Seuil, 1979), 86.
23 „Gleichzeitigkeit von Elektrotechnik und Mythos, Atomzertrümmerung und Scheiterhaufen".

establishes a direct connection to current events, providing in sometimes astonishing detail an exact picture of the new situation. As a fundamental textual layer, it provides factual justification for the development of Kraus's argument. It is indeed remarkable to what extent Kraus is able to document censorship, propaganda, torture, political assassination, persecution of the Jews, and random violence as defining the German state of exception. The text provides in this regard a continuation and radicalization of the critique of violence and of the violent use of language of the "troglodytes" that had been conducted in *Die Fackel* for several years already. Incidentally, this is also an aspect containing multiple connections to the use of documentary material in the *Kriegsfackel* and *The Last Days of Mankind*. Sometimes, those connections are quite literal: to provide just one example among others, the phrase "every cliché a hand grenade"[24] (DW: 71) of 1933 brings inevitably to mind a passage in "In these Great Times" which reads: "The newspaper dispatch is an instrument of war like a grenade, which has no consideration for circumstances either."[25] In general, the implicit or explicit connection to Kraus's own war writings is repeatedly present in the text of 1933, including through self-quotation, in contexts where the meaning of the allusion is made clear by that text itself. Consider another example: "Well, is it so that all motives of the war times come to life since the bullet went out through the other ear of humankind?"[26] (DW: 74).

The documentary quotation is of evident significance as the basis of polemical commentary, which is at the same time triggered and underpinned by it. A close analysis would, however, also pay special attention to the overall literary form of the composition. The interplay between the authorial voice and the quoted fragments, the foreign body that is *incorporated* in different ways, provides a variety of rhetorical effects that have in common the kind of semantic explosion that is characteristic of dialogic discourse. In retrospect, following a line of thought that is omnipresent in his reflections on the misreading of his writings by an audience that, to his view, is unable or unwilling to understand the specificities of an aesthetic use of language, Kraus would name his fear that his text could be understood as a mere political pamphlet as one of the reasons for not having published *Dritte Walpurgisnacht*. The literary nature of the composition is overdetermined by the extensive use of literary quotations and allusions from various sources, mainly Goethe, of course, but also Shakespeare and others, including – quite prominently, and perhaps unexpectedly, August von Platen.

---

24 "jedes Schlagwort eine Handgranate".
25 Zohn, *In These Great Times*, 78. "Die Depesche ist ein Kriegsmittel wie die Granate, die auch auf keinen Sachverhalt Rücksicht nimmt".
26 "Ja werden den seit die Kugel der Menschheit beim andern Ohr hinausging, alle Motive der Kriegszeit lebendig?".

This is a textual layer that requires a reader who is particularly alert and who is able to identify not just the source, but also the original context. The meaning of a phrase such as e.g. "The forest of Birnam is approaching",[27] towards the end of *Dritte Walpurgisnacht* (DW: 326), will be lost, if the *Macbeth* allusion is not only identified, but also understood as an announcement of the imminent end of the tragedy, with the fall of the bloodthirsty tyrant.

In the second part of my essay, I would like to concentrate on this textual layer, since resorting to literary memory is an essential component of the strategy that, despite the confrontation with absolute violence, supports the relationship between the authorial self and language in a meaningful way. In this regard, despite everything that is qualitatively new in *Dritte Walpurgisnacht*, Kraus's literary strategy remains essentially in line with the poetics of quotation that he had consolidated for many years as an essential principle of satiric composition. In the essay "Sittlichkeit und Kriminalität", "Public Moral and Criminality" of 1902, one can find the famous sentence "Shakespeare hat alles vorausgewußt", "Shakespeare has foreseen it all" (F115: 3), following an initial montage of quotations from *Measure for Measure* and *King Lear*. This sentence has been interpreted a bit too often, in a rather ludicrous way, in literal terms, as the affirmation of a blind belief in some kind of prophetic vision of the dramatist, nurtured by Kraus's allegedly blind conservative belief in the power of literary tradition. As a matter of fact, one should take that famous sentence not as the proclamation of a solution, but as the formulation of a problem. Approaching Kraus's relation to literary tradition, Kurt Krolop once remarked that the text of tradition is, evidently, not taken by Kraus "as a pre-prophecy, but as pre-satire".[28] In other words, the question is not about some kind of sacral relation to literary tradition, but, rather, its practical deployment in contemporary terms as a strategic weapon of satire. As a verbal utterance firmly placed within cultural memory, the "knowledge" of Shakespeare may build a common ground, literally a commonplace, for the satirist's argument to be articulated and conveyed to an audience, but it does not stand by itself; it is, rather, entirely contingent on its appropriation by the discourse of satire. Under this light, quotation by no means simply implies the transmission of preformed knowledge; knowledge, instead, is that which is produced by the very act of repetition within the new contextual framework. This is the meaning of the allusion in *Dritte Walpurgisnacht*, introducing the quotation of the ironic letter sent by Kraus to the Westdeutscher Rundfunk concerning his trans-

---

27 "Der Birnamwald rückt heran."
28 Kurt Krolop (1987): "Ebenbild und Gegenbild. Goethe und 'Goethes Volk' bei Karl Kraus," in *Sprachsatire als Zeitsatire bei Karl Kraus. Neun Studien* (Berlin: Akademie-Verlag, 1987), 197. "nicht als Vor*verheißung*, sondern als Vor*satire*".

lation of Shakespeare's sonnets, "that in Shakespeare everything that is actual, including my own statement, already appears"[29] (DW: 158).

It is important to keep in mind this essential strategic meaning of the use of literary quotation throughout *Die Fackel* to make sense of the dense intertextual web structuring *Dritte Walpurgisnacht*. One could pinpoint the underlying assumption of this extended polemic by paraphrasing the programmatic sentence of 1902. Yes, "Goethe has foreseen it all". Kraus would write in "Warum die Fackel nicht erscheint", "Why Die Fackel Is not Being Published" (F890–905: 81), that "the most German event – quite worthy of the superlative – is preformed in every respect in a miraculous way in the most German poem."[30] In its sheer abundance of quotations structuring the whole composition of the text, *Dritte Walpurgisnacht* builds the unmistakable climax of Kraus's Goethe reception. The "Third" in the title, while being an evident allusion to the Third Reich, implies, at the same time, that the text presents itself as a kind of sequel to Goethe's drama, as a projection of the Faustian motif into the contemporary situation, in a way that seems as "incommensurate" as its model itself. As already mentioned, it would be misleading, here as elsewhere in Kraus, to interpret the use of literary tradition as simply the search for a positive counterpart to a contemporary situation in the form of a retreat into purely aesthetic values. This is an interpretation that is implied by the first extensive treatment of the topic of Kraus's relation to literary tradition, the book *Das Ja des Neinsagers*, by Werner Kraft. Kraft's title is, indeed, misleading as regards the use of literary quotation by Kraus in general and in *Dritte Walpurgisnacht* in particular. The use of the Goethe matrix signifies the continuation of satire with other means, a continuation which, as I implied in my earlier observations, does not leave that matrix untouched; instead, it becomes itself the object of critical scrutiny. In particular, the topos of violence as a vitalistic, necessary, fateful force and the corresponding notion of history as a senseless nightmare is repeatedly approached through the means of Goethe's text itself, enabling the development of a meaningful correlation between the logics of absolute violence governing the politics of the Third Reich and the Faustian metaphysics of the deed.

The pre-Hellenic, chaotic-apocalyptic world of the classical Walpurgis night presents itself as a space where a reflection on violence can be presented in an exemplary manner as the phantasmagoric chaos inherent to the conflict of elementary forces. The epigraph – the collage of quotations extending over three pages – gives expression to this in a very clear way. The several omissions of orig-

---

29 "dass bei Shakespeare schon alles Aktuelle wie auch meine Stellungnahme vorkomme".
30 "Das deutscheste Ereignis – dem der Superlativ ziemt – ist wunderbarer Weise Zug um Zug im deutschesten Gedicht präformiert."

inal text passages result in a strong compression of the words of the sorcerer Erichtho in the scene "The Fields of Pharsalos". The voice of the timeless mythical figure offers the perspective of a perpetual return of history as a history of violence – "how often has it repeated itself already" (DW: 9). The phantasmagorical setting of the classical night of Walpurgis – also in its occasional grotesque peculiarities – presents itself as the scene of a nightmare, which, by being projected into the present of the year 1933, offers an adequate setting for the presentation of everything that Kraus has to say about Nazism after all. This does not project the present into some mythical distance; on the contrary, the dynamics of intertextual play, the constant, often surprising alternation between literary allusion and documentary connection, presents National-Socialism in both its singularity and its exemplary significance.

There are many examples of this. Let us take the first Goethe quotation in *Dritte Walpurgisnacht* (apart from the epigraph), which refers to the episode of Philemon and Baucis in the 5$^{th}$ act, scene "Palace", of Goethe's drama. The quotation is of the cynical words of Mephisto on the tragic fate of the two old people who, having purportedly been only dislocated to a new home, have in reality been murdered: "a nice new place will reconcile them to any violence they suffer" (DWN: 16).[31] In Kraus's text these words comment cryptically on the fate of those who have been deported to a concentration camp ("it happened overnight; and in every subsequent night you live in expectation"[32] [DW: 16]). The abysmal irony of the application of the allusion to current events is apparent; it is confirmed by the authorial voice, which, at the same time, alludes in retrospect to the way in which, in the drama, Faust's naiveté makes him objectively guilty: "Order starts to reign; if one closes one's ears no more moaning can be heard"[33] (DW: 17). As a matter of fact, the figure of Faust in Kraus's essay is thoroughly ambivalent – among other aspects, his associates, the three thugs Raufebold, Habebald and Haltefest, appear as the incarnation of Nazi henchmen (this is yet another possibility of the literary quotation: the use of characters who, embodying themselves paradigmatic types, instantaneously illuminate the meaning of a contemporary context).

One of the most relevant literary quotations in *Dritte Walpurgisnacht* is not, however, taken from Goethe, but rather from Shakespeare's most apocalyptic drama, *King Lear*, which is one of the main sources of Shakespeare quotations throughout the whole *Die Fackel*. In the initial pages Kraus refers to "the Shake-

---

31 J. W. Goethe, *Faust*, trans. Stuart Atkins (Princeton: Princeton University Press, 2014), 284. "Nach überstandener Gewalt / versöhnt ein schöner Aufenthalt."
32 "Über Nacht geschah es; und jede weitere Nacht lebst du in Erwartung."
33 "Ordnung beginnt zu herrschen; hält man sich die Ohren zu, hört man kein Stöhnen mehr."

spearean formula that combines pain and hope in such a beautiful way"³⁴ (DW: 30); he is referring to Edgar's lines in the 1ˢᵗ scene of the 4ᵗʰ Act, a quotation he used several times, and in which he found expressed a precarious combination of apocalyptic despair and desperate hope:

> O gods! Who is 't can say 'I am at the worst'?
> I am worse than e'er I was.
> And worse I may be yet: the worst is not
> So long as we can say 'This is the worst'.³⁵

It should be noted that the Schlegel-Tieck version used by Kraus dislocates the lines from an allusion to a personal condition ('I am at the worst' / I am worse than e'er I was) to the expression of a general predicament (Gott, wer darf sagen: schlimmer kann's nicht werden'? / 's ist schlimmer nun als je.) (DWN: 30), which certainly suits better Kraus's intentions. In any case, the ambivalence of the interaction between hope and despair in Edgar's lines is entirely based on the tragic consciousness of the possibilities and limits of language: language can give expression to the most terrible extremes of violence, thus demonstrating in the process that the uttermost limits have not yet been fully reached, the limits where there would only be silence and that coincide with the space where absolute violence would have irrevocably asserted itself with no fear of being in any way challenged. At the same time, the quotation feeds implicitly from the hope that it may perhaps never come to the worst, since, in the end, language is able to constitute itself in the process of permanently pushing and dislocating those limits. The quotation from *King Lear* thus has strategic significance for a text in which the question of overcoming silence and the stubborn refusal to leave the last word to naked violence plays a permanent role.

*King Lear* is also the source of other cryptic or non-cryptic quotations in *Dritte Walpurgisnacht*. There is, for example, the central mention: "Gloucester formulated the principle of the *Führer*: 'Tis the time's plague when madmen lead the blind."³⁶ (DW: 282) Or I could refer to another case, which provides a good example of the use not just of pathos, but also of irony, the quotation of the words of the Fool in the 4ᵗʰ scene of the 2ⁿᵈ act, providing literally foolish examples of a world turned upside down (DW: 136). The Fool's eccentric vision, however, which is given prominence in other passages in *Die Fackel*, where the Fool

---

34 "die shakespearesche Formel [. . .], die Schmerz und Trost so schön verbindet."
35 "Gott, wer darf sagen: schlimmer kann's nicht werden'? / 's ist schlimmer nun als je. / Und kann noch schlimmer gehn, 's ist nicht das Schlimmste / Solang man sagen kann: dies ist das Schlimmste."
36 "Gloster ersah das Führerprinzip: 's ist Fluch der Zeit, dass tolle Blinde führen."

and his counterpart, the mad king, appear in several instances as satirical masks, is here a more occasional reference. Indeed, the central place is given to the tragic tone. And here another Shakespearean reference occupies a central position, namely *Macbeth*, the tragedy that plays the most prominent role in Kraus's Shakespeare canon in his last years as, in Kraus's words, "the greatest and, unfortunately, most contemporary of Shakespeare's dramas"[37] (F912–915: 70–71). Frank Leschnitzer recalls a public reading in Prague in April 1933 in which Kraus "jumping suddenly off his chair, in a stronger ton of accusation than ever before and full of confidence, shouted loud Malcolm's words: The night is long that never finds the day!"[38] In *Dritte Walpurgisnacht* the most central quotation from *Macbeth* occurs already near the end, expressing the desperate situation of a country entirely permeated by the rule of violence and invoking the dire situation of each and everyone who, at any given moment, may become the object of that violence:

> Alas, poor country,
> Almost afraid to know itself! It cannot
> Be called our mother, but our grave [. . .][39]
> (DW: 282)

The counterpart to the Lear quotation on the ambiguous relationship between language as a final hope against despair is to be found at the conclusion of Kraus's essay. The already mentioned allusion to *Macbeth* sets the scene by invoking quite forcefully the figure of vengeance and retribution: "The forest of Birnam is approaching" (DW: 326). The crescendo in pathos culminates in a last *Faust* quotation from the civil war scenes in the 4$^{th}$ Act (On a Foothill):

> So let this ghost that's risen up against us,
> that dubs itself the Emperor and claims our lands,
> that calls itself the army's duke, our princes' liege,
> be thrust by my own hand into the underworld!
> (DW: 327)[40]

---

37 "Shakespeares [. . .] größtem | und leider gegenwärtigstem Drama."
38 Leschnitzer, Franz, "Der Fall Karl Kraus (1934–1964), in F. Leschnitzer, *Von Börne zu Leonhard oder Erbübel – Erbgut?* (Rudolstadt: Greifenverlag, 1966), 125. "Jäh aufspringend, anklägerischer als je zuvor und zuversichtlich Malcolms Worte rief: So lang ist keine Nacht / Dass endlich nicht der helle Morgen lacht!"
39 "Das arme Reich / Kennt kaum sich selber mehr. Nicht unsre Mutter / Kann's heißen sondern unser Grab [. . .]".
40 *Faust*, 264. "Sei das Gespenst, das gegen uns erstanden, / Sich Kaiser nennt und Herr von unsern Landen, / Des Heeres Herzog, Lehnsherr unsrer Großen, / Mit eigner Faust ins Totenreich gestoßen!"

This last quotation, as I just mentioned, must be read as a counterpart to the *Lear* quotation in the initial part of the essay. The tone is completely different: it is an affirmative, confident tone. Edward Timms reminds us quite pertinently that these words by the Emperor refer to a secondary action in the drama which does not provide an answer to the central question of the relation between nature, violence, and morality.[41] From this perspective, the use of this final *Faust* quotation would simply express some kind of irrational wishful thinking with no actual foundation in the current course of events. Be that as it may: precisely as wishful thinking, the final quotation in *Dritte Walpurgisnacht* visibly reinforces the confidence in the unbroken possibilities of language. The appropriation of the Emperor's words through the authorial voice has a distinctly performative quality, representing the mobilization of the most primordial core of satire, the figure of the imprecation and the curse. Such a figure is able to bring together simultaneously the inescapable ambiguity of the connection between the impotence of the subject and the power of language, and, at the same time, the assertion of the possibility of survival of the subject in language, which, in the end, constitutes the red thread governing the whole of Kraus's confrontation with National-Socialism.

From a certain perspective, it is hard not to read *Dritte Walpurgisnacht* as the expression of a failure. This, in some sense, it is. And, from our most comfortable retrospective point of view, such a text and those that were yet to follow, in the first place "Warum *Die Fackel* nicht erscheint", may indeed appear as some kind of tragic epilogue to the satirist's career, some sort of "Abgesang". However: right at the start of that amazing tour de force entitled *Dritte Walpurgisnacht*, one can read that the Nazi dictatorship has everything under control except language. I tend to read this allusion to "eine Diktatur, die heute alles beherrscht außer der Sprache" (DW: 13) not just as a relatively obvious ironic reference to the notoriously clumsy command of German by many Nazi dignitaries, but also as an expression of hope, hope in the survival of language and, concomitantly, of the humanity of the human being in dark times. If the experience of absolute violence appears to suffocate the voice of a satirist who feels stunned on the head by the course of events, salvation lies not in silence, but in the intertextual play the satirist proves able to mobilize, drawing from the energy of his masterful verbal virtuosity and his intimacy with the manifold verbal material that constitutes the solid foundation of his textual composition, thus demonstrating once again that that which cannot be said does not have to be silenced. Albeit in a most precarious manner, literary writing thus proves able to fulfil yet again its most essential, paradoxical role of naming the unnameable.

---

41 Timms, Edward, *Karl Kraus, Apocalyptic Satirist. The Postwar Crisis and the Rise of the Swastika* (New Haven: Yale University Press, 2005), 507.

# References

Benjamin, Walter. "Karl Kraus." *Gesammelte Schriften*. Ed. Rolf Tiedemann and Hermann Schweppenhäuser, vol. 4. Frankfurt am Main: Suhrkamp, 1980. 334–367.

Brecht, Bertolt. "Über die Bedeutung des zehnzeiligen Gedichtes in der 888. Nummer der Fackel," *Werke. Große kommentierte Berliner und Frankfurter Ausgabe*. Ed. Werner Hecht et al., vol. 14. Berlin und Weimar: Aufbau; Frankfurt am Main: Suhrkamp, 1993.

Canetti, Elias. "Karl Kraus. Schule des Widerstands." E. Canetti, *Das Gewissen der Worte*. Frankfurt am Main: Fischer, 1982. 42–53.

Compagnon, Antoine. *La seconde main ou le travail de la citation*. Paris: Seuil, 1979.

Goethe, J. W. *Faust*. Trans. Stuart Atkins. Princeton: Princeton University Press, 2014.

Kraft, Werner. *Das Ja des Neinsagers. Karl Kraus und seine geistige Welt*. München: Text+Kritik, 1974.

Kraus, Karl. *In These Great Times*. Trans. Harry Zohn. Manchester: Carcanet, 1984.

Kraus, Karl. *Dritte Walpurgisnacht*. Ed. Christian Wagenknecht. Frankfurt am Main: Suhrkamp, 1989.

Krolop, Kurt. "Ebenbild und Gegenbild. Goethe und 'Goethes Volk' bei Karl Kraus." *Sprachsatire als Zeitsatire bei Karl Kraus. Neun Studien*. Berlin: Akademie-Verlag, 1987. 192–209.

Krolop, Kurt, "Ästhetische Kritik als Kritik der Ästhetik." *Reflexionen der Fackel. Neue Studien über Karl Kraus*. Wien: Verlag der Österreichischen Akademie der Wissenschaften. 53–71.

Lachmann, Renate. "Ebenen des Intertextualitätsbegriffs." *Das Gespräch*. Ed. Karlheinz Stierle und Rainer Warning. München: Fink, 1984. 133–163.

Leschnitzer, Franz. "Der Fall Karl Kraus (1934–1964)." *Von Börne zu Leonhard oder Erbübel – Erbgut?*. Rudolstadt: Greifenverlag, 1966. 88–131.

Ribeiro, António Sousa. "Karl Kraus e Shakespeare. Uma poética da citação". PhD diss., University of Coimbra, 1991.

Ribeiro, António Sousa. "Uma estética da compaixão. A Primeira Guerra Mundial na literatura europeia.", in M. C. Carvalho et al. (eds.), *Concordância e diferença*. Coimbra: Instituto de Estudos Filosóficos, 2024, 277–290.

Scharang, Michael. "Zur Dritten Walpurgisnacht," *Literatur und Kritik* n° 213/214 (1987): 152–156.

Timms, Edward. *Karl Kraus Apocalyptic Satirist. Culture and Catastrophe in Habsburg Vienna*. New Haven: Yale University Press, 1986.

Timms, Edward. *Karl Kraus, Apocalyptic Satirist. The Postwar Crisis and the Rise of the Swastika*. New Haven: Yale University Press, 2005.

Ari Linden
# Jargon, Journalism, and Heideggerese: Adorno and Kraus

Worte können sein wie winzige Arsendosen: sie werden unbemerkt verschluckt, sie scheinen keine Wirkung zu tun, und nach einiger Zeit ist die Giftwirkung doch da.[1]

While Kraus perceived the phenomenon early, he was not alone in devoting significant attention to the perversions of language under the National Socialist regime. Indeed, linguistic critiques of National Socialist ideology – or "language critique as ideology critique" – can be identified in the work of other German-Jewish writers of both the pre- and postwar eras.[2] Victor Klemperer's *LTI – Notizbuch eines Philologen* (1947), an impassioned and, at times, potently satirical critique of the transformation and decay of language under the Third Reich, provides one such example of this phenomenon. Told from a first-hand perspective, Klemperer's study examines common abbreviations, phrases, words, and metaphors employed wittingly and unwittingly by the Nazis for the purpose of obscuring the destructive ends of this regime, for emboldening acts of violence by disguising them as acts of heroism.[3] Even the title of Klemperer's work – "*LTI*" ("*Lingua Tertii Imperii*") – functions as a parody of the Nazi predilection for both abbreviations and self-aggrandizement.[4] Hannah Arendt's seminal work of 1963, *Eichmann in Jerusalem: A Report on the Banality of Evil*, also draws attention to the language of the regime by focusing on the utterances of one of its most infamous functionaries. "Officialese" (*Amtssprache*), Arendt writes, is the language spoken by Eichmann, and it "became his language because he was genuinely incapable of uttering a single sentence that was not a cliché."[5] On the one hand, this is a characterization *in*

---

[1] Viktor Klemperer, *LTI: Notizbuch eines Philologen*. Leipzig: Reclam, 21.
[2] The quoted phrase is derived from the title of the volume *Sprachkritik als Ideologiekritik: Studien zu Adornos* Jargon der Eigentlichkeit, eds. Max Beck and Nicholas Coomann, Würzburg: Königshausen & Neumann 2015.
[3] Klemperer devotes one chapter, for example – "Boxen" – to the way sports metaphors seamlessly migrated to the domain of war: "Im Dritten Reich legt man es stark auf die Verdeckung dieses Unterschieds [zwischen Sportspiel und blutigem Kriegernst] an." *LTI*, 244.
[4] Anne Peiter's *Komik und Gewalt* is one of the few works of scholarship that devotes one full chapter to the relationship between Kraus and Klemperer, focusing on the interconnectedness of comedy and violence in these respective critiques of Nazi discourse. See Peiter, *Komik und Gewalt: Zur literarischen Verarbeitung der beiden Weltkriege und der Shoah*, Vienna: Böhlau 2017, 143–210.
[5] Hannah Arendt, *Eichmann in Jerusalem: A Report on the Banality of Evil*, New York: Penguin 2006, 48.

*nuce* of Eichmann's problem: he could not *think* on his own, which means he could not speak on his own.⁶ But more broadly, Arendt points to an entire linguistic apparatus, a system of "language rules" that both obscured the brutal reality of the situations or events to which they referred (in the use of terms such as "resettlement," "evacuation," and "special treatment") and lent these actions or processes a certain legitimacy.⁷ The fantasy could be sustained, Arendt implies, as long as the language informing it remained internally consistent.

While both Klemperer and Arendt merit a study of their own (in conjunction with Kraus), the focus of this essay will be on the language critique of the Frankfurt School critical theorist Theodor Adorno, whose work has a more direct, but often unacknowledged relationship to Kraus.⁸ More specifically, I will argue that Adorno's late essay, *Jargon der Eigentlichkeit* (1964), contains profound resonances with Kraus's *Dritte Walpurgisnacht* in view of the broader discursive context of National Socialist rhetoric and ideology. While the importance of Kraus for Adorno has been documented, the relationship between their texts – and these two in particular – has received relatively little scholarly attention.⁹ This relationship was, to be sure, one-directional: there was no actual dialogue between the two figures as Kraus never wrote on, to, or about Adorno. This one-directionality might partially explain why there have been only two comprehensive studies of this relationship to date, both by Irina Djassemy.¹⁰ One of Djassemy's essential claims – which I will both substantiate and complicate – is that Kraus's approach to Nazi society "'ahnt' mehr, als

---

6 For more on this topic see Martin Shuster, "Hannah Arendt on the evil of not being a person," in *Philosophy Compass*, July 2018, Vol. 13:7, 1–13.

7 Arendt, 85.

8 For a comparative analysis of Kraus and Arendt, see Björn Quiring's essay in this volume, "'A Contest Between Words and Deeds': Karl Kraus and Hannah Arendt on Proto-totalitarian 'Wahrlügen.'"

9 *Taking on the Stigma of Authenticity: Adorno's Critique of Genuineness* tendencies in both his writing and his theory/critique of (in)authenticity, for example, does not mention Kraus once, even though the satirist figures largely in Adorno's discussions of the polysemious notion of mimesis. See Jay, "Taking on the Stigma of Inauthenticity: Adorno's Critique of Genuineness," *New German Critique* Vol. 33:1 (97) 2006, 9–21. When Adorno and Kraus are brought together, it is usually in the context of Kraus's influence on Adorno's (and other prominent German Jewish intellectuals') reception of Heinrich Heine, encapsulated succinctly in Adorno's essay, *Die Wunde Heine*. See, for example, Ulrich Plass, *Language and History in Adorno's* Notes to Literature, Abingdon: Routledge 2012, 115–52, and Peter Hohendahl, *Prismatic Thought: Theodor W. Adorno*, Lincoln: University of Nebraska Press 1995, 105–117.

10 See Djassemy, *Der "Produktivgehalt kritischer Zerstörerarbeit": Kulturkritik bei Karl Kraus und Theodor W. Adorno*, Würzburg: Königshausen & Neumann 2002 and *Die verfolgende Unschuld: Zur Geschichte des autoritären Charakters in der Darstellung von Karl Kraus*, Vienna: Böhlau 2011. The former entails a detailed and considered analysis of this relationship; the latter focuses on the way

sie auf den Begriff zu bringen vermag, legt damit aber ein für eine Deutung im Sinne Adornos äußerst fruchtbares literarisches Zeugnis ab."[11] This is another way of stating that Kraus was not a speculative, sociological, or otherwise philosophical thinker, that his insights regarding fascism, the "culture industry," and the "dialectic of Enlightenment" tend to be phrased in the form of satirical pointes, aphorisms, and allusions, many of which resist seamless translation into discursive or conceptual language.[12] Nevertheless, it could be argued that Kraus's texts constitute the most concrete articulation of what Richard Schuberth calls an Adornian "Guerillakampf [. . .] gegen die Verdinglichung des Denkens."[13]

It is worth lingering on Schuberth's use of "reification" considering my own attempt to first investigate the Krausian inheritance within, and influence on Adorno's most sustained critique of pseudo-philosophical language and its relationship to fascist ideology. Adorno's critique of jargon – rooted in his philosophy of language – is, as we will see, inseparable from his critique of fascism. But Adorno's critique of jargon also illuminates what is at stake in Kraus's engagement with National Socialist rhetoric and its relationship to journalistic discourse. If, for Kraus, the Nazis (Goebbels above all) were "Leitartikler" whose success was in large part due to their ability to generate romantic and nativist impulses through the techniques of modern media, for Adorno, the distinctly modern "jargon of authenticity" and the various guises it assumes in mass culture have informed the conditions of possibility for fascist politics and thinking, and vice versa.

Writing, to be sure, at different historical junctures, both figures are nonetheless attuned to the reification – that phenomenon wherein the social and historical processes that congeal in the objectification of an object are *forgotten* in the determination of its meaning – entailed in journalism, jargon, and the language of Nazism. Both offer distinct but related ways to think critically about the relationship *among* these discursive modes, which otherwise might be treated as independent of each other. What, in other words, does journalistic language as Kraus views it share in common with jargon on Adorno's account? Without ignoring the differences in both the content of their claims and in their respective em-

---

the Adorno-inspired concept of the "authoritarian character" articulates itself in Kraus's important works, including *Die letzten Tage der Menschheit* and *Dritte Walpurgisnacht*.
11 Djassemy, *Die verfolgende Unschuld*, 234.
12 Walter Benjamin concluded something similar in 1931, when he wrote: "Daß [Kraus] der soziologische Bereich nie transparent wird – im Angriff auf die Presse so wenig wie in der Verteidigung der Prostitution – hängt mit dieser seiner Naturhaftung zusammen." Benjamin, *Gesammelte Schriften Band 2*, Frankfurt am Main: Suhrkamp 1991, 353. In this sense, Benjamin questions Kraus's credentials as a historical materialist and makes a more critical claim than Djassemy.
13 See Schuberth, "Blauer Dunst und Brauner Dunst," in *Sprachkritik als Ideologiekritik*, 98.

phases, I will furthermore argue that a significant common denominator emerges in their individual treatments of the philosopher Martin Heidegger, whose recourse to an ontology of language functions as a site of convergence between jargon, journalism, and fascist ideology. The combination of Adorno's philosophical polemic against Heidegger with Kraus's satirical response to Heidegger allows us to see more clearly the relationship adumbrated above and its implications for a more general critique of language under the regime of reification.

## Adorno on Authenticity and the Origin

There is no language critique in Adorno that is not rife with implications extending well beyond the domain of language *per se*.[14] *Jargon der Eigentlichkeit* thus relies on many of the recurring concepts and commitments that appear in Adorno's earlier work, the revisiting of which will help make his critique of the "jargon of authenticity" more intelligible. Given that this larger discourse in Adorno also contains significant allusions to Kraus, it is necessary to first address what Adorno generally means by "authenticity" as such, a concept that makes one of its earlier appearances in *Minima Moralia* (1951), written by Adorno while living in American exile. In a gloss entitled "Goldprobe," Adorno writes that terms such as "authenticity" or "genuineness" (often rendered *Eigentlichkeit* or *Echtheit*) were being circulated among various strains of contemporary existential philosophy and theology, and to dubious ends.[15] For Adorno, such terms index an appeal to the isolated ego that turns both inward and away from the world, and to a notion of the self that exists entirely independent of the social. He identifies this no-

---

14 The volume *Noten zur Literatur*, consisting largely of radio addresses delivered by Adorno to the postwar, West German public – the title of which already indicates a relationship between language and music – contains a number of essays on prominent literary figures (Goethe, Mörike, Eichendorff, Hölderlin, Heine, Valéry, Benjamin, etc.) and is a good place to start for perceiving how Adorno's theory of language, his literary criticism, his musicological critique, and his philosophical commitments all converge and/or can be seen as mutually constitutive of one another. See Adorno, *Gesammelte Schriften, Band 11: Noten zur Literatur*, Frankfurt am Main: Suhrkamp 2003.
15 For an excellent reading of Heideggerian authenticity – and its deficiencies – see Lambert Zuidervaart, "Truth and Authentication: Heidgger and Adorno in Reverse," in *Adorno and Heidegger: Philosophical Questions*, eds. Iain Macdonald and Krzysztof, Palo Alto: Stanford University Press 2007, 22–46. Zuidervaart's primary critique aligns with Adorno's (whose "empahtic experience" he also subjects to rigorous critique), namely, that Heideggerian authenticity relies exclusively on self-authentication and thus can never be tested intersubjectively, or in public. For Zuidervaart, Heidegger's account of authenticity "denies the objective mediation of the self" (41).

tion, however, as an "abstraction" that only arises in conjunction with what he calls modern, rootless, "exchange society" (*Tauschgesellschaft*) and the various forms of oppression such a society entails. "Echtheit," he writes, "ist nichts anderes als das trotzige und verstockte Beharren auf der monadologischen Gestalt, welche die gesellschaftliche Unterdrückung den Menschen aufprägt."[16] Gold, he claims, is commonly treated as a material source of value – becoming, under this optic, a fetish – when it is, from a dialectical perspective, merely an expression of a historically determined social relation; "authenticity" is likewise a fetish.[17] Adorno next identifies the claim of authenticity as fantastical and reactive, and thus as the expression of a *mis*recognition of the relation between ego and world. He continues:

> In [dem Begriff der Echtheit] steckt die Vorstellung von der Suprematie des Urpsrungs übers Abgeleitete. Die ist aber stets mit sozialem Legitimismus verbunden. Alle Herrensgeschichten berufen sich darauf, älter eingessesen, autochthon zu sein. Die ganze Philosophie der Innerlichkeit, mit dem Anspruch der Weltverachtung, ist die letzte Sublimierung der barbarischen Brutalität, daß, wer zuerst da war, das größere Recht habe, und die Priorität des Selbst ist so unwahr wie aller, die bei sich zu Hause sind.[18]

For Adorno, the ruling strata of all types derive their legitimacy from their claim to being the first ones on the scene; they turn a historical contingency, that is, into a necessary element of their dominion, suggesting that because (and only because) they have been here longest, they rule. Adorno then establishes a direct relationship between the "supremacy of origins" and what he calls the "philosophy of inwardness," another name for the (modern) philosophical appeal to the notion of authenticity. For Adorno, such philosophy has transformed what was once the ruling stratum's claim to being the *original* into the contemporary notion of authenticity or genuineness.[19] Yet it is worth noting how Adorno calls the resulting contempt for the world "professed" contempt (*der* Anspruch *der Weltverachtung*). For what such professed contempt conceals is silent complicity with the status quo, complicity that can only develop within one who has never experienced utter powerlessness or rootlessness, or who has suppressed this moment of their own consciousness. The ruling strata – in whom the notion of the origin is firmly lodged – is thus, for Adorno, at one with the philosopher of authenticity.

---

16 Adorno, *Gesammelte Schriften Band 4: Minima Moralia: Reflexionen aus dem beschädigten Leben*, Frankfurt am Main: Suhrkamp 2003, 175–76.
17 Ibid., 177.
18 Ibid., 176–77.
19 Adorno's use of the word "Sublimierung" in this passage, it should be noted, evinces the psychoanalytic dimension of this thought, which makes sense given his attempt to read authenticity as the expression of the modern re-routing of a more primary drive or impulse.

When Adorno insists on the untruth of this sense of the "self" and of the very feeling of being *at home* where one lives, he thereby questions not only the claim to authenticity, but any claim to being at home in a world that remains fundamentally inhospitable. Indeed, only the historical conquerors – most recently and saliently, the fascists – , those who are perennially suspicious of the migrant, refugee, or exile, can speak unflinchingly about the metaphysical need to locate such an authentic self. Extrapolating from these passages, we could argue that for Adorno, all modern nationalist discourse is fueled by the need to defend one's authenticity over and against all (perceived) latecomers, those subjects who are invariably barred from this mode of experience.[20]

The relationship between origins and authenticity is thus at stake for Adorno, which helps us better understand the reprisal of this thought in *Negative Dialektik* (1967), where Adorno situates it within a comprehensive critique of what he calls "Ursprungsphilosophien." This broad category, as defined by Adorno, includes not only German Idealism in its various iterations, but also contemporary phenomenology and other strands of ontology. Adorno argues here that the positing of an origin is tantamount to an assertion of power, or a covert appeal to philosophical imperialism that either absorbs difference or expels it altogether. This "identity-thinking" thus operates according to the logic of what we could call *Gleich-* or *Ausschaltung*: it either reduces the *non*-identical to a concept or expunges it from the realm of discursive intelligibility. At a crucial juncture in this text, Adorno once again invokes the significance of the concept of the origin – thus recalling *Minima Moralia* – but in this iteration, he mobilizes Kraus, whom he treats as an ally of sorts. Adorno writes:

> Die Kategorie der Wurzel, des Ursprungs selbst ist herrschaftlich, Bestätigung dessen, der zuerst drankommt, weil er zuerst da war; des Autochthonen gegenüber dem Zugewanderten, des Seßhaften gegenüber dem Mobilen. Was lockt, weil es durchs Abgeleitete, die Ideologie, nicht sich beschwichtigen lassen will, Ursprung, ist seinerseits ideologisches Prinzip. In dem konservativ klingenden Satz von Karl Kraus, 'Ursprung ist das Ziel,' äußert sich auch ein an Ort und Stelle schwerlich Gemeintes: der Begriff des Ursprungs müßte seines statischen Unwesens entäußert werden. Nicht wäre das Ziel, in den Ursprung, ins Phan-

---

[20] More famously, Kraus is the subject of another gloss entirely in *Minima Moralia* ("Juvenals Irrtum"), which pertains to Kraus's satire more than his language critique and which Adorno assesses rather negatively in light of recent historical events. Essentially, Adorno views satire as constitutively unable to think beyond the limits of the given world and is thus compelled to either idealize the irretrievable past, or, in Kraus's case, embrace the lesser of two evils. For a recent analysis of Adorno's reading of satire, see Ari Linden, *Karl Kraus and the Discourse of Modernity*, Evanston: Northwestern University Press 2020, 117–119.

tasma guter Natur zurückzufinden, sondern Ursprung fiele allein dem Ziel zu, konstitutierte sich erst von diesem her. *Kein Urpsrung außer im Leben des Ephemeren.*²¹

The resonances with the quote from *Minima Moralia* should be evident. Reading Kraus's verse against the grain, Adorno suggests that Kraus's equation of *Ursprung* and *Ziel* is to be read in non-static terms, and indeed, dialectically. For seemingly implied in Kraus's phrase is the fantasy of pure repetition or of primal return to some form of "good" nature, where, say, a wholly unmediated experience of *Blut und Boden* awaits – and in yet another incarnation of this thought, Adorno explicitly invokes the infamous National Socialist mantra.²² This fantasy, to be sure, would be consistent with the image of Adorno's 'bad' modernity thus far sketched out: that fruitless search for an origin and the claim to legitimacy such a search entails. On Adorno's reading (as with Benjamin's), however, Kraus's aphorism actually challenges the conventional notion of origin without disavowing the concept altogether.²³ For Adorno, the newcomer and the migrant – nonidentical, "ephemeral" figures – are redeemed by Kraus insofar as the sheer fleetingness of their existence undermines the authoritative claims of the autocthon and the settler, whose suppression of the migratory moment of their own history functions as a necessary condition of their dominion. Adorno thus invokes Kraus

---

21 Adorno, *Gesammelte Schriften Band 6: Negative Dialektik. Jargon der Eigentlichkeit*, Frankfurt am Main: Suhrkamp 2003, 158. Emphasis added. Kraus's aphorism – originally a verse from a 1913 poem by Kraus entitled "Der sterbende Mensch" – is part of a history of Kraus's own investment in the notion of the "origin" (*Ursprung*), references to which are littered throughout his poetry and essays during the teens. Benjamin also had a fondness for the aphorism as evidenced in his use of it as the epigraph above his fourteenth thesis in *Über den Begriff der Geschichte*, which introduces the difference between "empty time" and "now time" (*Jetztzeit*). See Benjamin, *Gesammelte Schriften Band 1*, Frankfurt am Main: Suhrkamp 1991, 701. Adorno invoked it at least three times in his oeuvre: once in *Ästhetische Theorie*, once in his essay on Thorsten Veblen, and once in *Negative Dialektik*. For a thorough engagement with Kraus's notion of the origin, including its uptake by some of these thinkers, see John Pizer, "'Ursprung ist das Ziel': Karl Kraus's Concept of Origin," in *Modern Austrian Literature*, Vol. 27:1 1994, 1–21.
22 In the introduction to *Zur Metakritik der Erkenntnistheorie*, Adorno's confrontation with Husserlian phenomenology, he yet again writes: "Der Faschismus suchte die Ursprungsphilosophie zu verwirklichen. Das Älteste, das was am längsten da ist, sollte unmittelbar, buchstäblich herrschen [. . .] Blut und Boden, die faschistisch konkretisierten und in der modernen Industriegesellschaft ganz schimärischen Ursprungsmächte und Herrschaft lief darüber hinaus, daß wer die Macht hat, nicht bloß der Erste, sondern auch der Ursprüngliche sein sollte." Adorno, *Gesammelte Schriften Band 5: Zur Metakritik der Erkenntnistheorie. Drei Studien zu Hegel*, Frankfurt am Main: Suhrkamp 2003, 28.
23 For a comprehensive reading of Benjamin and Kraus on the concept of the origin, see Christian Schulte, *Ursprung ist das Ziel: Walter Benjamin über Karl Kraus*, Würzburg: Königshausen & Neumann 2003.

to expose the conventional vision of origin as a fantasy projected by the ruling stratum in order to legitimize its rule. Adorno is clearly thinking here of the experience of exile, and, more urgently, of fascism and its culmination in Auschwitz.[24] But he is also thinking, I would argue, of Heidegger and of his variant of origins-philosophy – and what Adorno will eventually call the "jargon of authenticity."

While Heidegger's role in Adorno's corpus would require a separate study altogether, it should suffice to suggest for now that he is one of *Negative Dialektik's* primary antagonists.[25] Indeed, one of Adorno's strategies throughout is to show how Heidegger's philosophy of *Dasein*, even while responding to an actual metaphysical need, ultimately fails because its fetishization of language renders it insufficiently materialist and thus insufficiently attuned to the vicissitudes of modern existence. What is relevant for our purposes, however, are the moments where Kraus's linguistic practices appear as a foil to Heidegger's, insofar as these moments illuminate some of Adorno's own views on the relationship between language, history, and violence – in a word, on Adorno's understanding of linguistic reification. In a crucial passage, Adorno spells out what appears to be his fundamental problem with Heidegger's language, and in so doing, elaborates on his own approach to the subject. He writes:

> Die Kraft der Sprache bewahrt sich darin, daß in der Reflexion Ausdruck und Sache auseinander treten. Sprache wird zur Instanz der Wahrheit nur am Bewußtsein der Unidentität des Ausdrucks mit dem Gemeinten. *Heidegger weigert sich jener Reflexion*; er hält inne nach dem ersten Schritt der sprachphilosophischen Dialektik. Repristination ist sein Denken auch darin, daß es durch ein Ritual des Nennens die Gewalt des Namens wiederherstellen möchte.[26]

Heidegger's quasi-nominalistic language bespeaks, it appears, the *return* to a prelapsarian past in which thing and name had been harmoniously united. In failing to recognize the non-identical relation between expression and that which is expressed, it precludes its own participation in the realm of truth-content. Such language, for Adorno, is reified inasmuch as it lacks awareness of its internal dialectic and resorts to a false religiosity. By contrast, Kraus's language obtains what Adorno calls "signifikative Kraft" in "der stetigen Konfrontation von Aus-

---

**24** There are many lines and sections of the text that indicate how present Auschwitz was on Adorno's mind as he was composing it, but the last section of the text brings to the surface what is implicit throughout. Adorno writes, "Auschwitz bestätigt das Philosophem von der reinen Identität als dem Tod." *GS 6*, 355.

**25** Peter E. Gordon's *Adorno and Existence*, Cambridge: Harvard University Press 2016, and the edited volume *Adorno and Heidegger* are good places to start for this type of analysis. Most recently, see Espen Hammer, "Adorno's Critique of Heidegger," *A Companion to Adorno*, eds. Peter E. Gordon, Max Pensky, and Espen Hammer, New Jersey: John Wiley & Sons 2020, 473–486.

**26** *GS 6*, 117. Emphasis added.

druck und Sache."²⁷ If Heidegger treats language as a fetish, Kraus's language attends to the ever-changing relationship between the thing and its linguistic expression, which Adorno illustrates through his dialectical reading of Kraus's aphorism discussed above. We should recall that the aphorism was not only *about* the relationship between the origin and the goal, but also, for Adorno, *enacted* this very relationship through its expression. In stark contrast to Kraus's linguistic process, "Heideggers Verfahren," Adorno continues, "ist, nach Scholems Prägung, deutschtümelnde Kabbalistik."²⁸ Adorno suggests that Heidegger's language carries with it the stench of "teutonism," a statement which, in light of Adorno's overarching critique of the type of thinking that eventuated in Auschwitz, contains serious implications.²⁹

The fundamental difference between Kraus and Heidegger hinges on Adorno's understanding of linguistic reification and its relation to violence and authority. The "Gewalt des Namens" invoked above indeed hints at the way Adorno views Heidegger's language as reified, not only in its internal structure (namely, the way it *appears* as a natural expression of philosophical truth), but also in the type of thinking and action of which it is a symptom. Heidegger's language is unphased by the vicissitudes of history and ignores the way that material suffering – for Adorno, the *sine qua non* of all philosophy after Auschwitz – must imprint itself on any kind of language that aims to articulate our deepest metaphysical needs.³⁰ This is relevant because it reveals the extent to which Adorno might have been drawing on Kraus, however implicitly, every time he subjected Heidegger's language to critique. As will soon become evident, Heidegger's ontology for Adorno is an ontology of origins, and as such, it serves as the model for the very "jargon of authenticity" that Adorno views as deeply implicated in fascist thought and practice. It is thus not coincidental that it is in this essay where the Krausian inheritance in Adorno is most salient.

---

27 Ibid., 118.
28 Ibid. I have not tracked down the origin of the reference to Heidegger by Gershom Scholem on which Adorno is supposedly drawing.
29 In light of the recent publication of Heidegger's *Schwarze Hefte*, comments like the one above resonate even more in the context of Heidegger's antisemitism/ideological proximity to National Socialism. This is, indeed, part of the argument Adorno is making – it was Adorno who effectively inaugurated this critique. What distinguishes Adorno's from cruder, more recent dismissals of Heidegger as an irredeemable Nazi, however, is his attempt to think through Heidegger's philosophy immanently in an effort to identify the fascism inherent in its *method*.
30 For a thorough engagement with the question and fate of Adornian ethics after the Shoah, see Martin Shuster, *Autonomy after Auschwitz: Adorno, German Idealism, and Modernity*, Chicago: University of Chicago Press 2014.

## The Jargon of Authenticity

In *Jargon der Eigentlichkeit* Adorno offers sundry examples of jargon in order to qualify his claim that there is an intimate relationship between this phenomenon and the socio-political forms of life in which it blossoms.[31] Initially conceived of as a section within *Negative Dialektik* until Adorno determined that "jargon" merited a study of its own, Adorno's text can be divided into three interrelated claims. The first is that what he labels as jargon – the language that permeates contemporary ontology, existentialism, and theology (not only the concept of "Eigentlichkeit," but also word-concepts such as "Aussage," "Begegnung," "Entscheidung" and "Auftrag") – emits a religious or otherwise metaphysical aura that is denuded, however, of the social structures that once imbued such language with meaning.[32] Secondly, Adorno claims that while jargon sees itself as responding to the *inauthenticity* of "exchange society" – with all of its insecurity, mobility, and uprootedness – in actuality, it reveals itself to be all the more infected by the very social entanglements it claims to reject. Jargon has been appropriated by various domains of culture: business, education, popular psychology, etc., and has thereby succeeded in making transcendent the iniquities of modern society. But it is Adorno's targeted assaults on Heidegger that constitute the essay's most polemical aspect, since for him it is Heidegger who reveals most trenchantly the political implications of jargon even as his is the most coherent and compelling philosoph-

---

**31** For more on the history of this text – including its largely negative initial reception within the German academic sphere – see Beck and Cooman, "Adorno, Kracauer und die Ursprünge der Jargonkritik" in *Sprachkritik als Ideologiekritik*, 7–15.

**32** In an effort to reappraise Adorno's late polemic and suggest (as I do) that this text is not meant solely as an assault on Heidegger, but rather as a diagnosis of a larger cultural-philosophical problem, Max Beck and Nicholas Coomann argue that the roots of Adorno's position are to be located in Weimar Germany, and specifically in Siegfried Kracauer's critical review of Martin Buber and Franz Rosenzweig's 1929 translation of the Bible. In this review, Kracauer is suspicious of Buber and Rosenzweig's attempt to revitalize an ancient tongue (biblical Hebrew) and make foreign a modern one (German) because there is no critical impulse entailed in this process; one is confronted with a language that merely emits the aura of authority. Adorno was apparently attuned to this review and praised Kracauer for being receptive to this kind of proto-jargon of authenticity. While Buber plays a very minor role in Adorno's late text, Beck and Coomann argue – by pointing to the very first line of Adorno's text – that this accord between Adorno and Kracauer is not insignificant. Given that *Jargon* was published in 1964 and was written in part as a response to the collusion between fascism and such jargon, it is not surprising, however, that the two German Jewish author-translators recede into the background and are hardly mentioned. For more on this discourse, see *Sprachkritik als Ideologiekritik*, 7–27.

ical project among the various twentieth century variants of ontology. Heidegger was, indeed, a philosopher whom Adorno took very seriously.[33]

In the essay's opening salvo, Adorno outlines the basic structure of the "Authentics'" language and makes explicit its relationship to fascism:

> Vor allem besonderen Inhalt modelt ihre Sprache den Gedanken so, daß er dem Ziel von Unterwerfung sich anbequemt, selbst dort, wo er ihm zu widerstehen meint. Die Autorität des Absoluten wird gestürzt von verabsolutierter Autorität. Der Faschismus war nicht bloß die Verschwörung [. . .] sondern entsprang in einer mächtigen gesellschaftlichen Entwicklungstendenz. Die Sprache gewährt ihm Asyl; in ihr äußert das fortschwelende Unheil sich so, als wäre es das Heil.[34]

In jargon, language imposes itself on thought, irrespective of its content, thereby suppressing the non-identical or the sensuous-mimetic aspect of language even as the speaker's intention is to resist or penetrate through reified forms of thinking. What thus links jargon and the language of fascism, for Adorno, is the demand for *subordination* on the part of the listener or audience, already implicit in the structural relationship between thought and language that inheres in jargon. Adorno identifies this dimension of jargon as its mythical or religious residue, which is what he means in claiming that the authority of the absolute has been replaced or "overthrown" by absolutized authority. Jargon, it appears, has stepped in as a placeholder for the absence of metaphysical authority (i. e., Christianity) – much like fascism developed, Adorno implies, in response to a need for authority that had remained unfulfilled.[35] Recalling the earlier passage from *Minima Moralia*, we can thus see how Adorno would identify in both jargon and fascism a fetish character: both take control of language or the social totality by fiat, thus concealing the "powerful social processes" that inhere in their constitutions. If fascism found "refuge" in jargon, that is because jargon fetishized its ideology by expressing it in salvific terms. For Adorno, fascism's success in appealing to a large audience was in large part due to its redemptive language of plenitude and immediacy. Adorno is thereby not simply conflating jargon with fascist rhetoric or intimating a causal re-

---

[33] Espen Hammer writes: "The political dimension notwithstanding, [Adorno] also took Heidegger extremely seriously as a philosopher, reading him not only as a symptom of a decaying German philosophical tradition, unable to withstand the allure of fascist irrationalism, but as a philosopher worthy of being compared with such luminaries of Western philosophy as Aristotle, Kant, and Hegel." See Hammer, "Adorno's Critique of Heidegger," 473.
[34] *GS 6*, 416.
[35] This would not be the forum to delve into a reading of this essay as a contribution to the thesis of secularization in modernity, but it would not seem overly polemical to suggest that Adorno's abiding investment in the notion of disenchantment also rears its head in his critique of philosophical jargon.

lationship; he is identifying, rather, the social ether that gave rise to both a mass political movement and a widespread linguistic phenomenon well suited to the former's purposes.

Among the ways in which Adorno makes visible – or, rather, aural – these phenomena is in his identification of jargon's "intonation," a critique that should resonate with anyone familiar with Kraus's essay from 1912, "Der Ton," which could very well be lingering in the background. In this essay, Kraus focuses on the ways in which the homogeneous tone of journalistic language has permeated all communicative domains, such that any objective difference in the relative weight of events themselves is ultimately nullified by the uniform tone in which such events are mediated.[36] The dominant tone thus has both a dissimulating and a coercive function. Though not an identical argument, Adorno writes: "Was Jargon sei und was nicht, darüber entscheidet, ob das Wort in dem *Tonfall* geschrieben ist, in dem es sich als transzendent gegenüber der eigenen Bedeutung setzt, ob die einzelnen Worte aufgeladen werden auf Kosten von Satz, Urteil, Gedachtem."[37] Jargon's effectiveness, Adorno claims, relies on the authority with which it is delivered, and his use of the term "aufgeladen" underscores the authoritative dimension of the auratic word (in this instance, *Aussage*), which hovers over the sentence in which it is embedded. Jargon becomes familiar to us, even appears humanizing vis-à-vis the expressed inhumanity of modern society, as it conceals an inhuman expression. Adorno continues: "Das vorbegriffliche, mimetische Element der Sprache nimmt [der Jargon] zugunsten ihm erwünschter Wirkungszusammenhänge in Regie."[38] As reified, instrumental reason in the form of language, jargon represses the "preconceptual, mimetic" moment in language, the element that philosophy and poetry need to recall if they are, for Adorno, to live on after Auschwitz – the very element, indeed, that Adorno identifies in Kraus's language.[39] Aiming primarily to produce an *effect* in its audience, jargon is thus furthermore rendered in terms similar to the way Kraus conceives of journalistic language. By enacting a form of coercion with respect to the syntactical context of which it is a part, jargon reveals itself to have

---

36 F 357–359, 05.10.1912, 1. For an insightful analysis of this essay and how Kraus anticipates the aurality of radio in his critique of journalistic tone, see Burkhard Müller, *Karl Kraus: Mimesis und Kritik des Mediums*, Stuttgart: Metzler 1994, 243–372.
37 *GS 6*, 418.
38 Ibid.
39 In Adorno's essay on Kraus's volume *Sittlichkeit und Kriminalität*, he refers to Kraus's gestural, imitative language as part of his "undomesticated, mimetic impulse," which I take Adorno to be thinking of when he critiques jargon's suppression of language's preconceptual, mimetic element. *GS 11*, 385–386.

absorbed the violence of the social totality into its structure. These insights will become more relevant when we turn to select passages from *Dritte Walpurgisnacht*.

When Adorno actually does invoke Kraus – only one time in the entire essay – it is, once again, in the service of an argument against Heidegger, and in this case, the latter's concept of "Gerede." This is important because part of what Adorno wants to argue is that the jargon of authenticity is itself a form of chatter insofar as it is, for Adorno, *inauthentic* language, or language that fails in any substantial way to distinguish itself from the language of "das Man" if we are to remain within Heidegger's own conceptual terrain. Adorno first endorses what he views as Kraus and Heidegger's shared insight into the relationship between the "business of communication" and the "chatter" of which it consists, or the way that idle talk creates the parameters for what can be heard and understood in everyday discourse. Kraus's version of this, writes Adorno, is his repeated claim that "die Phrase gebäre heute die Wirklichkeit."[40] What distinguishes Heidegger's view from Kraus's, however, is that the former, for Adorno, treats *Gerede* as a "negative ontological presence" – as endemic to the "fallenness" of *Dasein* – rather than as a function of social-historical relations.[41] Adorno thus concludes:

> [Das Geschwätz] wird den Menschen aufgedrungen von einer gesellschaftlichen Verfassung, welche sie als Subjekte verneint, längst vor den Zeitungskonzernen. Heideggers Kritik aber wird ideologisch, indem sie unterschiedslos den emanzipierten Geist ereilt als das, was unter höchst realen Bindungen aus ihm wird. Er verurteilt das Gerede, aber nicht die Brutalität, mit der zu paktieren die wahre Schuld des an sich weit unschuldigeren Geredes ist. Sobald Heidegger das Gerede zum Schweigen verhalten will, klirrt seine Sprache mit der Rüstung.[42]

There are two issues at stake in this passage. For Adorno, Heidegger's ontology, far from providing the needed response to modern alienation that it proclaims, reproduces through "authenticity" the reification of the status quo and thus an apology for the violence that such existing conditions implicitly sanction. This is further confirmed when Heidegger takes on the mantle of social critic but misrecognizes the problem of "chatter." Chatter, for Adorno is innocent relative to the "brutality" of modern social unreason that informs the conditions of its possibility but is not reducible to it; Heidegger confuses the symptom for the condition when authenticity replaces the need for a social and historical account. Adorno's final

---

40 *GS 6*, 480.
41 In apparent disagreement with Adorno's assessment of Kraus, Cornelia Vismann has recently concluded in her essay on Kraus's "voice of the law" that Kraus's ultimate aim is another form of *Verschwiegenheit*: "Keine Wiederholung und Vervielfältigung des Geschwätzes, sondern ihre Refiguration, so daß sie das andauernde Gerede zum Schweigen bringt." Vismann, "Karl Kraus: Die Stimme des Gesetzes," *Das Recht und seine Mittel*, Frankfurt am Main: Fischer 2012, 724.
42 *GS 6*, 481.

point thus serves as a reading of Heidegger's language rendered in historical terms: Heidegger calls for the total negation of chatter in his demand for "Verschwiegenheit," which Adorno interprets as the absorption of the fascist privileging of authentic "quietude" over and against the liberal public sphere into Heidegger's linguistic apparatus. What Heidegger cryptically desires, for Adorno, is the termination of a certain form of life, the victory of "meaningful silence" over the "endless talk of the urban bourgeoisie," including the culture of intellectuals and Jews.[43] While Adorno and Kraus have their own critiques of this phenomenon, Adorno's point is that Heidegger's failure to be sufficiently attentive to the material basis of his ontology is indexed both in his language and in his philosophical diagnosis of modernity. His philosophy, and, in far cruder ways, the entirety of the jargon of authenticity, unwittingly mimes the social conditions it condemns. "Gewalt," Adorno concludes, "wohnt wie der Sprachgestalt so dem Kern der Heideggerschen Philosophie inne."[44]

These various strands of Adorno's critical project and their dialogue with Kraus come to a head when Adorno offers a meta-psychological etiology of the resentment of those who perceive themselves to be on the losing end of the processes of modernity and the seemingly uprooted society these processes have produced. Such subjects – whom, in texts such as *Minima Moralia* and *Negative Dialektik*, Adorno identifies as the self-proclaimed "original" inhabitants of a given society – experienced social progress as a "verdict" against them; their memory of such a verdict, in turn, manifests itself today in jargon and its claims of authenticity. This is precisely where jargon is tantamount to commodified language qua social mystification, for its "Blasen," Adorno explains,

> lassen das wahre Objekt des Leidens verschwinden, die bestimmte gesellschaftliche Verfassung. Denn die auserwählten Opfer des Affekts wider die Beweglichkeit sind selber verurteilt [. . .]. Nur darum hat das Bestreben des Jargons, die Rancune des Seßhaften, Stummen in etwas wie ein metaphysich-moralisches Vernichtungsteil über den, der reden kann, zu wenden, soviel Erfolg, weil es prinzipiell bereits ausgesprochen, in Deutschland an Unge-

---

43 Hammer, 480.
44 Ibid., 502. Adorno's critique of *Gerede* in Heidegger issues into a critical examination of Heidegger's notion of *das Man*, which, Adorno argues, essentially absolves the individual of his responsibility, regardless of the circumstances: "Unter der Herrschaft des Man habe keiner etwas zu antworten," Adorno writes. *GS 6*, 481. Heidegger's philosophy is once again fulfilled historically under Nazism, and specifically the concept of the *Befehlsnotstand* that the torturers invoked as their state of emergency, which enabled them to commit their atrocities with perceived impunity. According to Adorno's logic, the "They" is construed as a leveling mechanism in Heidegger, and in certain of his formulations it effectively replicates the exchange relationship immanent to capitalist social relations by reducing it to a negatively ontological moment of Being.

zählten exekutiert ist; weil die Gebärde des Wurzelechten mit den geschichtlichen Siegern es hält. Das ist das Substantielle der Eigentlichkeit, der heilige Quell ihrer Kraft.[45]

By invoking the "chosen victims," Adorno is clearly referring primarily (though not exclusively) to the Jewish victims of the Shoah, those "mobile" and "uprooted" individuals who were deemed responsible for the ills of modernity and thus whose persecution was justified in the eyes of the executioners. Without in any way vindicating the perpetrators, Adorno suggests that jargon is partly responsible for obscuring the real source of suffering (the domination built in to the "constitution" of modern society) through its false promises of return and redemption; it is sublimated resentment that has become, in the twentieth century, fatal in its implications and effects. Thus, Adorno once again identifies the jargon of authenticity – as he had expressed elsewhere – as being of one piece with the "historical conquerors," i. e., the fascists.

What is at stake for Adorno is the intimate relationship between linguistic mystification and the impulse toward social and political domination, a relationship clearly at work in fascism. More specifically, Adorno shows the way jargon is both a function of, and a factor involved in (re)producing authority. It is an inclination toward reified speech which wants to be viewed as purified or freed from social and historical conditions. It is in this sense not mystified language as such, but language that 'coordinates' or 'aligns' with a given social reality even as it claims to repudiate that reality. Adorno shows how language – through both its aural evocation of authority and its hypotactic structure – and violence can be seamlessly coordinated with one another and are done so most effectively in Heidegger's philosophy. Understood historically and meta-psychologically, jargon is, for Adorno, continuous with fascism as both a politics and a mode of thinking. This claim is fundamental for arriving at a richer understanding not only of Adorno's larger critical project, but also of his indebtedness to Kraus, and, as I will ultimately show, of the deeper implications of some of Kraus's assertions in *Dritte Walpurgisnacht*. It is here where Kraus makes claims both about Heidegger's language and Nazi rhetoric, as well as the journalistic mode that functions as the mediating third term.

## The Blue and the Brown Mist

Denn wo Gespenster Platz genommen
Ist auch der Philosoph willkommen.[46]

---

**45** Ibid., 445.
**46** Kraus, *Schriften 12*, 68. Here he is quoting from Goethe's *Faust II*.

If there is ever a place where Kraus "ahnt" more than he conceptualizes it is in the brief but significant section in *Dritte Walpurgisnacht* in which he discusses the contemporary cultural and philosophical landscape in Germany. After enumerating various invocations of the "German spirit" and "German virtue" uttered by renowned cultural icons, Kraus disqualifies them – even Wagner – in the search for the "Treuhänder des nationalsozialistischen Gedankens."[47] Unlike Adorno, Kraus is not interested in tracking a genealogy of fascist thought from within the German literary and philosophical tradition, even suggesting that the desire to attribute cosmic meaning to the events unfolding by turning to this genealogy would only make sense if we understood the current context as "pathological" and somehow endemic to the German "spirit." Kraus refuses to think this way, which is not an unimportant distinction between him and Adorno, who finds something rotten at the core of Idealist/bourgeois thinking. Yet it is *dialectics* and *relationality* that Adorno is after in his critique, and this is what would separate Adorno's project from those whom Kraus subjects to ridicule, those who turn to tradition for legitimacy. For Kraus, to draw on this tradition in the way Nazi ideologues are doing is to rewrite it, for there is no possible way to embolden the actions of the Nazis or to attribute to them motivations other than lust for power and enslavement, avarice and envy. Rather, when Kraus addresses the role of German philosophy in the fomentation of Nazi ideology, it is for the purpose of highlighting the extent to which all contemporary domains of the social have been "coordinated," even within the highest ranks of intellectual life. What stands before us, Kraus claims, is the

> Betrieb einer Büromantik von Befreiungskriegen zum Zweck der Sklaverei. Gewimmel von Verwendbaren: Belletristen, Gesundbeter und nun auch jene Handlanger ins Transzendente, die sich in Fakultäten und Revuen anstellig zeigen, die deutsche Philosophie als Vorschule für den Hitler-Gedanken einzurichten.[48]

For Kraus, the combination of ruthless efficiency and romantic ideology ("Büromantik") has convinced not only the literati and the faith healers; a new wave of university professors is also committed to discerning from the history of German thought a trajectory that aligns with the politics of the present moment. These are the figures who meddle in the "transcendent," as if merely by uttering the word the phenomenon could be made tangible, a very Adornian thought.[49]

---

47 *Schriften 12*, 70.
48 *Schriften 12*, 71.
49 Toward the end of *Negative Dialektik*, Adorno makes references to the pseudo-philosophical attempts to produce "transcendence" or derive transcendent meaning from the Shoah. In so doing, he invokes Kraus yet again in support of his claim: "Wer Transzendenz dingfest macht, dem kann mit Recht, so wie von Karl Kraus, Phantasielosigkeit, Geistfeindschaft und in dieser

Thus, while Kraus exposes flagrant contradictions between the Nazis' appropriation of Kant and (especially) Nietzsche and their actual philosophical doctrines, he makes one exception: the "neudeutscher Denker" Heidegger. If there is any consonance between the reigning political and philosophical regimes, Kraus continues, "Da ist etwa der Denker Heidegger, der seinen blauen Dunst dem braunen gleichgeschaltet hat und klar zu erkennen beginnt, die geistige Welt eines Volkes sei 'die Macht der tiefsten Bewahrung seiner erd- und bluthaften Kräfte als Macht der innersten Erregung und weitesten Erschütterung seines Daseins.'"[50] Quoting from Heidegger's Rectoral Address of 1933, "Die Selbstbehauptung der deutschen Universität," which the philosopher delivered upon assuming the position of Rectorship of the University of Freiburg,[51] Kraus identifies a direct "coordination" between the "blue mist" of Heidegger's language and the "brown mist" of Nazi discourse (blue indexing the pseudo-romantic impulses in Heidegger's language, and brown, the color of the uniforms worn by the SS).[52] Kraus's aim is twofold. On the one hand, he points to the completely unironic tone of Heidegger's language, mocking the idea that the spiritual world of the German "Volk" could be summoned forth by recourse to blood and soil. On the other hand, he draws attention to the violent implications of these words themselves when viewed in their proper context. Hence his response: "Warum das Volk durch seine erd- und bluthaften Kräfte erregt und erschüttert sein muß und wie es dadurch auf einen grünen Zweig kommen könnte, das zu sehen ist natürlich mehr Sache des Glaubens als der Beweisführung..."[53] The basic insight that it would be difficult to demonstrate how the convulsion of primal energies will lead to spiritual fulfillment reveals Kraus to be highly attuned to the modes of experience both Heideg-

---

Verrat an der Transzendenz vorgeworfen werden." *GS 6*, 392. Adorno is presumably referring implicitly to the "Authentics" and their way of addressing Auschwitz. Above, Kraus is referring to the claims to transcendence that were implicit and explicit in Nazi rhetoric – and, as we will see, in the language of university professors.
50 *Schriften 12*, 71.
51 For an engagement with the transformative relationship between philosophy and politics Heidegger begins to articulate in this speech, see Andrea Hurst, "'To Know and not to do is not to Know': Heidegger's Rectoral Address," in *South African Journal of Philosophy* Vol. 21:1 2002, 18–34.
52 About this particular line, Schuberth concludes: "Eine Sentenz aus Kraus' *Dritter Walpurgisnacht*, mit der er 1933, lange vor der Autobahn, der Volksbeschäftigung, den Olympischen Spielen und der Wannseekonferenz nicht nur das wahre Wesen der Nazibarbarei bei dessen vielen Namen nannte, sondern, lange bevor Heideggerianer das Opus ihres Gurus von seiner politischen Verirrungen scheiden wollten, die Konvertibilität von blauem und braunen Dunst mit beiläufiger Geste als 'business as usual' entlarvte." *Sprachkritik als Ideologiekritik*, 92.
53 *Schriften 12*, 71.

ger and the Nazi regime are conjuring in this type of language. Heidegger's phraseology is not philosophical in any robust sense, but rather journalistic, since it merely validates the mechanisms of power and authority that have occasioned it. And yet his position of authority confirms that there is no thinking outside of this historical moment, that there is, in Adornian terms, no separation between reality and ideology.

When Kraus then quotes Heidegger enjoining students and faculty to act "im Sinne des fragenden, ungedeckten Standhaltens inmitten der Ungewißheit des Seienden im Ganzen," he turns directly to the *affective* dimension of Heidegger's language and its embeddedness in the larger political context in which it is articulated.[54] The call to a certain type of action amidst uncertainty leads Kraus to refer to Heidegger as one of the "Worthelfer der Gewalt" – not one who participates in the violence directly, but one who encourages it through suggestive language – along with the poet Gottfried Benn, whom Kraus subjects to an even more scathing defrocking. Its pretentions to profundity appear to Kraus, indeed, more symptomatic of a medical than a philosophical condition: a psychosis, he writes, that can be traced to an "epidemic of national spasms (*Starrkrampfanfall*) characteristic of those who strut their stuff on parade grounds or lecture platforms or are capable of doing both at once."[55] Such language, in other words, is of one piece with its surrounding political context. Yet there may be more to it if we briefly contextualize Heidegger's speech. Sandwiched between the two passages Kraus quotes above, Heidegger speaks of the true meaning of "Geist" as he conceives it:

> Denn 'Geist' ist weder leerer Scharfsinn, noch das unverbindliche *Spiel des Witzes*, noch das uferlose Treiben verstandesmäßiger *Zergliederung*, noch gar die *Weltvernunft*, sondern Geist ist *ursprünglich* gestimmte, wissende Entschlossenheit zum Wesen des Seins. Und die geistige Welt eines Volkes ist *nicht der Überbau* einer Kultur, sowenig wie das Zeughaus für verwendbare Kenntnisse und Werte, sondern sie ist die Macht der tiefsten Bewahrung seiner erd- und bluthaften Kräfte [. . .].[56]

---

54 *Schriften 12*, 72.
55 *The Third Walpurgis Night by Karl Kraus*, trans. Edward Timms and Fred Bridgham, New Haven: Yale University Press 2020, 42.
56 Martin Heidegger, *Gesamtausgabe 16: Reden und andere Zeugnisse eines Lebensweges (1910 – 1976)*, ed. Hermann Heidegger and Vittorio Klostermann 2000, 112. Emphasis added. Jean-Luc Nancy does not cite from this address in his short but insightful reading of Heidegger's *Schwarze Hefte*, and yet it is easy to identify affinities between the passage above and some of the sentiments about which Heidegger is more explicit in his private "notebooks." While this is not the proper forum to explore Heidegger and antisemitism, for more on this discourse, see Nancy, *The Banality of Heidegger*, trans. Jeff Fort, New York: Fordham University Press 2017. For a comprehensive reading of Heidegger's relationship to Nazism and Judaism or Jewishness, see Elliot

The affinity between Heidegger's language and the more explicitly antisemitic epithets espoused by Nazi ideologues is salient: implicitly Jewish, destructive-analytic intellectualism is contrasted against the creative-productive German spirit; abstract reason against *original* essence or being; and the notion of a cultural superstructure against the more elementary class-transcending energies preserved in blood and soil.[57] By naming the ostensibly un-German influences on Germany's intellectual life, one could argue that he solders a dimension of his philosophy to the ideology of his political moment – precisely what Adorno claims in *Jargon*. Kraus, too, is critical of the bourgeois public sphere, but he is quick to sniff out continuity under the guise of reaction and rupture. He has, like Adorno, identified in Heidegger the dubious longing for an irretrievable origin or a mode of authenticity (the "erd- und bluthaften Kräfte") that must be wrested from the corrupting forces of modernity. Yet the stakes of this Adornian ideology critique cannot be fully understood without turning, finally, to Kraus's key assertions about the relationship between journalism and Nazi discourse and his attempt to de-reify the language of the Third Reich.

## From the Phrase to the Deed

Early on in his essay, Kraus singles out Goebbels as the mastermind behind the success of this movement, the figure, he writes, whose language contains ethos, pathos, and "Mythos," the journalist *par excellence*. In a memorable passage, he writes:

> *Und doch hat sich eben im Tonfall der deutschen Welt nichts verändert.* Mit den gleichen Mitteln erfolgt die Verankerung dessen, was heute zu verankert ist, Vision ist Phrase, Rhythmus das alte Überbleibsel der Syntax, das der Expressionismus für kollektives Erlebnis festgelegt hat, und selbst verdrängte Komplexe, die doch zweifellos verdächtiger Herkunft sind, finden Unterkunft. Hat doch sogar der Führer, dessen Ausdrucksvermögen keineswegs von Gundolf geschult wurde und dessen Weltbild nicht so sehr durch Freud als durch Karl May geformt scheint, bereits den Minderwertigkeitskomplex beklagt, an dem die Nation leide.[58]

For Kraus, nothing in the domain of language has fundamentally altered with the rise of National Socialism. If the journalistic phrase is the vessel for the political

---

R. Wolfson, *The Duplicity of Philosophy's Shadow: Heidegger, Nazism, and the Jewish Other* (New York: Columbia University Press, 2018).
57 For a thorough, if idiosyncratic study of what Jay Geller calls the "Other Jewish Question" – by which he means the overlapping discourses in modern German thought on health, disease, and *Judentum*, see Geller, *The Other Jewish Question: Identifying the Jew and Making Sense of Modernity*, New York: Fordham University Press 2011.
58 *Schriften 12*, 55. Emphasis added.

imaginary, Expressionist poetry introduced a kind of pathos that can be easily reproduced by aping its rhythm. Even that which would, according to Nazi ideologues, be deemed to be of unsavory or impure origins – namely, psychoanalysis (or its Adlerian variant) – has made its way into Hitler's speeches and appeals to the German people to account for the suffering they have endured. Kraus's point is that it is virtually impossible to disambiguate National Socialist rhetoric from the modern ether whence it emerges. Hitler's, Goebbels's – and Heidegger's – language collectively relies on similar phraseology, since such phraseology has proven to be effective (because *affective*) in captivating an audience. The "blue" and the "brown" mist are also intimately related to the "black magic" of journalism, since all three modes of language on Kraus's account have coercive, instrumental ends. Hitler can promote a worldview shaped by Karl May so long as he has found the right linguistic husk with which to encase it, and as long as he presents it with the kind of self-authenticating authority that characterizes the most effective journalistic spin.

The rhetorical exponents of National Socialism are, for Kraus, editorialists who have consummated the transformation of the world into a reflection of the "Zeitungsbegriff" that created them, a transformation that began well before their ascendance to power. Unlike social democracy, Kraus suggests, National Socialism succeeded because it effectively combined the strategies of modern journalism with an atavistic appeal to blood and soil, thereby eliding profound social and cultural tensions. In Kraus's words, it had "nicht nur die Phrase, sondern er wollte auch den Inhalt; er hatte die Romantik und darum die bessere Organisation."[59] The Nazis created a mythology and therefore supplied the element decidedly missing from other political parties and movements. This mythology, in turn, was buffered both by their journalistic techniques as well as acronymic inventions such as "SA" and "SS," "Formen der Ausschaltung einer Sprache, die, solange sie sich nicht vollends auf Zeichendeutung reduziert, hinreichend Spielraum für Gleichschaltung gewährt."[60] The double-meaning entailed in the word "Zeichendeutung" links the pre-modern act of divination to the bureaucratic language of signs or characters that constituted Nazi jargon. Kraus's point, however, is that such a self-legitimizing deployment of language is calculating and clever enough to remain credible, while also mystifying enough to radiate authority. It is, more importantly, a use of language that dissolves all social tensions and thus masks its own reification.

---

59 *Schriften 12*, 241.
60 *Schriften 12*, 130.

Both Kraus and Adorno insist on the mystification inherent to the journalistic cliché (for the former) and philosophical jargon (for the latter), both of which have informed the conditions of possibility for a world in which the language of fascism could find refuge. If Adorno is more concerned with the mimetic relationship between the syntax of jargon and the authoritarian structure of fascism, Kraus is more inclined to identify how the empty word (*Wort*) and the violent deed (*Tat*) had, under National Socialism, collapsed into one another – in other words, how hyperbolic or metaphorical language could no longer be distinguished from the harrowing violence it once merely anticipated. As Kraus writes: "In allen Gebieten sozialer und kultureller Erneuerung gewahren wir diesen Aufbruch der Phrase zur Tat."[61] Simply stated, Adorno and Kraus provide us with a framework to better understand the relationship between the political regimes of modernity and the discursive modes that inform the conditions of their possibility. Both figures argue, in other words, that whoever *owns the language* of a particular historical moment also controls the levers of power. The task is to identify how this mono-language is expressed in different genres that remain fundamentally linked to one another.

The convergence of Kraus's literary critique and Adorno's philosophical critique leads, however, to one concluding insight. Kraus's style throughout *Walpurgisnacht* and elsewhere is never reducible to a straightforward argument. It is in the spirit of his own views on language – especially language under National Socialism – that his language itself represents an attempt to transcend the icy reification of modern discourse and thereby arrive at a *thought*. The few remarks Kraus makes in response to Heidegger are illuminating not so much on account of their 'reading' of the philosopher, but in the way in which they are embedded in his essay: surrounded by a discussion of the most renowned representatives of the modern German cultural and philosophical tradition, an interrogation of the constant reference to one's own nation and its supposedly distinct virtues, and a focus on the problems that arise when that nation confuses a mass psychosis with an "awakening." In bringing together strands of myth and cultural inheritance with the ostensibly rational thinkers leading the way, and in foregrounding the tensions and contradictions inherent in his present moment, Kraus offers his own "dialectic of Enlightenment" without spelling it out as such. This is, indeed, why bringing Kraus's text in dialogue with Adorno is so fruitful: they are both in their own medium addressing the relationship between myth and reason and therefore both affirming and, at the same time, undermining the Enlightenment project in light of National Socialism.

---

61 *Schriften 12*, 141.

# References

Adorno, Theodor W. *Gesammelte Schriften Band 4: Minima Moralia: Reflexionen aus dem beschädigten Leben*. Frankfurt am Main: Suhrkamp, 2003.
Adorno, Theodor W. *Gesammelte Schriften Band 5: Zur Metakritik der Erkenntnistheorie. Drei Studien zu Hegel*. Frankfurt am Main: Suhrkamp, 2003.
Adorno, Theodor W. *Gesammelte Schriften Band 6: Negative Dialektik. Jargon der Eigentlichkeit*. Frankfurt am Main: Suhrkamp, 2003.
Adorno, Theodor W. *Gesammelte Schriften, Band 11: Noten zur Literatur*. Frankfurt am Main: Suhrkamp, 2003.
Arendt, Hannah. *Eichmann in Jerusalem: A Report on the Banality of Evil*, New York: Penguin 2006, 48.
Beck, Max and Coomann, Nicholas (Eds.). *Sprachkritik als Ideologiekritik: Studien zu Adornos Jargon der Eigentlichkeit*. Würzburg: Königshausen & Neumann, 2015.
Benjamin, Walter. *Gesammelte Schriften Band 1*. Frankfurt am Main: Suhrkamp, 1991.
Benjamin, Walter. *Gesammelte Schriften Band 2*. Frankfurt am Main: Suhrkamp, 1991.
Djassemy, Irina. *Der "Produktivgehalt kritischer Zerstörerarbeit": Kulturkritik bei Karl Kraus und Theodor W. Adorno*. Würzburg: Königshausen & Neuamann, 2002
Djassemy, Irina. *Die verfolgende Unschuld: Zur Geschichte des autoritären Charakters in der Darstellung von Karl Kraus*. Vienna: Böhlau, 2011.
Geller, Jay. *The Other Jewish Question: Identifying the Jew and Making Sense of Modernity*. New York: Fordham University Press, 2011.
Gordon, Peter E. *Adorno and Existence*. Cambridge: Harvard University Press, 2016.
Hammer, Espen. "Adorno's Critique of Heidegger," *A Companion to Adorno*. Eds. Peter E. Gordon, Max Pensky, and Espen Hammer. New Jersey: John Wiley & Sons, 2020. 473–486.
Heidegger, Martin. *Gesamtausgabe 16: Reden und andere Zeugnisse eines Lebensweges (1910–1976)*. Ed. Hermann Heidegger. Frankfurt am Main: Vittorio Klostermann, 2000.
Hohendahl, Peter. *Prismatic Thought: Theodor W. Adorno*. Lincoln: University of Nebraska Press, 1995.
Hurst, Andrea. "'To Know and not to do is not to Know': Heidegger's Rectoral Address," *South African Journal of Philosophy* Vol. 21:1 (2002): 18–34.
Jay, Martin. "Taking on the Stigma of Inauthenticity: Adorno's Critique of Genuineness," *New German Critique* Vol. 33:1 (97) (2006): 9–21.
Klemperer, Viktor. *LTI: Notizbuch eines Philologen*. Leipzig: Reclam (1998).
Kraus, Karl. *Schriften Band 10: Die letzten Tage der Menschheit. Tragödie in fünf Akten mit Vorspiel und Epilog*. Frankfurt am Main: Suhrkamp, 1986
Kraus, Karl. *Schriften Band 12: Dritte Walpurgisnacht*. Frankfurt am Main: Suhrkamp, 1989.
Linden, Ari. *Karl Kraus and the Discourse of Modernity*. Evanston: Northwestern University Press, 2020.
Müller, Burkhard. *Karl Kraus: Mimesis und Kritik des Mediums*. Stuttgart: Metzler, 1994.
Nancy, Jean-Luc. *The Banality of Heidegger*. Trans. Jeff Fort. New York: Fordham University Press, 2017.
Peiter, Anne. *Komik und Gewalt: Zur literarischen Verarbeitung der beiden Weltkriege und der Shoah*. Vienna: Böhlau 2017.
Pizer, John. "'Ursprung ist das Ziel': Karl Kraus's Concept of Origin," *Modern Austrian Literature* Vol. 27:1 (1994): 1–21.
Plass, Ulrich. *Language and History in Adorno's Notes to Literature*. Abingdon: Routledge, 2012.
Schuberth, Richard. "Blauer Dunst und Brauner Dunst," *Sprachkritik als Ideologiekritik: Studien zu Adornos Jargon der Eigentlichkeit*. Eds. Max Beck and Nicholas Coomann. Würzburg: Königshausen & Neumann, 2015. 90–107.

Schulte, Christian. *Ursprung ist das Ziel: Walter Benjamin über Karl Kraus*. Würzburg: Königshausen & Neumann, 2003.
Shuster, Martin. "Hannah Arendt on the evil of not being a person," *Philosophy Compass* Vol. 13:7 (July 2018): 1–13.
Shuster, Martin. *Autonomy after Auschwitz: Adorno, German Idealism, and Modernity*. Chicago: University of Chicago Press, 2014.
Timms, Edward and Bridgham, Fred (Eds.). *The Third Walpurgis Night by Karl Kraus*. Trans. Edward Timms and Fred Bridgham. New Haven: Yale University Press, 2020.
Vismann, Cornelia. *"Karl Kraus: Die Stimme des Gesetzes," Das Recht und seine Mittel*. Frankfurt am Main: Fischer, 2012.
Wolfson, Elliot R. *The Duplicity of Philosophy's Shadow: Heidegger, Nazism, and the Jewish Other*. New York: Columbia University Press, 2018.
Zuidervaart, Lambert. "Truth and Authentication: Heidgger and Adorno in Reverse," *Adorno and Heidegger: Philosophical Questions*. Eds. Iain Macdonald and Krzysztof. Palo Alto: Stanford University Press, 2007, 22–46.

Björn Quiring
# "A Contest Between Words and Deeds": Karl Kraus and Hannah Arendt on Proto-Totalitarian "Wahrlügen"

We know that Hannah Arendt knew the work of Karl Kraus, since she mentions him repeatedly, in a respectful, if somewhat distanced, manner. She calls Kraus a great writer and sets him on par with Franz Kafka and Walter Benjamin.[1] As with other literary sources, such as Proust, Joseph Conrad and Brecht, she uses Kraus' texts primarily as historical documents, but she also grants them a certain role in theory formation. It is not easy to determine to what degree Kraus influenced Arendt in this regard; the direct references are sparse. In her book *The Origins of Totalitarianism* (1951), Arendt explicitly refers to Kraus, but only as a chronicler of Viennese society life, concentrating on his positions regarding the "Jewish question" at the time of the Habsburg monarchy and the First Republic.[2] However, she does not investigate his attitude toward National Socialism. Only in the correspondence with Karl Jaspers, she briefly quotes Kraus' "Mir fällt zu Hitler nichts ein" ("Concerning Hitler, there is nothing that comes to my mind"), thus demonstrating that she was basically informed about Kraus' work on the subject.[3] The letter was written in 1965, so we do not know whether she had read the posthumously published *Dritte Walpurgisnacht* (*Third Walpurgis Night*) in the 1950s or the 1934 *Fackel* essay "Warum die *Fackel* nicht erscheint" ("Why the *Fackel* Is Not Coming Out") in which this sentence is quoted, or if her knowledge stems from another source. Are there concrete indications of Kraus' influence on the theories expounded in *The Origins of Totalitarianism*? And can their two studies of the Nazi regime be set in relation to each other and thereby be deepened and expanded? For example, can Kraus' wealth of concrete examples serve to flesh out Arendt's diagnoses that are occasionally a bit too sweepingly general?

In an attempt to answer these questions, I would like to begin with one of the most obvious similarities between the findings of Kraus and Arendt: both of them contradict the prevalent commonplace according to which National Socialism is a despotic form of government with a strictly enforced hierarchy that prescribes a function to all of its members with bureaucratic rigidity. Contrariwise, Kraus in-

---
1 E.g., Hannah Arendt, *Men in Dark Times*, New York: Harvest/Harcourt, 1968, pp. 172, 183, 186.
2 Hannah Arendt, *The Origins of Totalitarianism*, New York: Harvest/Harcourt, 1973, pp. 65–66.
3 Hannah Arendt and Karl Jaspers, *Correspondence 1926–1969*, ed. Lotte Köhler and Hans Saner, New York: Harvest/Harcourt, 1992, p. 592.

sists on the lack of fixed rules within the Nazi state and the consequent tendency of its representatives both to contradict themselves and to get in each other's way, on a theoretical as well as on a practical level. Kraus emphasizes that the rule of Nazi law is not hindered by these incoherencies, as long as the most brutal force triumphs reliably.[4] In addition, Arendt points out that this form of apparent self-sabotage is not a defect in the system, but a systematically induced confusion: the proliferation of competing agencies and of 'double binds' within the National Socialist state creates an institutionalized chaos which allows the *Führer* to reign more unrestrictedly, since only he is able to regulate the resultant contentions.[5]

At first sight, however, their common discoveries lead Kraus and Arendt to diametrically opposed conclusions: Arendt's central thesis is that the totalitarian state is to be understood as an invention of the twentieth century, as a completely new form of government which must be distinguished from mere tyranny. Kraus, on the other hand, tends to represent the Third Reich as a catastrophic relapse into troglodytic times, as suggested, for example, by the numerous quotations from Shakespeare and Goethe in the *Dritte Walpurgisnacht*, which describe various forms of primitive barbarism, but are also applicable to the Nazi era. Kraus even goes so far as to overcome his declared hostility against the "psycho-anal" worldview[6] by attributing the sadistic violence of the Nazis to traumatic childhood fixations and the resultant regressions: he describes SA men as individuals whose "sexual youth witnessed and retained the mystifying conjunction of pain and lust."[7] Kraus sees the ideology of the Nazis as a flimsy pretext for the lustful unleashing of archaic violence, the great "idea of having no idea."[8] Arendt, on the other hand, emphasizes that the citizens of totalitarian states generally want to believe in the officially promulgated ideologies, despite their evident internal contradictions. These ideologies fulfill a fundamental need, since they allow the members of the commonwealth to imagine that they have merged into a new form of pseudo-unity. They offer what Arendt characterizes as fictions of an absolutely consistent and comprehensible world.[9] Totalitarianism claims to have found the eternal laws that govern existence, and decorates this grand claim with scraps gleaned from the natural sciences. Politics is subsumed to the inevitable course of a natural history of which totalitarian rulers and their underlings con-

---

4 See e. g. Karl Kraus, *Dritte Walpurgisnacht*, ed. Christian Wagenknecht, Frankfurt a. M.: Suhrkamp 1989, pp. 178–180.
5 See e. g. Arendt, *Origins of Totalitarianism*, p. 397–405.
6 See e. g. Karl Kraus, "Die letzte Nacht" in *Die Fackel* 613–621 (1923), p. 71.
7 Kraus, *Dritte Walpurgisnacht*, p. 216.
8 Kraus, *Dritte Walpurgisnacht*, p. 33.
9 Arendt, *Origins of Totalitarianism*, pp. 352–354.

sider themselves to be the executive organs. Above all, this political enforcement of an all-embracing cosmic law involves the annihilation of those whom nature has declared to be on the losing side in the struggle for existence. Every act of violence against these inferiors confirms the official ideology and calls for new acts of violence, until mankind, in the words of Arendt, "is in itself only an exponent of the laws that are executed in it."[10]

Kraus does not introduce this perspective in the *Walpurgisnacht*, which may be due to the fact that his text only describes the Nazi regime in its initial stages, before the Night of the Long Knives in June 1934. This first phase of the Nazi regime was a time of somewhat awkward propaganda that accompanied the still rather unorganized violence of the SA torture cellars. Relying on his characterization of the Nazi regime as a dictatorship that "has gained command of everything in Germany except of the German language",[11] he uses his well-established satirical methods to attack its spokesmen, first and foremost by unmasking them through citations. Written and oral statements of the National Socialists are subjected to a "refutation of their thinking through their language",[12] which demonstrates their constant failure to live up to their own pretensions. In addition to recording amusing, but somewhat predictable examples of their profound orthographical and grammatical ineptitude, which throws a strange light on their a-vowed Teutonomania, Kraus focuses on the Nazis' symptomatic logical errors, for example, in the statements they use to vindicate their acts of violence. He characterizes the argumentative pattern by which they habitually justify themselves with the words:

> Man hat nichts getan, aber der andre ist dran schuld; es ist nichts geschehn und er hat es getan; man bezichtigt den, der die Wahrheit sagt, der Lüge, auf der man ertappt wurde.[13]

> They've done nothing but somebody else is the culprit; nothing happened but he's done it; when caught out telling a blatant lie, they blame those who speak the truth.[14]

Kraus's symptomatic reading of these official statements enables him to draw conclusions about the actual situation in Germany from the propaganda in the Nazi newspapers, thus coming to know quite accurately the atrocities about which the German people later claimed to have known nothing. In the words of Kraus:

---

**10** Hannah Arendt, *Elemente und Ursprünge totaler Herrschaft*, München/Berlin: Piper, 2016, p. 948. This sentence was added when Arendt translated the book into German.
**11** Kraus, *Dritte Walpurgisnacht*, p. 12.
**12** Kraus, *Dritte Walpurgisnacht*, p. 132.
**13** Kraus, *Dritte Walpurgisnacht*, p. 186–187.
**14** Karl Kraus, *The Third Walpurgis Night: The Complete Text*, trans. Fred Bridgham and Edward Timms, New Haven/London: Yale University Press, 2020, p. 132.

> Genügt denn nicht zur Vergewisserung ihres Tuns, was sie reden und wie sie leugnen?[15]
>
> Doesn't what they say and the way they deny suffice to enlighten us about their actions?[16]

However, Kraus himself soon notes that there is a fundamental problem with his attempt to expose and attack these developments with his old satirical methods: in the *Walpurgisnacht*, he occasionally hints that the Nazi discourse achieves something genuinely new, a "formation that is proper to their species" which "adapts language to the need for a radical dishonesty."[17] The Nazis are not interested in the question whether their propositions conform to the traditional norms of truth and logical coherence, because their rhetorical goals are ultimately different. For this reason, the demonstration of their logical, performative and formal self-contradictions cannot produce the social friction that satire needs in order to become effective – as it did, for example, in the case of Imre Békessy. Kraus' tried and tested instruments fail him, and he therefore draws the familiar resigned conclusion: "Kein Wort, das traf" ("No word that hit its mark").[18]

This diagnosis of a boundless mendacity connects his texts, *mutatis mutandis*, with those of Arendt. And the closer one looks, the more striking the similarities between their conceptions become: Arendt argues that the Nazis invented a new form of lying to secure their ideology: "One can say that to some extent fascism has added a new variation to the old art of lying – the most devilish variation – that of lying the truth".[19] Occasionally, she also calls this variation "Wahrlügen" ("truthlying").[20] Arendt uses the term to describe the tendency of the Nazis to affirm a lie and to remake reality in its image.[21] Perhaps "lying" is not the most appropriate term in this context; nor is "fiction", which Arendt also frequently uses.[22] Her late work *The Life of the Mind* suggests that the totalitarian project could also be understood as a violent materialization of a dominant metaphor. According to Arendt, a secondary result of Hans Blumenberg's metaphorological studies is the demonstration that many pseudo-scientific ideologies "owe their plausibility to the seeming evidence of metaphor".[23] Basically, "Wahrlügen" violently enforces these seeming evidences until reality conforms to them. For exam-

---

15 Kraus, *Dritte Walpurgisnacht*, p. 108.
16 Kraus, *Third Walpurgis Night*, p. 72. Translation modified.
17 Kraus, *Dritte Walpurgisnacht*, p. 126–127.
18 Kraus, "Man frage nicht", in *Die Fackel* 888.4 (1933), p. 4.
19 Hannah Arendt, "Approaches to the 'German Problem'", in: *Partisan Review* 12 (1945), p. 98.
20 Hannah Arendt, "Das 'deutsche Problem'", in *Zur Zeit: Politische Essays*, München: dtv, 1989. p. 29.
21 See e.g. Arendt, *Origins of Totalitarianism*, p. 350.
22 See e.g. Arendt, *Origins of Totalitarianism*, pp. 392, 421.
23 Arendt, *The Life of the Mind*, San Diego/New York: Harvest/Harcourt, 1978, p. 113.

ple, Nazism conceives all social interaction as a natural struggle of higher and lower races, and transforms society until it coincides with this conception. A main component of this transformation is the production of population segments who, by means of their systematic degradation, disenfranchisement and impoverishment, are forced to take the role of the demonstrably "lower races".[24] As can be gleaned from this example, the medium by which totalitarianism creates the truthful lie is violence, constantly inscribing itself into all bodies and objects. In designating the elimination of political opponents as "power propaganda", Arendt portrays Nazi violence as a kind of speech act that, while not really establishing new truths, generates complete indifference to the distinction between truth and lies in the German citizenry.[25]

What Kraus calls "radical dishonesty" can be regarded as a precursor to this "Wahrlügen", the practice of which was not yet fully developed at his time. Kraus already comes to suggest that a strange agglomeration of words and deeds develops under the Nazis, which can no longer be grasped with the conventional categories of truth and falsehood: in the centre of their discourse, he locates a certain

> Etwas, das immer auch ein anderes ist, fließend und flimmernd, gleitende Relativität am laufenden Zungenband, umso reizvoller, als sie doch das Absolute bejaht, ja aufs Ganze geht, das sogar das Totale ist.[26]

> something, always shifting, fluid and flickering, a continuous slippery relativising of meaning running off the tongue, all the more attractive for affirming the Absolute, even aspiring to the wholeness of Totality.[27]

In his article "Warum die Fackel nicht erscheint" as well as in *Die Dritte Walpurgisnacht* he describes one of the preliminary stages of "Wahrlügen" as a "turn of the stock phrase into action" („Aufbruch der Phrase zur Tat").[28] By this turn, various discursive commonplaces are given a concrete, material form by violent means. Empty words are "refilled with the blood [. . .] that once was their content."[29] Dead metaphors such as "rubbing salt into open wounds" are re-actualized as torture

---

[24] See also Klaus Theweleit, *Male Fantasies*, Vol. 2: *Male Bodies: Psychoanalyzing the White Terror*, trans. Chris Turner, Erica Carter and Stephen Conway, Minneapolis: University of Minnesota Press, 1989, p. 46.
[25] Arendt, *Origins of Totalitarianism*, p. 344.
[26] Kraus, *Walpurgisnacht*, pp. 162–163.
[27] Kraus, *Third Walpurgis Night*, p. 113. Translation modified.
[28] Kraus, *Walpurgisnacht*, p. 141. See also Karl Kraus, "Warum die Fackel nicht erscheint", in *Die Fackel* 890 (1934), p. 96.
[29] Kraus, *Walpurgisnacht*, p. 138.

methods by the stormtroopers.³⁰ The result is a strange depletion of language in which the conventional, "innocent" use of these stock phrases becomes impossible. In the words of Kraus: "The buzzword quickens and dies off."³¹

Kraus analyzes another subcategory of Nazi parlance to which the distinction between honesty and mendacity is found to be inapplicable: the denial that is at the same time a confession, as well as a recommendation. Kraus speaks of a "state morality based on bragging with all the things that did not happen."³² And he outlines the incoherent argumentation that the National Socialists tend to use when they are accused of employing atrocious violence against their political opponents: in the first place, they state that they know nothing about the violent attacks, secondly that nothing whatsoever happened to the victims, and thirdly, that the victims just received the rough treatment they deserved.³³ This form of denial is not just an indirect confession, but also an indirect message to the fellow party members that such attacks, which by definition do not occur, will not be punished either. In this respect, these denials encourage the acts that are denied and help to propagate them. Kraus writes about the typical Nazi personality:

> Daß er aber auch die Dinge nicht glaubt, die er sieht, ja nicht einmal die, die er tut; daß er nicht weiß, was er tut, und sich darum gleich selbst vergibt, das zeugt von einem Gemüt ohne Falsch, dem die Andersgearteten wohl ausweichen, aber nicht mißtrauen sollten. Da ihm die Gabe ward, nicht lügen zu können, und weil es doch auch unmöglich wäre, so viel zu lügen wie der Tatbestand erfordern würde, so kann nur ein mediales Vermögen im Spiele sein, das solchem Wesen die Dinge, die aus Illusion erschaffen sind, wieder durch Illusion entrücken hilft.³⁴

> But that he doesn't believe the things he has seen either, nor even those he has done; that he doesn't know what he is doing and promptly exonerates himself for that very reason, that points to a disposition incapable of falsehood, someone whom those differently constituted should avoid but not mistrust. Given the ability never to tell a lie, let alone the overwhelming multitude of lies required by the facts of the case, he must possess some

---

30 Kraus, *Walpurgisnacht*, p. 140.
31 Kraus, *Walpurgisnacht*, p. 141.
32 Kraus, *Walpurgisnacht*, p. 185.
33 Kraus, *Walpurgisnacht*, p. 183 et passim. An obvious parallel is an old joke quoted by Freud when describing the workings of the unconscious, concerning a man who was accused of having returned a borrowed kettle in a damaged condition. He "asserted, first, that he had given it back undamaged; secondly that the kettle had a hole in it when he borrowed it; and, thirdly, that he never borrowed a kettle [. . .] at all." Sigmund Freud, *The Interpretation of Dreams*, in *The Standard Edition of the Complete Psychological Works*, Vol. 4, ed. and trans. James Strachey, London: Hogarth Press, 1953, p. 119.
34 Kraus, *Walpurgisnacht*, p. 184.

mediumistic faculty that enables him to absolve himself by an illusion of the things that illusion created in the first place.³⁵

In these sentences, Kraus anticipates Arendt's conception of "Wahrlügen". And for this "contest between words and deeds"³⁶ he holds responsible the hegemony of clichés that already dominated public discourse before the Nazis came to power. This is one of the points on which it is interesting to read Arendt and Kraus in tandem: while Arendt ascribes the rise of totalitarianism primarily to a collapse of the public sphere in the aftermath of imperialism and economic crisis, Kraus understands it as the result of a pervasive corruption of language, instigated by various interest groups. And on this basis, he affirms that the journalistic discourse of the early 20$^{th}$ century bears the greatest responsibility for National Socialism. More than Arendt, he insists on a continuity between the Weimar Republic and Nazi Germany, between the language use of a decaying democracy and that of a totalitarian state. In the 1910s and 1920s, Kraus already polemicizes against the constant feedback loop between "deeds that generate reports and reports that generate deeds".³⁷ In 1914, he characterizes the "great times" at the outbreak of the First World War as a period "when pens are dipped in blood and swords in ink".³⁸ Therefore, National Socialism can be understood as the "fulfilment"³⁹ of the language depletion the press had effected in the preceding decades. Kraus insists on this continuity:

> Jenseits aller Frage, mit welchem Humbug sie [die Nationalsozialisten] die Masse nähren – sie sind Journalisten. Leitartikler, die mit Blut schreiben; Schwätzer der Tat.⁴⁰
>
> Over and above the humbug with which they [the National Socialists] nourish the masses, they are journalists. Editorialists who write in blood, blathering with their fists.⁴¹

According to Kraus, the Weimar Republic was already marked by a strong tendency to "Wahrlügen", which the Nazis only had to adopt and radicalize.⁴² Occasionally, Arendt also reflects on a certain unacknowledged affinity of bourgeois society with National Socialism; but Kraus analyzes their latent complicity in

---

35 Kraus, *Third Walpurgis Night*, p. 130. Translation modified.
36 Kraus, *Walpurgisnacht*, p. 177.
37 Karl Kraus, "In dieser großen Zeit", in *Die Fackel* 404 (1914), p. 1.
38 Karl Kraus, "In dieser großen Zeit", p. 1.
39 Kraus, *Walpurgisnacht*, p. 307.
40 Kraus, *Walpurgisnacht*, p. 307.
41 Kraus, *Third Walpurgis Night*, p. 226. Translation modified.
42 Kraus, *Walpurgisnacht*, p. 55: "Und doch hat sich eben im Tonfall der deutschen Welt nichts verändert. Mit den gleichen geistigen Mitteln erfolgt die Verankerung dessen, was heute zu verankern ist [. . .]."

more detail and comes to the conclusion that the common ground of the two groups is a specific use of language. From this hidden collusion springs the helplessness of established Weimar politicians and journalists when confronted with Nazi discourse: because their underlying agreement with their declared enemy is neither acknowledged nor analyzed, their efforts to distance themselves from Hitler and his minions end in grotesque, helpless performances.

Surprisingly, the exemplary failings that Kraus enumerates in this context are not so much those of reactionaries, who preferred the Nazis to the Communists anyway, but above all those of the German Social Democrats. He repeatedly insists that the principal credit for the victory of the "swastikastics" ("Hakenkreuzler") goes to the maneuverings of Social Democractic Party representatives.[43] In the essay "Hüben und Drüben" ("Over Here and Over There"), he adds:

> Wir müssen uns endlich klar werden, daß es, seitdem sich Menschheit von Politik betrügen läßt, nie ein größeres Mißlingen gegeben hat als das Tun dieser Partei, und daß die Entehrung sämtlicher Ideale, die sie benützt haben, um mit der Bürgerwelt teilen zu können, vollendet ist.[44]
>
> We finally have to come to terms with the fact that, ever since mankind has been betrayed by politics, there has never been a more disastrous failure than the deeds of this party, and that the violation of all its ideals, that it has misused in order to share the spoils with the bourgeoisie, is now complete.

That Kraus describes the Social Democratic Party as a "state-licensed institution for the consumption of revolutionary energies"[45] is mainly due to the fact that this party tends to sublate social tensions into a historical-determinist phantasm of inevitable working class victory, rather than to fight them out politically. Kraus avers that Social Democracy as well as National Socialism behave parasitically towards both conservative and revolutionary interest groups by seemingly harmonizing them in a pseudo-synthesis that is based on empty phrases. That is why he regards the former party as a prefiguration of the latter. He explains this extensively in the essay "Warum die Fackel nicht erscheint"[46] which should be read together with *Die dritte Walpurgisnacht*, since it has much more to impart than

---

43 Karl Kraus, "Hüben und Drüben", in *Die Fackel* 876 (1932), p. 1. See also Karl Kraus "Hüben und Drüben", in: *Hüben und Drüben: Aufsätze 1929–1936*, ed. Christian Wagenknecht, Frankfurt a. M.: Suhrkamp, 1993, p. 165.
44 Kraus, "Hüben und Drüben", p. 1/165.
45 Kraus "Hüben und Drüben", p. 7/170.
46 Karl Kraus, "Warum die Fackel nicht erscheint", pp. 1–315.

Kraus' sympathy – deplored by Walter Benjamin and others[47] – for the methods of Dollfuss. In this text, Kraus blames the sellout of Social Democracy on the internal dynamics of the party system, in which all political parties must focus on providing employment and income for their fellow members. Here Kraus' analysis is once more in line with Arendt's: insofar as the parties with revolutionary and reformist aspirations increasingly concern themselves with the preservation of their members' positions within society as it is, they tend to adapt to the social structures which they officially aim to transform.[48] Kraus sees the Social Democratic surrender of internationalism after 1914 as a result of this development and therefore speaks occasionally of the "National Social Democracy" in Germany and Austria.[49] As early as 1932, Social Democratic journalists occasionally wrote texts for Nazi newspapers, and Kraus saw this as a confirmation of his verdict. The phrases that he imputes to the Social Democratic apologist of this opportunistic behaviour resemble the incoherent, self-subverting arguments used by the Nazis:

> Wie, ihr könnt glauben, daß sie ein Hakenkreuzlerblatt ist und daß ein Sozialdemokrat an so einem mitarbeitet? Erstens ist sie bloß ein Blatt des Finanzkapitals, zweitens arbeitet er nicht mit, denn drittens hat er soeben die Mitarbeit aufgegeben, weil es ein Hakenkreuzlerblatt ist und ein Sozialdemokrat so etwas nicht tut, ihr Herren, wenn man ihm draufkommt!<sup>50</sup>

> What, can you seriously believe that this is a Nazi newspaper and that a Social Democrat would ever contribute to it? Firstly, it's only a newspaper of the financial capitalists, secondly, he doesn't contribute to it, because, thirdly, he has just renounced his contributorship, because it is a Nazi newspaper, and a Social Democrat would never do something like that, gentlemen, if he gets caught.

Kraus condemns the Social Democratic press in general when he writes:

> Man glaubt, wenn man durch einen Monat diese Publizistik der Rechtfertigung verfolgt hat, das Delirium eines Wettlaufs aller Einzellügen mitzumachen, die einander das kurze Bein stellen.[51]

> When one has followed this vindicatory journalism for one month, one gets the impression that one witnesses a delirious foot race of aggregate lies that keep tripping up each other.

---

47 See e.g. Walter Benjamin, *Briefe*, Vol. 2, Frankfurt a. M.: Suhrkamp, 1978, p. 623. See also Walter Benjamin, *Gesammelte Schriften* 2.3, Frankfurt a. M.: Suhrkamp, 1991, p. 1085.
48 Arendt, *Elemente und Ursprünge*, p. 676–677. The passage was added when Arendt translated the book into German.
49 Kraus, "Warum die Fackel nicht erscheint", p. 172.
50 Kraus, "Hüben und Drüben", p. 9/172.
51 Kraus, "Warum die Fackel nicht erscheint", pp. 231–232.

Thus, Kraus declares that the Social Democrats also fail to abide by the norms of logical coherence. And even in their case, one cannot just call the result a lie, because it sets out to transform the world in their image, even if these changes are much less ambitious than those of the Nazis. Kraus demonstrates that the defensive Social Democratic delirium has a fairly exact complement in the aggressive delirium of the National Socialists, and that one delirium feeds on the other: while the Nazis enact a truly radical revocation of all civilizational standards and declare it as necessary for the maintenance of law and order,[52] the discourse of the Social Democrats revolves around the invocation of a profound social revolution which they at the same time consistently prevent and abort. In Kraus' formulation: Social Democracy keeps advertising itself as the pathway toward a freedom it has already "frittered away".[53] As a symptom of this "double profiteerism" ("Doppelverdienertum")[54], he quotes a Social Democratic editorial which consoles the worker comrades who have been disappointed by a setback in their fight for the right of free assembly and for better working conditions, with these words:

> Man löse ihre Organisationen auf – morgen muß doch die Fabriksirene die Arbeiter wieder versammeln.[55]

> Their organisations may be dissolved – but tomorrow the factory siren must nonetheless reassemble the workers.

Kraus comments:

> Welche Vorstellung von der Gottgewolltheit einer politischen Macht, die sogar noch mit dem Verzicht auf den Generalstreik imponiert! [. . .] Die Gewißheit, daß die Fabriksirene die Arbeiter wieder versammeln wird, nachdem man sie entrechtet hat, als Raumgewinn zu imaginieren: solche Verzückung taktischer Nüchternheit ist selten.[56]

> What a conception of the divinely preordained allocation of political power that dazzles even with the avoidance of a general strike! [. . .] To interpret as a territorial gain the certainty that the factory siren will reassemble the workers, after they have been deprived of their rights: this rapture of tactical sobriety is a rare thing.

As in the case of the Nazis, this delirium is based on a belief in the overarching laws of history and nature that move things inexorably toward their destined

---

52 Kraus, *Walpurgisnacht*, p. 173. "Der Nationalsozialismus hat überhaupt keine andere Waffe als den umgekehrten Spieß, mit der der Bürger die Ordnung verteidigt."
53 Kraus, "Warum die Fackel nicht erscheint", p. 2.
54 Kraus, "Hüben und Drüben", p. 9/172.
55 Kraus, "Hüben und Drüben", p. 23/185.
56 Kraus, "Hüben und Drüben", p. 23–24/185.

aim. However, unlike the Nazis, the Social Democrats do not actively strive to enact these laws, but are contented with watching them unfold from the sidelines, leaving the travails of the class struggle to the laws' own sublime mechanics. Because this conscientious opportunism, which presents itself as the art of the possible, leaves the political tasks at hand undone, the Social Democratic passivity plays into the hands of the Nazis. Accordingly, in the *Walpurgisnacht*, Kraus poses the rhetorical question whether the Social Democrats do not already have a mindset that is "is in line with the mindset that concretizes metaphors".[57] The question is also motivated by the circumstance that the Social Democratic functionaries' betrayal of their ideals and of the working class is accompanied by their self-deception: like many insulated elites, the Social Democratic party officials begin to believe in their own lies, and Kraus often indicates that the mediatization of 20$^{th}$-century politics is chiefly to blame for this delusion. In this context, his aphorism should be remembered: "How is the world governed and led into war? Diplomats lie to journalists and believe it when they see it printed."[58]

Such feedback mechanisms can also be regarded as a preliminary stage of "Wahrlügen": Arendt's analysis of totalitarian rule includes an examination of the nested echo chambers in the National Socialist Party organization, in which totalitarian propaganda is constantly confirmed by its own proliferation.[59] Moreover, she points out that these mechanisms reinforce the impression of the respective functionaries that they have the silent majority and the powers of nature and history on their side.[60] The National Socialists share this sense of invulnerability in their function as executive organs of a supreme necessity with many Social Democratic policymakers. Kraus remarks that the centre-left parties in general and the Social Democrats in particular seem to assume that they enjoy the protected status of historical monuments.[61] The reason why this belief in their own infallibility had a fatal effect towards the end of the Weimar Republic is presented in more detail by Arendt than by Kraus: she addresses the general problem that parliamentary democracy usually only reaches a certain percentage of the population and can only involve a part of it in the political process.[62] In this respect, the concept of "popular sovereignty" is a fiction. As long as the economic situation of a state can secure the prosperity of its wider population, this deficit poses no problem. But when the wealth of a nation disintegrates in a time of economic crisis, it becomes

---

57 Kraus, *Walpurgisnacht*, p. 257.
58 Karl Kraus, *Nachts*, Leipzig: Kurt Wolff, 1918, p. 114.
59 Arendt, *Origins of Totalitarianism*, pp. 366–369.
60 See, e.g., Arendt, *Origins of Totalitarianism*, pp. 366.
61 Kraus, *Walpurgisnacht*, p. 250.
62 Arendt, *Origins of Totalitarianism*, pp. 311–313.

clear that only a fraction of the population actually considers itself to be truly represented by the established parties and interest groups within "their" representative democracy, and that this fraction tends to diminish rather than increase under the pressure of bad times. This disintegration of social cohesion essentially deprives the political parties of their legitimacy as representatives of the people. This is all the more problematic since politicians in their echo chambers barely notice this disintegration and either continue to believe in their own fictions (while the citizens are already disillusioned) or hope that the development will reverse itself and the Great Cause will eventually come to be appreciated again.[63] Finally, however, they must realize that, in Arendt's words,

> the unorganized masses whose apathetic, passive support they had counted on were no longer apathetic and no longer supportive, but emerged wherever they saw an opportunity to express their general hostility towards the whole system.[64]

This isolation of the rulers and this alienation of the masses are both conditions for the success of totalitarian propaganda and for the totalitarian destruction of the public sphere; the Nazis replace cumbersome political negotiations with the pseudo-reconciliation of shared resentments that seems to unite the atomized masses against a common enemy.[65]

It is notable that National Socialist rhetoric often represents all expressions of these resentments as liberating articulations of a suppressed truth which the mendacity of the ruling elite had concealed from the populace for far too long. The world of the bourgeois is denounced as a cloud-cuckoo-land from whose dreams the Nazi has finally awakened.[66] This uncharacteristic passion for the at-

---

[63] "Zwar überlebten sie ihren eigenen Zusammenbruch erheblich besser, als das Volk den Auseinanderfall der Klassengesellschaft überlebte, weil ja jede von ihnen ihren eigenen Parteiapparat entwickelt hatte, dem von sich aus, wie allen menschlichen Institutionen, eine gewisse Vitalität eignete. [. . .] Was aber die Parteimitglieder anlangte, so bestand die Bedeutung dieser überlebenden Parteien vor allem darin, daß sie garantieren schienen, daß alles irgendwann einmal wieder in seine alte Ordnung zurückfallen würde; mit anderen Worten, was die Parteimitglieder zusammenhielt, waren nicht so sehr gemeinsame Interessen als die ihnen gemeinsame Hoffnung, die Parteien würden diese Interessen wieder zum Leben erwecken." Arendt, *Elemente und Ursprünge*, pp. 676–677. These sentences were added when Arendt translated the book into German.
[64] Arendt *Elemente und Ursprünge*, p. 677. This sentence was added when Arendt translated the book into German.
[65] Arendt, *Origins of Totalitarianism*, p. 475.
[66] Regarding this metaphor, see also Anja Lobenstein-Reichmann, *Houston Stewart Chamberlain: Zur textlichen Konstruktion einer Weltanschauung, Eine sprach-, diskurs- und ideologiegeschichtliche Analyse*, Berlin: de Gruyter, 2008, S. 343–351.

tainment of truth may at first appear surprising, but it can partly be explained by the set of issues delineated above: Kraus and Arendt argue that the Nazi discourse appears attractive to the disillusioned masses because its lies are so disarmingly obvious and deliberate. The blatant, strategic lie seems to be more "realistic" and, as it were, more honest than the mendacity of the old order, since the shameless liars at least do not appear to fool themselves about the true state of affairs.[67]

Because of all these unacknowledged affinities between Social Democracy and National Socialism in the early 1930s, the efforts of the former to repudiate the latter must turn out strangely inept. Kraus speaks of a "ban" under which the Social Democrats seem to have been placed[68] and which renders their official fight against the Nazis so ham-fisted, complacent and small-minded, that it almost eliminates itself. The "Sozis" convey the impression that they

> bis zum letzten Hauch von Mann und Führer zur Redensart stehn, deren Inhalt oder einziger Sinn doch nur das Blut sein kann, das wir mit Recht nicht sehen können – das weckt auf die Dauer [. . .] die Vorstellung einer politischen Jammergestalt, die mit allem phraseologischen und taktischen Aufwand doch nicht der lebendigen Entschlußkraft des einen Sätzchens fähig wäre, das die politische Sachlichkeit, die psychologische Sicherheit und die formale Präzision hatte, einen Bann zu brechen.[69]

> up to the last breath of man and mountebank stick to an empty phraseology whose content can only mean the shedding of blood, despite the fact they cannot bear to see it – in the long run [. . .] this conjures up the image of a pitiable political figure who, for all the energy expended on phrasing and tactics, is still incapable of the strength of purpose to make a single short sentence come alive, one that has sufficient political objectivity, psychological assurance and formal precision to break a spell.[70]

According to this diagnosis, the Social Democrats succumb to a mimetic capture which drives them to refashion themselves as "social nationalists"[71] and thereby to implicitly endorse the standpoint of their declared opponents. Kraus therefore also designates them as "lemures shoveling their own graves".[72]

---

67 Kraus, *Walpurgisnacht*, p. 298. Kraus compares the corruption in Germany before 1933 with corruption after 1933 and concludes that the new regime's "openness in all forms of bribery, partisanship, and personal enrichment at the expense of the state" provides a "lavish contrast" to "the hidden sponsorships of the former system."
68 Kraus, *Walpurgisnacht*, p. 236.
69 Kraus, *Walpurgisnacht*, pp. 235–236.
70 Kraus, *Third Walpurgis Night*, p. 171. Translation modified.
71 Kraus, "Hüben und Drüben", p. 11/173–174. "Es gibt – und dies ist leider Gottes die stärkste aller Gegebenheiten, die wir herbeigeführt haben – es gibt Nationalsozialisten: da bleibt uns nichts übrig, als Sozialnationalisten zu werden, und uns zu gebärden, als wären wir die echten."
72 Kraus, "Hüben und Drüben", p. 6/170.

These continuities between the stock phrases of the "post-democratic" Weimar republic and the totalitarian "Wahrlügen" make the pathos of many Krausian utterances appear less hyperbolic: under these auspices, his whole work can be read as the chronicle of a world heading toward totalitarianism. If nothing came to his mind when he looked at Hitler's reign, the reason might be that he indirectly had already said everything about it, or at least about the gigantic void in which it was formed.[73] In this respect, Kraus' lapse into silence around 1933 should be regarded in continuity with the programmatic silence which he himself propagated, even in his most eloquent texts. One thinks of his commentary on the outbreak of the First World War: "Wer etwas zu sagen hat, trete vor und schweige!" ("Whoever has something to say, step forward and be silent!")[74] This form of silence can be quite voluble; it is only important that it interrupts the incessant background chatter of empty phrases. First and foremost, Kraus regards the resultant stillness as a breathing space in which a sense for the fragility of things and the contingency of perspectives can develop, a sense that he often designates as "imagination" ("Phantasie") and which he appraises as the foundation for every appearance of the truth.[75] The submission to the rule of the stock phrase leads to a congealment of thought habits and thus to a failure of the imagination, which Kraus calls "the calamity of all politics".[76] Accordingly, he unfolds his ideal of the public sphere as a place in which dramatic imagination can freely develop. However, Kraus ultimately does not conceive this sphere as a place of negotiations between equal citizens, but as that of an encounter between mimes and audiences.[77] Here Kraus and Arendt seem to diverge, since the latter insists on the need for a political space in which the members of a community can meet and come to an understanding on their past, present and future.[78] Kraus's ideal, on the other hand, is more dramatic than democratic: he tries to establish a harmony of reality and imagination, underpinned by a media ensemble with the theater at its centre. The social panorama that he designs in *Die Fackel* is, despite all its aggressive polemics, shaped by an effort to turn Viennese life into a happy farce in the spirit of Offenbach or Nest-

---

73 Kraus, *Walpurgisnacht*, pp. 307–308. "Zwar Trogloditen, haben sie doch die Höhle bezogen, als die das gedruckte Wort die Phantasie der Menschheit hinterlassen hat."
74 Kraus, "In dieser großen Zeit", *Die Fackel* 404 (1914), p. 2.
75 See e. g. Kraus, "Warum die Fackel nicht erscheint", p. 54.
76 Karl Kraus, "Ich und wir", in *Die Fackel* 743 (1926), p. 152.
77 See e. g. Walter Benjamin "Karl Kraus", *Gesammelte Schriften* 2.1, Frankfurt a. M.; Suhrkamp, 1991, pp. 356–359.
78 See Hannah Arendt, *The Human Condition*, Chicago/London: University of Chicago Press, 2018. On the blind spot of this conception, see e.g. James Bohman, "The Moral Costs of Political Pluralism: The Dilemmas of Difference and Equality in Arendt's 'Reflections on Little Rock'", in: Amy Allen (ed.), *Hannah Arendt*, Abingdon/New York: Routledge, 2016, p. 390.

roy, and thus to harmonize it *sub specie aeternitatis*.[79] Imagination is not only called upon to reveal the truth behind the veil of encrusted, empty phrases, but also to sublate these phrases within itself.

This partly explains why the *Machtergreifung* for Kraus was not only a humanitarian and cultural, but also an epistemic catastrophe. For in their own, perverted way, the Nazi stratagems are quite imaginative, as Kraus occasionally concedes: he states that National Socialism in its barbaric literalness has "romanticism" and is, for that very reason, better organized than Social Democracy.[80] In this context, the fact that Hitler around 1908 was as regular a visitor of the Burgtheater and of the Viennese operetta as Kraus can be regarded as symptomatic.[81] The Nazis used theatrical strategies that in many respects resembled those of Kraus; and with their help they unleashed a truly infernal mirth by, for example, first parodying institutions and then replacing the original by the parody. Arendt has analyzed these procedures, which the National Socialists seem to have employed quite systematically: in the constitution of the Nazi party's shadow cabinets, the prospective leadership positions were carefully filled with individuals whose qualifications predestined them to obstruct the official function of their office: criminals were appointed as ministers of justice, murderers as chairs of the medical association, and proven ignoramuses as ministers of science.[82] A similar effect is produced by the exuberant proliferation of offices with overlapping competencies and jurisdictions which the Nazis promoted and which appears as a persiflage of the very same sprawling bureaucracy that they constantly criticized.[83] When parody thus takes state power, the tensions and contrasts that satire needs in order to function disappear and its structures collapse. Kraus himself describes this implosion with the words:

> Es waltet ein geheimnisvolles Einverständnis zwischen den Dingen, die sind, und ihrem Leugner: autarkisch stellen sie die Satire her, und der Stoff hat so völlig die Form, die ich ihm einst ersehen mußte, um ihn überlieferbar, glaubhaft und doch unglaubhaft zu machen: daß es meiner nicht mehr bedarf und mir zu ihm nichts mehr einfällt.[84]

---

79 Walter Benjamin »Karl Kraus«, pp. 356–359.
80 Kraus, *Walpurgisnacht*, p. 241. "Sicherlich, der Nationalsozialismus ist von keinem andern oder doch einem ähnlichen antiquierten geistigen Rhythmus fett geworden, wie der Sozialismus mager. Aber er hatte nicht nur die Phrase, sondern er wollte auch den Inhalt; er hat die Romantik und darum die bessere Organisation."
81 J. Sydney Jones, *Hitler in Vienna, 1907–1913: Clues to the Future*, New York: Cooper Square Press, 2002, pp. 14, 58.
82 Arendt, *Elemente und Ursprünge*, p. 781. The passage was added when Arendt translated the book into German.
83 See e.g. Arendt, *Origins of Totalitarianism*, pp. 399–400.
84 Kraus, *Walpurgisnacht*, p. 28. See also Kraus, "Warum die Fackel nicht erscheint", p. 160.

> There is a mysterious collusion at work between the things that exist and those who question their existence: the former produce satire of their own accord, and their material assumes such grotesque forms – forms I once had to invent in order to make it transmissible and plausible, however implausible it was – that I am no longer needed, and my mind goes blank.[85]

To cite the satire that has been transposed into reality and to count on the social effectiveness of this procedure can no longer be regarded as a sensible strategy under these circumstances. But at the end of the *Walpurgisnacht*, Kraus nevertheless expresses his confidence that truth must ultimately prevail and that the regime of the tangible lie will not be able to change the nature of things and therefore will not endure. And as the basis of this assurance, he does not refer to a divine or natural agency, but to language itself which entangles the Nazis in performative and other contradictions. At least in and through the medium of language, true remembrance will therefore survive and condemn totalitarian rule.[86] This is the assumption underlying Kraus' concluding Goethean curse, which prophesies the fall of the Nazi empire:

> Wie lange noch! – Nicht so lange, als das Gedenken aller währen wird, die das Unbeschreibliche, das hier getan war, gelitten haben; jedes zertretenen Herzens, jedes zerbrochenen Willens, jeder geschändeten Ehre, aller Minuten geraubten Glücks der Schöpfung und jedes gekrümmten Haares auf dem Haupte aller, die nichts verschuldet hatten, als geboren zu sein! Und nur so lange, bis die guten Geister einer Menschenwelt aufleben zur Tat der Vergeltung:
>
>> Sei das Gespenst, das gegen uns erstanden,
>> Sich Kaiser nennt und Herr von unsern Landen,
>> Des Heeres Herzog, Lehnsherr unsrer Großen,
>> Mit eigner Faust ins Totenreich gestoßen![87]
>
> How long, O Lord! – Not as long as the memory shall endure of all those who suffered the indescribable things that were done here; the memory of all shattered hearts, all crushed wills, all violated honour, of every minute of happiness stolen from creation, and every harmed hair on the head of all those who committed no crime, apart from having been born! And only as long as it takes for the good spirits of this human world to rise up, seeking retribution:
>
>> And may the Phantom, which against us stands,
>> The self-styled Emperor, lord of our lands,
>> The army's Duke, our Princes' feudal head,
>> By our own hand be hurled among the dead![88]

---

85 Kraus, *Third Walpurgis Night*, p. 7. Translation modified.
86 Kraus, *Walpurgisnacht*, pp. 322–323.
87 Kraus, *Walpurgisnacht*, pp. 326–327.
88 Kraus, *Third Walpurgis Night*, p. 235. Translation modified.

Hannah Arendt, whose hindsight has to take the fact of Auschwitz and its implications into account, cannot adopt this optimism. Admittedly, she states that totalitarian rule "bears the germs of its own destruction" within itself; but she adds that this ruin might encompass the end of "the world as we know it".[89] "Wahrlügen" would then have reached its ultimate aim by the elimination of truth; for truth, according to Arendt, can only be imagined within the field of human communication.[90] In this respect, the triumphal march of totalitarianism has no inherent limits, as Arendt spelled out in her discussion with Eric Voegelin.[91] What keeps Kraus from coming to a similar conclusion seems to be his conception of language, which ultimately remains a theological one, insofar as it never loses its orientation toward the horizon of a final judgment.[92] This thesis has been treated in other contexts[93] and should be specified further; but it needs to be emphasized in this context that, according to Kraus' creed, even an inarticulate "cry out of stifling chaos" as well as the ensuing silence are bound to endure as instances of language, and thus as manifestations of truth.[94]

# References

Arendt, Hannah. "Approaches to the 'German Problem'" *Partisan Review* 12 (1945).
Arendt, Hannah. *Men in Dark Times*. New York: Harvest/Harcourt, 1968.
Arendt, Hannah. *The Origins of Totalitarianism*. New York: Harvest/Harcourt, 1973.
Arendt, Hannah. *The Life of the Mind*. San Diego/New York: Harvest/Harcourt, 1978.
Arendt, Hannah. *Zur Zeit: Politische Essays*. München: dtv, 1989.
Arendt, Hannah and Jaspers, Karl. *Correspondence 1926–1969*. Ed. Lotte Köhler and Hans Saner. New York: Harvest/Harcourt, 1992.
Arendt, Hannah and Voegelin, Eric. *Disput über den Totalitarismus: Texte und Briefe*. Ed. Hannah-Arendt-Institut für Totalitarismusforschung und Voegelin-Zentrum für Politik, Kultur und Religion. Göttingen: V&R unipress, 2015.
Arendt, Hannah. *Elemente und Ursprünge totaler Herrschaft*. München/Berlin: Piper, 2016.
Arendt, Hannah. *The Human Condition*. Chicago/London: University of Chicago Press, 2018.

---

89 Arendt, *Origins of Totalitarianism*, p. 478.
90 See e.g. Arendt, *Men in Dark Times*, p. 85.
91 Hannah Arendt/Eric Voegelin, *Disput über den Totalitarismus: Texte und Briefe*, ed. Hannah-Arendt-Institut für Totalitarismusforschung und Voegelin-Zentrum für Politik, Kultur und Religion, Göttingen: V&R unipress, 2015.
92 See e.g. Walter Benjamin "Karl Kraus", pp. 348–349.
93 See e.g. Christian Schulte, *Ursprung ist das Ziel: Walter Benjamin über Karl Kraus*, Würzburg: Königshausen und Neumann, 2003, p. 116. Burkhard Müller, *Karl Kraus: Mimesis und Kritik des Mediums*, Stuttgart: Metzler, 1995, p. 372.
94 Kraus, *Walpurgisnacht*, p. 14. See also Kraus, "Warum die Fackel nicht erscheint", p. 154.

Benjamin, Walter. *Briefe, Vol. 2*. Frankfurt a. M.: Suhrkamp, 1978.
Benjamin, Walter. "Karl Kraus", *Gesammelte Schriften 2.1*. Frankfurt a. M.: Suhrkamp, 1991.
Benjamin, Walter. *Gesammelte Schriften 2.3*. Frankfurt a. M.: Suhrkamp, 1991.
Bohman, James. "The Moral Costs of Political Pluralism: The Dilemmas of Difference and Equality in Arendt's 'Reflections on Little Rock'." *Hannah Arendt*. Ed. Amy Allen. Abingdon/New York: Routledge, 2016.
Freud, Sigmund. *The Interpretation of Dreams, in The Standard Edition of the Complete Psychological Works*, Vol. 4. Ed. and trans. James Strachey. London: Hogarth Press, 1953.
Jones, J. Sydney. *Hitler in Vienna, 1907–1913: Clues to the Future*. New York: Cooper Square Press, 2002.
Kraus, Karl. "In dieser großen Zeit" *Die Fackel* 404 (1914).
Kraus, Karl. *Nachts*. Leipzig: Kurt Wolff, 1918.
Kraus, Karl. "Die letzte Nacht" *Die Fackel* 613–621 (1923).
Kraus, Karl. "Ich und wir" *Die Fackel* 743 (1926).
Kraus, Karl. "Hüben und Drüben" *Die Fackel* 876 (1932).
Kraus, Karl. "Man frage nicht" *Die Fackel* 888 (1933).
Kraus, Karl. *Dritte Walpurgisnacht*. Ed. Christian Wagenknecht. Frankfurt a. M.: Suhrkamp, 1989.
Kraus, Karl. "Hüben und Drüben." *Hüben und Drüben: Aufsätze 1929–1936*. Ed. Christian Wagenknecht. Frankfurt a. M.: Suhrkamp, 1993.
Kraus, Karl. *The Third Walpurgis Night: The Complete Text*. Trans. Fred Bridgham and Edward Timms. New Haven/London: Yale University Press, 2020.
Lobenstein-Reichmann, Anja. *Houston Stewart Chamberlain: Zur textlichen Konstruktion einer Weltanschauung, Eine sprach-, diskurs- und ideologiegeschichtliche Analyse*. Berlin/Boston: de Gruyter, 2008.
Müller, Burkhard. *Karl Kraus: Mimesis und Kritik des Mediums*. Stuttgart: Metzler, 1995.
Schulte, Christian. *Ursprung ist das Ziel: Walter Benjamin über Karl Kraus*. Würzburg: Königshausen und Neumann, 2003.
Theweleit, Klaus. *Male Fantasies, Vol. 2: Male Bodies: Psychoanalyzing the White Terror*. Trans. Chris Turner, Erica Carter, and Stephen Conway. Minneapolis: University of Minnesota Press, 1989.

Galili Shahar
# Karl Kraus: Literature, Halacha, a Jewish Joke

## Prologue

We deal once more with Karl Kraus and his legacies as a thinker, a critic and an author, whose writings contributed to the discussion on the matter of law and justice around 1900. Kraus's essays gathered in the volume *Sittlichkeit und Kriminalität* (1908) attest to this enterprise.[1] In many of his articles, first published in his journal *Die Fackel* during the years 1902–1907, Kraus tales on trials and court-affairs in Vienna, exploring the corrupted juristic discourse and the false journalistic reportage. Kraus attacks the moralistic, hypocritical attitudes of court and media, and reveals the regressive, anti-feminine world-view of judges and journalists. In his essays "Zum Prozeß Klein" and "Theatermoral", alongside his notes "Montignoso" and "Verbrecher gesucht" – to mention only a few, Kraus presents his thesis on the criminalization of sexual affairs and the perverse legalization of erotic relationships. In his essays he refers also to the false pathos and wrong over-tons of the court sentences, pointing at their deceitful performative aspects. In Kraus's view, the Viennese court and the newspapers were performing a very bad play on Eros and morals, while staging prostitutes, actresses, Jews and others as evils, accusing and condemning in the name of the law. His writings can be read as a critique of judgment, in which Kraus deconstructs the language of the law – from within. For not only the content of Kraus's writings on the law was crucial, but also their form. Kraus's essays are written as reflections of sentences, appropriating the poetics of judgment – yet as a deformed, fragmented trope. Kraus, who writes "before the law", reveals the court as a humoresque. His accusations are severe, yet comic.

Kraus's writings are acts of judgment. However, how this writing on the matter of law and its performances in the Viennese court can be addressed as an act of literature? Furthermore: How these acts of writings are to be considered as a Jewish writing? In what sense Kraus's texts, his critical re-views of court accusations, his acts of judgment are expressions of being-Jewish?

Kraus, an Austrian author with a "weak Jewish background", who knew almost nothing about Judaism's major traditions – the Midrash, the Talmud and the

---

[1] Karl Kraus, *Sittlichkeit und Kriminalität*, München: Kösel Verlag, 1970.

Kabbalah, the liturgical prayers and songs, addressed in a few of his writings the "Jewish question" – in its modernist form, and discussed critically the Zionist enterprise. Regarding the Jewish affairs of his age Kraus acted as a bystander, as a spectator. His vocation as a critic, his devotion to acts of judgment, his playful, ironic approach – also in regard to the "Jewish question", was identified by a few of his readers as a phenomenon of "(Jewish-) self-hatred". We recall in this context Theodor Lessing's argument against Kraus:

> Karl Kraus ist ein gewaltiger Literat, und er würde ein Literat sein, ganz gleich, was er triebe und wo er sich befände. Aber seine Literatur ist gespeist von keuchendem Hasse gegen Literatur. Er schreibt Zeitung, um Zeitungen zu bekämpfen, und stellt sich in der Mitte der Zeit, um der Zeit zu sagen, wie sehr er sie verachte.[2]

Lessing's remark on Kraus belongs to the notorious attempt of categorizing Jewish intellectuals as "self-hatred", arguing about their mental distortions and inclinations towards self-destruction. A similar argument was made regarding other Viennese intellectuals of Jewish background, among them were Otto Weininger, Sigmund Freud, Gustav Mahler and Theodor Herzl. In his remark, however, Lessing refers to Kraus's literary work, arguing that Kraus reclaimed the literary form for destroying its major enterprises. Should this be considered as a Jewish form of writing?

The effort to discuss Kraus's writing as a signifier of the German/Austrian-Jewish literary project is not free of regressive considerations and false efforts. Our own discussion is also at risk of falling into pure generalizations. A reading of Kraus's work in the frameworks of German-Jewish literature should thus keep degrees of freedom and double-irony.

Our point of departure, in asking about the Jewish implication of Kraus's work, is found in a short text on Kraus by Walter Benjamin, published in 1928. Benjamin's text, serving as *Urzelle* of his great 1931 essay, is titled "Karl Kraus". Benjamin's essay calls the proper name of the critic, admitting not only its major theme – an attempt of a short intellectual biography of Kraus, but also calling his name as a gesture of incantation. In Benjamin's own view, Kraus's literary impact and his public effect were to be considered "demonic" – magical and destructive, yet associated with the language of creation. Kraus's enterprise as a critic, to follow Benjamin's major argument, should be understood, alongside its modernist attributes (Vienna around 1900), as associated with the mythical structure of language, performing the power of "judgment" in its demonic (creative/destructive) implications. Benjamin, in pronouncing Kraus's name, wishes, however, to call him back to the realm of divine justice, signed by a liturgical gesture – prayer and hymn. This, in Benjamin's view, was the main "Jewish" aspect, hidden in Kraus's writings.

---

2 Theodor Lessing, Der jüdische Selbsthass (1930), München: Matthes & Seitz, 1984, 43.

Benjamin's argument on the Jewish dimension in Kraus's writing on the law refers, however, to the Talmud. Kraus's interventions in the realm of the law, according to Benjamin, were of "Halachic" nature. Such an argument – on the Talmudic nature of Kraus's work, cannot be read without irony. Benjamin's interpretations of Jewish being, if one recalls his essay of Franz Kafka (1934) and his own autobiographical notes, like his short text titled "Agesilaus Santander" (1933), attest also to a comic register. There is something witty in Benjamin's suggestion to understand Kraus as a Talmudic scholar or as a choral singer. It reveals, however, through its ironies, the complexities of tradition, both in Kraus's and Benjamin's own work. Our question thus refers to this argument by Benjamin: How to understand properly Kraus's act of writing as a Talmudic intervention in the realm of the law?

This first question, however, is followed by a second one: What sounds Jewish in Kraus's work? This question will bring us to a short discussion of Franz Kafka's note on Kraus and the heritage of *Mauscheln* – the German-Jewish dialect, the language of the "mouse people". Kafka's remark on the Jewish accent in Kraus's play "Literatur. Oder Man wird doch da sehn", should also, like Benjamin's, be understood as an ironic note. These remarks on Kraus are read as "Jewish jokes".

This essay thus reflects Kraus's writings through a double mirror. Benjamin and Kafka provide us with ironic notes regarding the Jewish aspects of his writing, illuminating perhaps their own experience as Jewish authors in the realm of German letters.

## Halacha, Interruptions

In his short essay from December 1928, defined by him, in a note to Gershom Scholem, as "eine neue Kraus-Notiz" (Benjamin 1991, 624–625), a new note about Kraus, Benjamin argues about his task, namely "ein Versuch, seine jüdische Physiognomie zu zeichnen", an attempt of drawing his [Kraus'] Jewish physiognomy. Benjamin addresses the question regarding Kraus not only as a "Jewish question" and not merely as a matter of "a portrait", but rather as a physiognomic fact, as if something in the expression of Kraus's writing, a certain aspect in their "face" (appearance), admits its being-Jewish. Benjamin refers to the spiritual dimension of Kraus's work, yet associates it with a sensual aspect, evoking a criminal implication and an Anti-Semitic trope. In writing about Kraus's legacy as of Jewish implication, Benjamin had to refer to its Anti-Semitic con-text. However, there is no need to rush into false conclusions regarding Benjamin's note, as if it admits (again) a certain dialectic of "Jewish Self-hatred". This category does not exhaust the real complexity of Benjamin's argument. For what Benjamin refers to is rather an attempt of drawing a portrait, in which Kraus's Judaism is not a matter of fact. Referring to physiognomy implicates again the judicial aspect, to which Benjamin attaches a demonic interpretation.

Being-Jewish, in Benjamin's view, is not an essence – neither religious nor historical, but rather refers to a certain recollection, a constellation of tradition, in which remnants of a liturgical work are being in-act, accumulating in *Studium*, studies (in Hebrew/Aramaic – Talmud). Jewish is the proper name for tradition that suffers crisis, inversions and demonic adaptations, yet keeps its liturgical intentions and its (week) messianic powers. Jewish, however, is also a name for Benjamin's own effort of reading Kraus, a name for his methodological approach, evoking the idea of justice as hermeneutical conclusion. In other words: Jewish in Benjamin's sense implies an act of intervention. What is Jewish in Benjamin should be understood not as a "fact" but rather as a re-collection (memory and prayer), not as a measure of itself, but rather as a proportion. Jewish in reading of Kraus is not an image (Benjamin seems to acknowledge the Hebrew prohibition against the making of an image, *das Bilderverbot*), but rather its rupture, or – its shadows. In writing about "Jewish physiognomy" in Kraus case, Benjamin implies this concept, but in inversion. Benjamin refers to a comic interpretation of tradition in his works. It that sense, Benjamin tells a "Jewish joke" on Kraus. The joke, however, is of judicial implications. Let us recall the opening sentence of Benjamin's note:

> In [Kraus] ereignet sich der großartigste Durchbruch des halachischen Schrifttums mitten durch das Massiv der deutschen Sprache. Man versteht nichts von diesem Mann, solange man nicht erkennt, daß mit Notwendigkeit alles, ausnahmslos Alles, Sprache und Sache, für ihn sich in der Sphäre des Rechtes abspielt (Benjamin, 1991, 624)

The writings of Kraus should be read, according to Benjamin, as texts of "before the law", intended, submitted – to the court. For everything in Kraus's world belong essentially – without exception (*ausnahmslos*) to the realm of the law. Kraus's world, Benjamin writes, is lawful. However, Kraus's writing-act is understood as an act of breaking-through, *Durchbruch*, an intervention (perhaps, an invasion) of the *Halacha*. Kraus's work is read as a Talmudic interference in the realm of German court language. What should this mean?

*Halacha*, implying in Hebrew "a way-of-life", a walk, a guide, a path of being in the world, is first and foremost an event of learning, a study of the law, a debate regarding its border-lines and implications – discussions being documented in a multi-text, written in Hebrew and Aramaic. Talmud, in which Halacha is being at-act, includes also *Midrash* (exegesis) and *Aggadah* (tale). *Halacha* is interwoven with interpretations (and often – interruptions) of the *Mishna* (The Hebrew ancient codex), alongside tales – stories and anecdotes about scholars, rabbis and disciples of *Torah*, among them great teachers but also laymen and fools. The Halachic scripts, to which Benjamin refers, are read as a protocol of an ancient Jewish seminar. Many of the Halachic questions, the dissuasions about the judicial implications of the *Mishna*, are left in the Talmud unfinished, without a solution or decision, being often called into new, contradictory interpretations, into "different matter" (In Hebrew: *Dawar Hacher*), or concluded as a draw (in Aramaic: *Tikko*).

What *Halacha* thus implies is not only a major version of a Jewish law, but rather forms of life that are based on radical interventions in the realm of the law. Halacha is a method of studying, in which story-telling (*Aggadah*) interferes the procedures of judgment, creating de-tours, suspensions, and corrective acts.

When Benjamin compares Kraus's writing with these of *Halacha* and argues about its breakthrough into the realm of German letters, he implies a comparison with a Jewish literary corpus, in which the producers of studying the law are interrupted by the cause of literature (the *Aggadah*). *Halacha* implies a method of learning, based, however, on over-interpretations that often end in a *Sackgasse*. Furthermore: When Benjamin writes about the *Durchbruch des halachischen Schrifttums*, he refers also to a certain dimension of resistance of Hebrew/Aramaic in the realm of German language. What *Halacha* means here is not only an act of resistance in the realm of the law, but also an interruptive movement in the world of German language, performed by the ancient Semitic languages. In that sense Kraus's work is that of a Talmudic messenger, a critic and a judge in the Halachic meaning of the word, whose acts hold liturgical values. This reflection, following Benjamin, should be understood properly, namely not without its ironic self-reference. This attitude finds an echo in the second argument by Benjamin, referring to the nature of Kraus's writing:

> Man begreift seine sprachlichen Untersuchungen nicht, erkennt man sie nicht als Beitrag zur Strafprozeßordnung, begreift das Wort des Anderen in seinem Munde nur als corpus delicti, ein Heft der „Fackel" nur als Termin. Um ihn türmen sich die Prozesse. (625).

Kraus's writings are not only manifestations about the essence of language, but rather they refer to the language of the law: Every word Kraus writes in his essays is meant as an act of judgment: His writing is an accusation. The whole enterprise of language in Kraus's world is understood as *ein Urteil*, what he writes is always a "sentence".

## The Demon, Literature and the Day of Judgment

In Jewish tradition, however, in the writings of Talmud and Kabbalah, the measure of judgment, *Midat HaDin*, is being associated not only with divine justice, with the "proper measure", but also with exaggerations of divine power and with false implications of creative language. Judgment often transforms itself into evil, being identified with the work of the devil. What judgment implies is rather an inversion of justice into the abstract, universal language of the law. Demonic, however, is not only the abstraction (generalization and the denial of concreteness), or the violent implications of law-giving. Demonic is rather the ambiguous character of judgment. Demonic is a name proper for the irony, the dualities and mimicries in acts of judgment. In his writings Kraus transforms the court into a theatre, the trial into a play. The play, however, is demonic:

> Unter seinen selbstverhängten Urteilen tut ihm keines genug. Es gibt das beispiellose, zweideutige, echt dämonische Schauspiel des ewig Recht heischenden Anklägers, des Staatsanwalts, der ein Michael Kohlhaas wird, weil keine Justiz seiner Anschuldigung, keine seiner Anschuldigung ihm selber Genüge tut. (625)

Kraus's "sentence", his act of judgment and of writing is demonic not only because of its accusative dimension, its charges, the accusation (Anklage) against judges, prosecutors and journalists. It is rather its ambiguous (*zweideutig*) implications, in which his cases are being transformed into an endless play of destruction. Nothing is more demonic than the double implication of the word itself (the ability to say "yes" and "no" in the same word). This, however, the double, endless procedure, is Halachic. Kraus, to follow Benjamin's argument, applies the Talmudic act of interruption in the realm of court: Every sign in Kraus's corpus is a "different matter" (*Dawar Hacher*).

Demonic thus in not only the power of judgment, the fall and punishment of man – in the name of the law, but also the interruptions, the inversions of meaning in the realm of language, as every sign, every sentence turns to something else.

Kraus's acts of judgments, however, are performative. They belong not only to courts and to halls of justice but also to the theatre and to the stages of German literature. Not in vain Benjamin refers in his note to Heinrich von Kleist's novella and to its main protagonist, Michael Kohlhaas. Kohlhaas is known for his war for justice and his enterprises of revenge, destroying cities by a declaration of a (false) "divine mandate". Kohlhass is without doubt a messenger of the Day of Judgment in the realm of new German literature. His final act of revenge, however, performed just before his execution, is a "literary" one: Kohlhaas performs his revenge against the sovereign by swallowing a piece of paper, on which a prophecy is supposed to be written, the name of a last descendant of the ruling house. Acts of judgment in Kraus's work are not to be separated from a certain literary canon and from the deconstructive possibilities of the play, *das Spiel*. Kraus, Benjamin argues, like Kohlhass, will find no satisfaction, no end in his acts of judgment. He rather writes his essays and court reviews as performances of the Last-Day. His play is left yet without solution. Kraus's theater is not eschatological, it rather transforms its forms of violence into an endless game. This game, we argue, belongs to the demonic sphere.

## Justice, a Jewish *salto mortale*

The discussion on the demonic, destructive aspects of the power of judgment, brings us closer to what Benjamin calls in his later essay on Kraus, the Jewish *salto mortale*, namely the leap from the realm of judgment into that of justice. In Hebrew, it refers the move from *Din* into *Tzedek*. This movement is understood as the difficult of all, for it demands an interruption in the state of law, a permanent revolution of values, to which Kraus was devoted, being performed, however, beyond the major work of judgment, beyond, perhaps, irony itself. In Hebrew this realm of justice is being identified with the measure of *Rachamim*. The word can be translated as "compassion", yet not to be wrongly interpreted as "pity" or "grace" (in the Christian theological sense). Justice depends a certain construction in being, called after a feminine limb of birth and of care (*Rechem*). The "Jewish leap" is thus of gender implication too. What justice implies demands a metaphysical structure that reveals itself in the inversions of judgment.

How this experience, the move from the realm of judgment into justice, is being implicated in Kraus's work? Benjamin writes:

> Die sprachliche und sittliche Silbenstecherei dieses Mannes meint nicht Rechthaberei, sie gehört zu der wahrhaft verzweifelten Gerechtigkeit einer Verhandlung, in der die Worte und Dinge, um ihren Kopf zu retten, das verlogenste Alibi sich ersinnen und unaufhörlich durch den Augenschein oder die nackte Rechnung widerlegt werden müssen. (625)

Kraus's work belongs to the tradition of justice, yet history made him into *ein Ankläger*, prosecutor, a critic. His major writings are left thus as acts of judgments, as interventions in the realm of the law. However, the secret of Kraus's work, its hidden essence, is liturgical:

> Ein Dasein, das, eben hierin, das heißeste Gebet um Erlösung ist, das heute über jüdische Lippen kommt. (625)

Benjamin listens to the hidden voice of Kraus, being concealed in his acts of judgment and by his demonic play of accessions. It is rather the work of prayer, a prayer for the creatures, a call for all which was created, to be saved and to reach correction in being. Neither the law itself, judgment and acts of revenge, nor the power for decision on the state of exception, is the essence of Kraus's sentence, but rather the plea for the poor creatures. This is how Benjamin ends his short portrait of Kraus, it ends with his image as a Jewish prayer. What sense does it make?

Benjamin's interpretation of Kraus's work, one can argue, is itself of Talmudic nature. What Benjamin suggests in his note on Kraus is a form of over-interpretation, a reading in which the portrait of the author is being transformed into a demonic image. Benjamin hints, however, at radical possibilities being concealed in Kraus's acts of judgment. The implications of these interruptive acts in the realm of the law, hold the potential of justice. Benjamin thus listens to a secret voice in Kraus's writings, and names it as a remnant of Jewish prayer.

## Prayer, *Mauscheln*

More should be said on the work of prayer – the gesture with which Benjamin signed his short note on Kraus. The liturgical task Benjamin relates to Kraus is of Talmudic nature. In the final section of his 1931 essay, Benjamin recalls this liturgical act, referring to the *Unmensch*, the inhuman, a "new angel", as he writes:

> . . . ein neuer Engel. Vielleicht von jenen einer, welche, nach dem Talmud, neue jeden Augenblick in unzähligen Scharen, geschaffen werden, um, nachdem sie vor Gott ihre Stimme erhoben haben, aufzuhören und in Nichts zu vergehen. Klagend, bezichtigend oder jubelnd? Gleichviel – dieser schnell verfliegenden Stimme ist das ephemere Werk von Kraus nachgebildet. Angelus – das ist der Bote der alten Stiche. (Benjamin 1991a, 367)

The new angel is formed as a liturgical body, created for singing before God's throne. This angel is mentioned in the tractate *Chagiga*, the book the Festival Offering in the Talmud, telling about the angels being born form God's breath (according to another Midrash, they are being born from the river of fire, נהר דינור), for singing the song of glory. It tells:

> כל יומא ויומא נבראין מלאכי השרת מנהר דינור, ואמרי שירה ובטלי, שנאמר
> "חדשים לבקרים רבה אמונתך"

Midrash Rabba, a late Talmudic exegesis to the Torah, adds to this the following:

> לעולם אין כת של מעלה מקלסת ושונה אלא בכל יום בורא הקדוש ברוך הוא כת של
> מלאכים חדשה והן אומרים שירה חדשה לפניו והולכין להם

According to this version every day God creates new angels to sing new song before his throne, and then to perish. The life of the new angel is poetic but short. The song of the angel, Benjamin comments, might be a lament or a song of glory.

Important is this alone: the angel embodies a voice of a prayer, despaired but celebrated. What the angel sing is the song of Exile, in which the sorrows of destruction and homelessness are interwoven with expressions of joy and hopes of salvation.

This prayer, however, how should it sound? According to the tradition (like the Zohar and the *Hekhalot* literature), the songs of the angels are mighty and no human ear should bear it. The voice of the heavenly creatures is beyond all measures. In a few sources, following the Prophetic scriptures, the sound of the angelic prayer is called a "great noise" (in Hebrew: *Rahash Gadol*). In other sources it is compared with a whispering, with breathing alone.

Following Benjamin's note, asking about the implications of Kraus's work as a Talmudic intervention in the realm of the German law, we reach the question regarding the Jewish prayer and its voices. In this context one recalls Richard Wagner's "thesis" on how Jewish prayer sounds. In his infamous essay on *Judentum in der Musik* Wagner identifies "with horror" the voice of the Jewish prayer and the synagogical songs as "gurgle, yodel and cackle". He hears the Jewish song of prayer as a disharmonic vocal texture, as a great noise, an evidence of the Jewish unmusical character, itself an outcome of an Exilic being. Wagner's statements, anti-Semitic of their kind, correspondent, however, the traditional argument about the creaturely, earsplitting nature of the angelic prayer. This should not surprise us. The Jewish prayer, because of its unfamiliar, disharmonic sound, ruptures and interferes the false harmonies of European music. Wagner, who denied the radical implications of the Semitic vocal, reject all together its traditions. The Jewish prayer does sound "creaturely"; its effects – the cry, the yell, twittering and whispering, are significant matters of its liturgical tasks.

How does this note refer, however, to Kraus's work? In what sense his writing sounds "Jewish"?

We have to reconsider these questions not without irony. While arguing about the liturgical remnants of Kraus's work – following Benjamin's suggestion, or asking about its vocal implication – as a "Jewish noise", we refer to these analogies not as facts, but rather as comic interpretations. Comic is also Franz Kafka's remark on Karl Kraus, referring to his writings as an example of *Mauscheln* – the German-Jewish dialect.

Kafka's note, included in a letter to Max Brod from June 1921, written while staying at a sanitarium in Matilary, Slovakia, begins with a report on his health issues, deals also with the question of German-Jewish literature, or the matter of *Mauscheln*. In his short note, Kafka not only reflects the debate between Karl

Kraus, Franz Werfel and the Prague circle, referring to Kraus's satirical operetta "Literatur. Oder Man wird doch da sehn", but rather explores his own view on the impossibilities of the German-Jewish literary project. Kafka uses, however, the German pejorative term *Mauscheln*, marking the German-Jewish body-language, considered as an Eastern, foreign, Yiddish-like jargon, to define the essence of Kraus's work and the Jewish writing as such. *Mauscheln*, in this context, is the name of a creaturely body (*eine Maus*), implying certain liturgical implications (Moses). *Mauscheln* is a name for the improper Jewish usage of German language.

Yet, Kafka's remarks on Kraus's work begin also with *ein Witz*, a joke, a wit – revealing the wisdom of Kraus's work:

> Der Witz ist hauptsächlich das Mauscheln, so mauscheln wie Kraus kann niemand, trotzdem doch in dieser deutsch-jüdischen Welt kaum jemand etwas anderes als Mauscheln kann. (Kafka 1995, 336)

*Mauscheln*, Kafka writes, is the principle of German-Jewish literature, being represented by Kraus. For nobody can *mauscheln* like him. The meaning of *Mauschlen*, Kafka writes, is the following:

> Anmaßung eines fremden Besitzes, den man nicht erworben, sondern durch einen (verhältnismäßig) flüchtigen Griff gestohlen hat und der fremder Besitz bleibt, auch wenn nicht der einzigste Sprachfehler nachgewiesen werden kann. (336)

*Mauscheln* is the way Jewish authors misuse German language. In their hands, German is *ein fremder Besitz*. The Jewish way of handling the German language is that of estrangement. It essence, however, depends a certain relationship between the act of writing the gestures – the (Jewish) body language:

> Das Mauscheln ist eine organische Verbindung von Papierdeutsch und Gebärdensprache

*Mauscheln* thus involves dramaturgical figures of expression (radical, exaggerated, intensive gestures). It is not only to argue, following Kafka, that German-Jewish writing, represented in Kraus's work, deals often with bodies and gestures, but rather that the gestures cause ruptures and distortions of rhythm, bringing language into disorder. *Mauscheln* is a Jewish body-language which brings literature into an unfamiliar mode. Kraus's contribution to the world of German letter, defined by Benjamin as Halachic intervention, is characterized by Kafka as *Mauscheln*. Both interpretations are comic, referring to the interrupting element, hinting at a certain traditional effect. In Kafka's view, *Mauscheln* is rather based on "(das) Verhältnis der jungen Juden zu ihrem Judentum". The complicated, despaired relations of young Jews (mainly young males) to Judaism (more precisely: to the Judaism of their fathers), is the condition that Kraus's work brings into expression. The Jewish voice, however, is a lament, and find its manifestation in Kraus's operate in the cry "oi". This short, minor speech-act, the last gesture of the grandfather in Kraus' operetta, who, at the end of the operetta, reveals what *Mauscheln* is.

In Kafka's view, the essential element in Kraus' work is the creating of poetical textures that express the Jewish condition – the foreignness, rootlessness and anxiety of being a Jew. These poetical textures are of dramaturgical nature – they are written as gestures and based on a radical, intensive language-body. *Mauscheln* is the language of a theatrical body – a body of exaggerated gestures and foreign sounds. This body, however, is of creaturely nature. This is how Kafka describes in his letter the body of the Jewish author:

> Weg vom Judentum, meist mit unklarer Zustimmung der Väter (diese Unklarheit war das Empörende), wollten die meisten, die deutsch zu schreiben anfingen, sie wollten es, aber mit den Hinterbeinchen klebten sie noch am Judentum des Vaters und mit den Vorderbeinchen fanden sie keinen neuen Boden. Die Verzweiflung darüber war ihre Inspiration. (337)

The image of a creaturely body, the body of a young Jewish author who searches in despair for "einen neuen Boden", while turning away from Judaism, is the image of *Mauscheln*. Kafka mentions in this context the "three impossibilities" of the Jewish writing:

> (Die) Unmöglichkeit, nicht zu scheiben, (die) Unmöglichkeit, deutsch zu schreiben, (die) Unmöglichkeit, anders zu schreiben. (337–338)

> The impossibility, not to write, the impossibly, the write in German, the impossibility, to write differently.

The impossibilities, or the paradoxes of Jewish writing, Kafka mentions in his letter, are grounded in the rootlessness and anxieties of a collective body – the body of *Mauscheln*. *Mauscheln* is the name for the poetics of anxiety, rooted in a certain historical, sociological and psychological context of Jewish being around 1900.

*Mauscheln*, however, can be understood also as the expression of what literature is. What Kafka sees as the essential element in Kraus' work – a poetical texture of anxiety and despair, also hints at the foundational tensions of modernist literature. *Mauscheln* expresses the impossible possibly to write in an age of destruction and radical transformations. This too, one can argue, was the major contribution of German-Jewish authors to world-literature: the attempt to escape the worlds of their fathers and to transform themselves into the world of German letters, brought about a poetic texture of crisis, expressing the fragility of human state.

Kafka's remarks on Kraus, *Mauscheln* and the German-Jewish literature, we argue, are comic. They reveal the matter of writing associated with the exaggerations of gestures and deformations of body-languages. Furthermore: Kafka's notes on Kraus can be studied first as reflections on his own writing. His remarks on *Mauscheln* are revealed as valid once we turn to read the story *Die Verwandlung*, or to discuss the nature of *Odradek* and the textual/vocal implications of *Josefine, die Sängerin*.

With this image, a vocal one, Benjamin signs his portrait, dedicated to Karl Kraus, a portrait of critic, a man of harsh judgment, a prosecutor, who nevertheless made his vocation into a prayer. This, we recall, should be considered according to Benjamin as a Halachic act, an interruption in the realm of German language, in the sake of creation.

# References

Benjamin, Walter. "Eine neue Kraus-Notiz" [1928]. *Gesammelte Werke, Vol. II.2*. Frankfurt am Main: Suhrkamp Verlag, 1991. 624–625.
Benjamin, Walter. "Karl Kraus" [1931]. *Gesammelte Werke, Vol. II.1*. Frankfurt am Main: Suhrkamp Verlag, 1991a. 334–367.
Kafka, Franz. *Briefe 1902–1924*. Frankfurt am Main: Fischer Tachenbuch Verlag, 1995.
Kraus, Karl. *Sittlichkeit und Kriminalität*. München: Kösel Verlag, 1970.
Lessing, Theodor. *Der jüdische Selbsthass (1930)*. München: Matthes & Seitz, 1984.

Katharina Prager

# „Wir Anhänger des Geistes sind in einer tragisch-komischen Position ..." – Biografische Perspektiven auf Karl Kraus zwischen 1933 und 1936

## Vorbemerkung zum Biografischen bei Kraus

Karl Kraus las gern Biografien. Nicht nur die Programmzettel seiner Vorlesungen aus den 1930er Jahren belegen umfangreich, dass er sich für das Leben Jacques Offenbachs und Johann Nestroys wie auch für das verschiedener Schauspieler und Schauspielerinnen interessierte. Schon als ganz junger Mann hatte er den von ihm verehrten Gerhart Hauptmann um „biographisches Material"[1] gebeten, um sein Stück *Die Weber* besser einordnen zu können, oder Freundinnen wie Berthe Maria Denk zur Niederschrift ihrer Memoiren angeregt.[2] Die weitgehende Zurückweisung auto/biografischer Zugriffe auf seine eigene Person wiederum gehörte zu seiner (oft sehr witzigen) Selbstinszenierung und -stilisierung als Satiriker, deren Strategien er um 1911 nochmals neu überdachte.[3] „Ich mische mich nicht gern in meine Privatangelegenheiten",[4] schrieb er um diese Zeit – oder: „Einer, der's gut mit mir meint, vermißte meine Biographie. [...] Mein Lebenslauf fühlt sich nur wohl dabei, wenn er [...] nicht durch Beachtung aufgehalten wird."[5] 1919 verweigerte er die Beantwortung eines biografischen Fragebogens mit der Begründung, dass „Fragen nach den Geburtsdaten [...] nicht das Geringste mit den Werken eines Autors [...] zu schaffen haben."[6] Um dieselbe Zeit allerdings unterstützte er auch Leopold Lieglers Anliegen, eine Kraus-Biografie zu verfassen, oder bewarb Berthold Viertels biogra-

---
1 Gerhart Hauptmann an Karl Kraus, 27.02.1892, Staatsbibliothek Preußischer Kulturbesitz, Autogr. I/1145/2, zit. nach Schick, Sophie: Karl Kraus. Fragmente einer Biographie, o. J., B 268.365, Wienbibliothek im Rathaus (in Folge: WBR), 20.
2 Strigl, Daniela, „Frauenverehrer", „Liebessklave", „Gott und Teufel" – zu Karl Kraus' erotischer Biographie. In: Katharina Prager (Hg.): Geist versus Zeitgeist: Karl Kraus in der Ersten Republik, Wien 2018, 166–181.
3 Vgl. Kuono, Eiji, Die Performativität der Satire bei Karl Kraus. Zu seiner „geschriebenen Schauspielkunst". Berlin 2015 und Stocker, Brigitte, Rhetorik eines Protagonisten gegen die Zeit. Karl Kraus als Redner in den Vorlesungen 1919 bis 1932, Wien 2013, 51–56.
4 F 326–328, 08.07.1911, 46.
5 F 341–342, 27.01.1912, 30.
6 Brief des Verlags *Die Fackel* an Prof. Maria Janitschek, 07.09.1919, H.I.N. 238.970, Handschriftensammlung (in Folge: HS), WBR.

fischen Essay *Karl Kraus. Ein Charakter und die Zeit* (1917/1921). Kraus' Freundinnen und Freunde wie auch die Forschungsmonokultur, die schon zu Lebzeiten um Kraus entstand und vorerst vor allem hagiografisch Relevanz behauptete, mussten sich also mit den Kraus'schen Ambivalenzen um Selbst/Archivierung, Selbst/Historisierung und Auto/Biografisierung herumschlagen. Im Bann des massiven Werkes – das abseits der 23.000 Seiten der *Fackel* mehrere Sammlungen von Essays und Lyrik sowie fünf Dramen und zahlreiche Nachdichtungen umfasste, zu dem aber auch 700 Vorlesungen, zahlreiche Radiobeiträge und über 200 Rechtsfälle gezählt werden können – war und ist es zum einen allein aus forschungspragmatischen und zeitlichen Gründen immer schwer, den Blick noch mit derselben Genauigkeit dem Zeitgeschehen um Kraus zu widmen. Zum anderen behauptete Kraus selbst so konsequent die Wahrhaftigkeit und Faktizität seiner Perspektive, dass oft nicht notwendig erschien und teilweise noch erscheint – ja, sogar als kleinliche Ketzerei verstanden werden konnte und kann –, mit Blick auf den lebensgeschichtlichen Kontext Kraus' Ambivalenzen oder Widersprüchen nachzugehen.[7] Mit einer derartigen Abwehr des Biografischen und damit der Einflüsse von Personen und Ereignissen kann auch „Ideologie" um „große Männer" produziert werden, die als Genies aus sich selbst erscheinen, und der ohnehin immer latent vorhandene „Geniekult in den Geisteswissenschaften" weiter befördert.[8]

Gerade für historisch und lebensgeschichtlich derart bewegte Zeiten wie das Jahr 1933 und die folgenden Jahre bis zu Kraus' Tod ist es daher notwendig, noch viel mehr biografische Quellen aufzusuchen und in Beziehung zu setzen; nicht nur um Kraus' Arbeit an der *Dritten Walpurgisnacht,* aber auch das Werk an sich besser zu verstehen. Im Folgenden soll also der Kontext und nicht der Text zentral gesetzt werden. Auf Basis der weitgehend unbekannten Materialien seiner engsten Freunde Berthold Viertel – meine Forschungen zu Viertel bilden den Ausgangspunkt und die Grundlage dieser Betrachtung – und Ludwig Münz,[9] aber auch anhand der Briefe an Sidonie Nádherný von Borutín, die in den späten 1960er Jahren einen „neuen" Karl Kraus sichtbar werden ließen,[10] unter Einbezie-

---

7 Vgl. Prager, Katharina, „Einer, der's gut mit mir meint, vermißte meine Biographie" – Anti/Biographische Affekte um Karl Kraus, in: BIOS – Zeitschrift für Biographieforschung, Oral History und Lebensverlaufsanalysen. Leverkusen 2015, 266–280.
8 Etzemüller, Thomas: Biographien. Lesen – erforschen – erzählen, Frankfurt am Main 2012, 13; Köhne, Julia Barbara: Geniekult in Geisteswissenschaften und Literaturen um 1900 und seine filmischen Adaptionen, Wien/Köln/Weimar 2014.
9 Vgl. Prager, Katharina: Berthold Viertel. Eine Biographie der Wiener Moderne. Wien / Köln / Weimar 2015; Jansen, Irene, Berthold Viertel. Leben und künstlerische Arbeit im Exil, Wien 1992.
10 Pfäfflin, Friedrich (Hg.): Karl Kraus, Briefe an Sidonie Nádherný von Borutin, 2 Bd, Göttingen, 2005; Canetti, Elias (2005): Der neue Karl Kraus, in: Friedrich Pfäfflin (Hg.): Karl Kraus, Briefe an Sidonie Nádherný von Borutin. 1913–1936. Bd. 1–2 Göttingen 2005, Bd. 2, 9–36.

hung weiterer Zeugnisse „aus großer Nähe"[11] sowie mit Blick auf die rechtlichen Auseinandersetzungen zwischen 1933 und 1936[12] sollen hier multiperspektivisch und mikroanalytisch einige bisher nicht miteinander verbundene biografische Mosaiksteine der Jahre 1933 bis 1936 – die Entstehungszusammenhänge und die Folgen der *Dritten Walpurgisnacht* – zusammengesetzt werden.

## Das Jahr 1933

Am 14. Jänner 1933 hielt der Regisseur und Schriftsteller Berthold Viertel, der im Sommer 1932 aus Amerika zurückgekommen war, einen Vortragsabend im Offenbachsaal des Wiener Musikvereins. Er hielt „eine große, prinzipielle Rede" mit dem Titel *Heimkehr nach Europa*, las Gedichte und Kleinigkeiten aus dem amerikanischen Tagebuch vor. In seiner einstündigen Rede sprach er über seine Jugend in Wien, seine Prägung durch Karl Kraus und die *Fackel*, den Ersten Weltkrieg, seine Regiekarriere im Deutschland der Weimarer Republik, über Hollywood, wo er ab 1928 Filme gemacht hatte, und schließlich über das aktuelle „europäische Erlebnis", das er bedrohlich fand.[13] Im Publikum saßen etwa 150 Menschen, Weggefährtinnen und Weggefährten aus Viertels Kindheit und Jugend – unter ihnen auch der Kunsthistoriker Ludwig Münz und eben Karl Kraus.[14] Fast allabendlich trug Kraus im Jänner 1933 sonst selbst im Offenbach-Saal sein „Theater der Dichtung" vor und so war also schon der Ort des Vortrags eine klare Positionierung für Viertel, der aber ohnehin in Wien noch immer als „der Busenfreund vom Kraus" galt.[15]

Elf Jahre jünger als Kraus, hatte Viertel schon als Vierzehnjähriger die *Fackel* zu lesen begonnen und sich gleich in Leserbriefen an ihren jungen Herausgeber gewandt. 1905 wurde er nach der von Kraus produzierten Aufführung von Wedekinds Büchse der Pandora seinem Idol vorgestellt und gehörte fortan mit Franz

---

11 Pfäfflin, Friedrich, Aus großer Nähe. Karl Kraus in Berichten aus Weggefährten und Widersachern, Göttingen 2008.
12 Böhm, Hermann (1995–1997): Karl Kraus contra ... : die Prozeßakten der Kanzlei Oskar Samek in der Wiener Stadt- und Landesbibliothek, hrsg. von Herwig Würtz, bearb. u. kommentiert von Hermann Böhm, Wien, Bd. 1–4; vgl. auch Karl Kraus: Rechtsakten der Kanzlei Oskar Samek. Wissenschaftliche Edition, hg. v. Johannes Knüchel und Isabel Langkabel, auf Grundlage der Vorarbeiten Katharina Pragers, unter Mitarbeit von Laura Untner, Andrea Ortner, Ingo Börner und Vanessa Hannesschläger (Wien 2022) URL: https://www.kraus.wienbibliothek.at/.
13 Berthold Viertel, Heimkehr nach Europa, in: Kaiser/Roessler/Bolbecher (Hg.), Viertel, Cherub, 1990, 280.
14 Berthold Viertel an Salka Viertel, 15./16.1.1933, 78.862/1, K34, A: Viertel, DLA.
15 Berthold Viertel an Salka Viertel, o. D. [Jänner 1933], 78.862/2, K34, A: Viertel, DLA.

und Gustav Grüner, Ludwig Münz und Oskar Kokoschka zur jungen Garde, die sich im Café Central um Kraus scharte.[16] Ab 1908 schloss er sich immer enger an Kraus an, wurde sein Mitarbeiter und Vertrauter. Er stritt mit ihm über einige seiner Haltungen und Texte – besonders über *Heine und die Folgen* –, ließ sich aber dennoch gern von Kraus schriftstellerisch erziehen. Als Viertel begann, als Regisseur Karriere zu machen und an Stefan Großmanns Wiener Freier Bühne zu arbeiten, wurde die Freundschaft wohl erstmals stärker strapaziert, denn Kraus polemisierte seit 1900 gegen Großmann, der für ihn eine schlimme Mixtur aus Kunst mit Kommerz, Korruption und Cliquenwesen verkörperte. Ludwig Münz, der ebenfalls ein enger Freund geworden war, „unterbrach" aufgrund von Viertels Volksbühnentätigkeit die Freundschaft mit diesem sogar kurzfristig ganz.[17] Münz nahm seine Zugehörigkeit zu Kraus immer schon ernster, stand Kraus auch dadurch, dass er stets in Wien lebte, alltäglich näher und widmete dem „K[raus]'schen Werk" einen großen Teil seines Lebens.[18] Viertel schätzte Münz als „hochbegabt" und „sensibel", sah ihn aber auch als „einen Puristen in Kunst und Literatur, der derart kritisch sei, dass er damit seine eigene Produktivität behindere".[19] Münz wiederum bezeichnete Kraus (Viertel gegenüber) als „Wahlvater unserer Jugend".[20] Und tatsächlich waren Viertel und Münz spätestens ab 1918 jene Freunde, die Kraus am „am nächsten" standen,[21] denen er Bücher widmete und mit denen er sich sogar duzte. Beide unterschieden sich aber vor allem darin, dass Viertel vieles lockerer nahm, als es im Kraus-Kreis üblich war, und so hatte Kraus Viertel immer wieder einiges nachzusehen – etwa einige kriegerisch-patriotische Gedichte, die dieser 1914 im ersten Überschwang verfasst hatte; oder auch sein stetes Engagement im Theater- und Filmbusiness von Berlin bis Hollywood in den 1920er-Jahren. Viertel positionierte sich zwar immer wieder als „Krausianer", wenn er etwa zum 25-jährigen Jubiläum der *Fackel* und zum 50. Geburtstag ihres Herausgebers 1924 mit seiner Berliner „Truppe" dessen Einakter Traumtheater/Traumstück inszenierte, er arbeitete aber eben auch für den Kraus verhassten Max Reinhardt oder beschloss 1927 nach Hollywood zu gehen, um seine Schulden in den Griff zu kriegen.[22] Viertel fand schon Ende der 1920er-Jahre Kraus' „Vorwürfe" und „Verhöre" zunehmend schwierig, wusste aber, dass Kraus

---

16 Pfäfflin, Aus großer Nähe. 100.
17 Vgl. Jansen, Viertel, 105.
18 Jansen, Viertel, 107.
19 Salka Viertel, Das unbelehrbare Herz, 1970, 137.
20 Jansen, Viertel, 87.
21 Vgl. Otto Soyka, Begegnungen mit Karl Kraus, in: *Die Schau* 19/20, Oktober 1953, 21; Salka Viertel 1969, in: Pfäfflin, Nähe, 228.
22 Vgl. Prager, Viertel, 268–290.

ihn und seine Familie „liebte". Es strengte ihn jedoch an, wenn dieser in Deutschland war, „eine Woche hindurch jede Nacht [zu] sitzen und [zu] debattieren, wobei die völlige Aussichtslosigkeit, einem der geistigsten Männer, die leben, den Weg über die Palisaden seiner selbstgebauten Festung hinweg zu den Tatsachen der Zeit zu zeigen, niederschmetternd wirkt. [...] Was nützt da alle Liebe: nur mit Mühe [...] wieder ein Bruch vermieden!"[23] In diesen Jahren setzte ein schleichender Prozess der Verdüsterung und Resignation bei Kraus ein, der sich immer mehr gegen sein Publikum zu kehren begann und besonders in seinen „Rechenschaftsberichten" und „Rückblicken" auf sein Lebenswerk manifest wurde. In diesem Zusammenhang erklärte Kraus auch seinen – immer wieder unterbrochenen – Rückzug aus der politischen Sphäre.[24]

Kraus kam die Familie Viertel nicht in Hollywood besuchen, obgleich er seinen Besuch angekündigt hatte. Erst im August 1932 trafen Kraus und Viertel nach vierjähriger Trennung wieder in Paris zusammen, wo Kraus angeblich diagnostizierte: „Es ist alles in Ordnung mit Berthold. Selbst diese Filmhölle hat ihm nichts anhaben können."[25] Berthold Viertel war in jenem Herbst und Winter wieder in Wien, weil sein Vater im Sterben lag. Regelmäßig dürfte er nun auch seinen „Wahlvater" wiedergesehen haben, und seine Frau Salka Viertel fragte aus Hollywood: „Hast Du Karl Kraus noch immer so in den Knochen?"[26] – „Karl Kraus einen Tag länger und wir hätten uns auf ewig zerstritten", antwortete Berthold Viertel, erschöpft von einem noch älter gewordenen Kraus.[27] Zurückblickend wusste er aber auch: „Man kommt aus Amerika, aus einer anderen Welt. Natürlich kann man nicht verlangen, dass der Mensch, der zuhause geblieben ist, um des Besuches willen sein tägliches Leben ändert."[28]

Anfang des Jahres hatte Irma Karczewska nach langjährigen Depressionen Selbstmord begangen. Sie hatte 1905 als 15-Jährige in der denkwürdigen Wiener Aufführung von Wedekinds Büchse der Pandora mitgespielt und war damals als „Kindweib" in (nicht nur aus heutiger Sicht) problematische sexuelle Beziehungen zu Kraus und anderen verwickelt gewesen, die ihr Leben noch lange bestimmten. Die Aufbruchszeit um 1900, über die Viertel im Offenbach-Saal sprach und die sicher auch an Karczewskas Tod erinnerte, lag Anfang 1933 also schon

---

23 Berthold Viertel an Salka Viertel, o. D. [August 1927], 78.856/12, K34, A: Viertel, DLA.
24 Fischer, Jens Malte: Karl Kraus. Der Widersprecher, Wien, 2020, 744–772.
25 Überliefert durch Heinrich Fischer 1961, in: Pfäfflin, Nähe, 129.
26 Salka Viertel an BV, 2. Oktober 1932, 78.910/13, K45, A: Viertel, DLA.
27 Berthold Viertel an Salka Viertel, 9. Dezember 1932, 78.860/23, K34, A: Viertel, DLA.
28 Berthold Viertel an Ludwig Münz, 14. November 1935, 78.849/4, K42, A: Viertel, DLA.

sehr fern. Anspannung lag in der Luft, denn jenseits der Grenze drohte Deutschland „unserem [!] Hitler [...] anheimzufallen, wie eine reife Frucht."[29]

Die „Hitlerdiktatur" wurde in den Briefen und Gesprächen dieser Tage bereits vorausgeahnt und dennoch kam es als Schlag, als Adolf Hitler am 30. Jänner Reichskanzler wurde. Kraus hielt an diesem Abend seine 645. Vorlesung – Shakespeares *Coriolanus* – im Offenbach-Saal. Berthold Viertel reiste sogar an ebendiesem Tag nach Berlin, denn er hoffte Verhandlungen um einen Regieauftrag zu einem positiven Abschluss zu bringen: „Ich verließ Wien, als die Nachmittagszeitungen eben Hitlers Berufung [Machtergreifung] gebracht hatten. In Wien, das märchenhaft im Schnee lag, war es so friedlich gewesen."[30]

In den nächsten drei Wochen wurde Viertel zum Augenzeugen der nationalsozialistischen Machtübernahme in Deutschland: „Es steht wohl in meinen Sternen geschrieben, daß ich all das hier jetzt durchmachen soll."[31] In dieser Zeit wurde rasch klar, dass Viertel als Jude nicht mehr „berechtigt" war, beim deutschen Film zu arbeiten. Er war also gleich persönlich mit dem nun offiziellen Antisemitismus der neuen Machthaber konfrontiert, und er erlebte auch in zahlreichen anderen Zusammenhängen den neuen Stil in Deutschland:

> Das ganze George-Grosz-Album, alle Sternheim-Figuren sind in Bewegung – das marschiert mit dröhnender Musik und Flaggen und trampelt die letzten Reste von Natur und Kultur nieder. [...] Die neue Zucht, die da jetzt auferlegt wird, wird eine Zukunft haben (wenn sie eine hat), die eher an den dreißigjährigen Krieg anknüpft als an das, was wir unter deutscher Kultur verstanden haben. [...] Das jüdische Problem wird wieder aktuell wie im Mittelalter – und wir gehören nach Palästina! – Sichtbar wächst den Juden wieder der gelbe Fleck! – Noch kein Pogrom – aber die Menge belagert die jüdischen Geschäfte, um keine Käufer hineinzulassen.[32]

Es kann nicht genau nachvollzogen werden, was Berthold Viertel alles sah und wahrnahm – ihm war rasch klar, dass es in Deutschland kein Telefon- und Briefgeheimnis mehr gab und so beschrieb er Salka Viertel erst aus Wien brieflich ausführlicher, was er empfand, wissend:

> Die deutsche Katastrophe kann sich niemand vorstellen, der sie nicht in Deutschland mitgemacht hat. Ich weiß nicht, was für Nachrichten Du in Hollywood gehabt hast, wahrscheinlich sogar übertriebene – und doch können sie Dir das Wesentliche nicht gesagt haben. Das wirst Du erst sehen, wenn ich es Dir mündlich schildere.[33]

---

29 Berthold Viertel, Heimkehr nach Europa, in: Kaiser/Roessler/Bolbecher (Hg.), Viertel, Cherub, 1990, 276.
30 Berthold Viertel an Salka Viertel, 30. Jänner 1933, 78.862/8, K34, A: Viertel, DLA.
31 Ebenda.
32 Berthold Viertel an Salka Viertel, 9. März 1933, 78.862/10, K34, A: Viertel, DLA.
33 Berthold Viertel an Salka Viertel, 20. März 1933, 78.862/12, K34, A: Viertel, DLA.

Alles in allem schockierten ihn die alltäglichen Vorkommnisse aber derart, dass er es – was genau der Auslöser war, bleibt im Dunkeln – in den Tagen um dem Reichstagsbrand sehr plötzlich als notwendig empfand, fluchtartig die Stadt in Richtung Prag zu verlassen – nicht ohne zuvor auch Freundinnen und Freunde wie Alfred Polgar von der Dringlichkeit eines raschen Aufbruchs überzeugt zu haben: „In Prag war ein richtiges Flüchtlingslager. Da waren Ernst Deutsch und Aufricht und Polgar und Wolffenstein und Arnold Zweig etc. Alles auf der Flucht: Brecht und Weill und Kerr und Theodor Wolff, die Brüder Mann, Pfemfert etc. etc."[34]

Anfang März war Viertel zurück in Wien – wo er sich zur Reichstagswahl als der eigentlichen Machtübernahme und zu den politischen Entwicklungen in Österreich vorerst nicht äußerte, wohl wiederum aus Sorge, dass seine Briefe mitgelesen werden könnten:

> Grausig, grausig, grausig! Mehr lässt sich nicht sagen […] Was habe ich mich in diesen letzten 5 Wochen aufgeregt, gegrämt, geängstigt. Trotzdem war es wichtig, das mitzumachen, es mit eigenen Ohren zu hören, mit eigenen Augen zu sehen. […] Man glaubt es sonst nicht, weiß innerlich nicht Bescheid, fasst falsche Entschlüsse, denkt und schreibt falsche Dinge. – In Wien kommt bald mindestens ähnliches. Es ist eine Welle.[35]

Nur zwei Tage nach dem nationalsozialistischen Wahlsieg in Deutschland hatte der österreichische Bundeskanzler Engelbert Dollfuß am 7. März 1933 aufgrund eines formalen Abstimmungsfehlers den österreichischen Nationalrat für handlungsunfähig erklärt. Er sprach von der „Selbstausschaltung des Parlaments" und schlug, mit den Notverordnungen des „Kriegswirtschaftlichen Ermächtigungsgesetzes" von 1917 regierend, im Laufe der nächsten Monate einen immer stärker autoritären Kurs in Richtung eines korporatistischen Staates ein. Dazu gehörten Zensur, Aufhebung der Versammlungsfreiheit und in weiterer Folge auch die Wiedereinführung der Todesstrafe.[36] Es ist davon auszugehen, dass Viertel und Kraus im März die Praxis ihrer alltäglichen Treffen wieder aufnahmen und er ihm seine Eindrücke schilderte. Auch Brecht, der mit beiden Männern befreundet war, war Anfang März mit seiner Familie in Wien. Kraus soll ihn mit den Worten „Die Ratten besteigen das sinkende Schiff" begrüßt haben.[37] Es kann als wahrscheinlich gelten, dass man – zu dritt – die Ereignisse in Deutschland besprach.

---

34 Berthold Viertel an Salka Viertel, 9. März 1933, 78.862/10, K34, A: Viertel, DLA.
35 Berthold Viertel an Salka Viertel, 10. März 1933, 78.862/11, K34, A: Viertel, DLA.
36 Vgl. Bernhard Hachleitner, Alfred Pfoser, Katharina Prager, Werner Michael Schwarz (Hg.), Die Zerstörung der Demokratie. Österreich, März 1933 bis February 1934. Wien/Salzburg: Residenz 2023.
37 Vgl. Pfäfflin, Nähe, 298.

Mitte März starb Kraus' jüngste Schwester Marie Turnovsky, der Kraus innerhalb seiner Familie am nächsten gestanden hatte. Aus Deutschland kamen weitere Schreckensnachrichten – Ende März etwa von den ersten Konzentrationslagern wie Oranienburg, wohin Freunde wie Erich Mühsam gebracht wurden.[38] Viertel und Kraus waren sich in diesen Märzwochen wohl einig, dass eine Welt untergegangen war: „Wenigstens der größte Teil von dem, was durch ein Leben hindurch unsere Welt gewesen ist."[39] Womöglich waren sie sich auch recht einig in ihrer Einschätzung, dass Österreich ebenfalls bedroht war. In einem Brief an Salka Viertel heißt es:

> Dabei brennt mir hier der Boden unter den Füßen. Ich fürchte das politische Erdbeben, das auch hier herrscht und daß ich zu spät abreise, zu spät, um abzureisen! ‚Falsch geflohen!', rief Stephan Ehrenzweig aus, als er in Wien ankam und sah, wie es hier steht. [...] Aber ich leide an der phantastischen Angst, durch gesperrte Bahnen, durch einen über Nacht ausgebrochenen Krieg endgültig von Dir abgetrennt zu sein. [...] und in Wien – wer weiß, ob Wien in 3 Monaten nicht verflucht ähnlich aussieht?[40]

Ende März brach Kraus in die Tschechoslowakei auf, wo er Sidonie Nádherný in Janowitz besuchte, Max Lobkowicz in Raudnitz und schließlich eine Vorlesungsreise durch Brünn, Mährisch Ostrau, Olmütz und Prag anschloss. Viertel brach um dieselbe Zeit nach Paris auf und meinte in einem weiteren Brief an Salka Viertel erleichtert:

> Also in Paris, in Freiheit! Der entsetzliche moralische Druck, der auch die Tage von Wien belastete, ist zunächst aufgeschoben, ich atme wieder normal. [...] Die ganze Zeit war Wien beunruhigt durch die Diktatur des kleinen Dollfuß – ‚Millimetternich' nennt man ihn in Wien – die jeden Augenblick in bewaffneten Generalstreik oder sofort in die Hitlerei umschlagen könnte. Täglich rüdeste Nazidemonstrationen. Die Erklärung Mussolinis gegen den Anschluss und die entsprechend laue Behandlung der österreichischen Frage durch Hitler in seiner R.T.[Reichstag-]Eröffnungsrede hat zunächst eine gewisse Beruhigung geschaffen. Trotzdem passiert man aufatmend die österreichische Grenze. [...] Meine enorme Unruhe hat sich gelegt. Ich hatte wohl das kommende Weltgewitter in den Knochen. Nun es auf Deutschland niedergegangen ist, bin ich viel ruhiger. Aber ich glaube, daß es eine Welle ist, die über die ganze Welt geht [...]. Könnte ich so gut handeln wie sehen, dann wäre mir leichter als mir oft ist. Überall Autarkie, überall Ausländerabwehr – und für die Juden beginnt eine internationale Verschärfung der Diaspora, die den Gedanken an eine Auswanderung jedes Juden, der ein wenig Geld besitzt, nach Palästina nahelegt (auch uns, mein Herz! Wirklich!!).[41]

---

38 Vgl. Krieghofer, Gerald: „Die Menschheit weiß immer noch nicht, was gesehen ist und jeden Augenblick geschieht" – Kraus nach 1933. In: Katharina Prager (Hg.): Geist versus Zeitgeist: Karl Kraus in der Ersten Republik, Wien 2018, 206–219.
39 BV an Salka Viertel, 20. März 1933, 78.862/12, K34, A: Viertel, DLA.
40 Ebenda.
41 Berthold Viertel an Salka Viertel, 27. März 1933, 78.862/13, K34, A: Viertel, DLA.

Ich habe Viertel hier deshalb so ausführlich zu Wort kommen lassen, da von Kraus selbst aus dem März 1933 – abseits von spärlichen, nicht sehr inhaltsreichen Korrespondenzstücken und Berichten anderer – keine Einschätzungen der Situation überliefert sind. Es kann aber davon ausgegangen werden, dass er die Eindrücke Viertels, Brechts und des Netzwerkes um sie wahrnahm, diskutierte und dass bereits dieser andauernde Austausch ein wichtiger, aber bisher zu unbekannter Impuls für die „große Arbeit"[42] an der Dritten Walpurgisnacht war, für die Kraus zu dieser Zeit schon Material sammelte. Mit Christian Wagenknecht ist anzunehmen, dass Kraus bereits im März/April erste Einfälle notierte – zwei Konvolute im Umfang von ca. 350 Notizblättern sind überliefert, wurden von Gerald Krieghofer digital aufgearbeitet und wären noch genauer auf einen solchen Austausch hin zu untersuchen.[43] In Prag begegnete Kraus zudem Anfang April selbst etlichen Flüchtlingen aus Berlin (wie etwa Heinrich Fischer) oder tauschte sich mit dem Germanisten und Diplomaten Marcel Ray – einem Vertrauten seiner späten Jahre – aus.[44]

Kurz nach seinem 59. Geburtstag also, im „Gefühl manifester Bedrohung", begann Kraus mit seinem „Versuch zu einer geistesgemäßen Verarbeitung der Eindrücke" in Form der Niederschrift seines wohl ungewöhnlichsten „politischen-satirisch-polemischen Textes", der die ersten Monate des Nationalsozialismus in Deutschland dokumentieren und analysieren sollte. Auf über 300 Seiten montierte und kommentierte Kraus – „durchwaltet" von klassischen Zitaten Goethes und Shakespeares – Zeitungsberichte zu Folterungen, Reaktionen von Journalisten und Intellektuellen (etwa Martin Heidegger und Gottfried Benn), Lügen der Propaganda, Goebbels' Mentalität, erste Konzentrationslager, den Nazi-Terror in Österreich und vieles mehr.[45] Ebenfalls Anfang Mai ließ er seinen Reisepass verlängern und zur Ausreise in die USA erweitern.[46] In diesem Monat erscheint Kraus nun wirklich extrem zurückgezogen, doch weiterhin erhielt er, abseits seiner eigenen Lektüre der (internationalen) Zeitungen offenbar auch „Dokumente" von Sidonie Nádherný:

> Die große Arbeit (ob sie auch herauskommen wird?) ließ mir – und läßt mir eigentlich – keine Minute. Aber sie hindert nicht, an dich zu denken. Dank auch für die interessanten Dokumente (ich revanchierte mich mit etlichen, hauptsächlich zum Judenpunkt, der den

---

42 B 996 (21./22. Mai 1933), in: Pfäfflin, (Hg.): Karl Kraus, Briefe, 646.
43 Vgl. Christian Wagenknecht, Entstehung und Überlieferung, in: Kraus, Karl: Dritte Walpurgisnacht, zitiert nach: Karl Kraus: Schriften, hg. von Christian Wagenknecht, Bd. 12, Frankfurt a. M. 1989, 331–343, 335. Vgl. auch: Kraus 1933, Notizblätter aus den Jahren 1930–1936, mit Notizen zur „Dritten Walpurgisnacht", zur „Sprache", https://kraus1933.ace.oeaw.ac.at
44 B 996 (21./22. Mai 1933), in: Pfäfflin, (Hg.): Karl Kraus, Briefe, 646.
45 Vgl. Kraus, Dritte Walpurgisnacht.
46 Reisepass von Karl Kraus, 24. September 1929. WBR, HS, H.I.N.-171160.

Kerlen* jetzt schon sehr peinlich zu werden scheint). Bitte aber: keine mehr, weil ich in den Wust bereits ersticke und leider alles anregt. [...]

*Das hiesige Vorgehen gegen sie ist überraschend gut und energisch; nur die Dummheit der Sozialdemokraten ist störend (wenngleich nicht aufhaltend).[47]

Im selben Brief, in dem Kraus ähnlich wie Viertel nur in Andeutungen spricht, gibt er auch an, einen „trostlosen" Brief von Tilly Wedekind erhalten zu haben. Diese war seit 1930 mit Gottfried Benn liiert, der sich in Reden im April und Mai 1933 im Berliner Rundfunk zum Nationalsozialismus bekannt hatte und in der zweiten Rede auf Vorwürfe des bereits geflüchteten Klaus Mann reagierte. In der *Dritten Walpurgisnacht* wird Benn zum Prototyp für den Verrat der Intellektuellen.[48]

Weiterhin war international ein (auch untereinander) in engem Austausch stehendes Netzwerk um Kraus – Brecht lud ihn nach Dänemark ein, Albert Bloch nach Kansas. Franz Pfemfert und Helene Kann telegrafierten aus Karlsbad, wo „viele interessante Menschen" um Kanns Schwester Grethe Bermann zusammengekommen waren. Der Diplomat Camill Hoffmann und sein ehemaliger Anwalt Botho Laserstein sorgten sich in Berlin um ihn und brachen für ihn „eine Lanze". Anfang August flog Karl Kraus nach Paris, um nochmals Marcel Ray zu treffen – wem er hier und bei seinem zweiten Paris-Aufenthalt im Oktober letztlich alles begegnete, bleibt im Dunkeln. Sicher ist, dass er auf dem Rückweg nach Wien Ludwig von Ficker in Innsbruck besuchte. Insgesamt hielt er sich während des Sommers immer wieder länger in Janowitz auf, wo er Mitte August das anspielungsreiche und vielfach missgedeutete Gedicht *Man frage nicht* verfasste.[49]

Man frage nicht, was all die Zeit ich machte.
Ich bleibe stumm;
und sage nicht, warum.
Und Stille gibt es, da die Erde krachte.
Kein Wort, das traf;
man spricht nur aus dem Schlaf.
Und träumt von einer Sonne, welche lachte.
Es geht vorbei;
nachher war's einerlei.
Das Wort entschlief, als jene Welt erwachte.[50]

---

47 B 997 (4./5. Juni 1933), in: Pfäfflin, (Hg.): Karl Kraus, Briefe, 646.
48 Vgl. Kraus, Dritte Walpurgisnacht, XXX; Fischer, Widersprecher, 824–829.
49 Vgl. Pfäfflin, Nähe, 298–301 und Pfäfflin, (Hg.): Karl Kraus, Briefe, 644–650.
50 F 889, Juli 1933, 4.

Weiterhin stand die *Walpurgisnacht* offenbar im Zentrum seiner Tätigkeit – „Schwerste Arbeit"[51] telegrafierte er wenige Tage nach der Niederschrift von *Man frage nicht* nochmals. Eine Woche später starb der Architekt Adolf Loos, einer der wichtigsten Freunde und Weggefährten von Kraus – am 25. August hielt er eine kurze Rede am Grab.[52] Auf den Tod dieses dritten nahestehenden Menschen innerhalb von neun Monaten folgte kaum eine Woche später die Ermordung des Schriftstellers Theodor Lessing im tschechischen Marienbad durch deutsche Agenten. Lessings Ermordung gehörte wahrscheinlich zu den maßgeblichen Gründen, warum sich Kraus letztlich gegen die Veröffentlichung der *Dritten Walpurgisnacht* als *Fackel*-Heft 888–907 entschied. Anfang Oktober erschien nach über neun Monaten Schweigen nur die schmale *Fackel* 888 mit der Grabrede auf Loos und dem bekannten Gedicht *Man frage nicht*.[53] Kurz darauf reiste Kraus über Paris an die Côte d'Azur und kam erst Mitte November nach Wien zurück.[54] Wie Helene Kann berichtete, versuchte er dort seinem üblichen Kreis aus dem Weg zu gehen.[55] Obgleich in diesem Jahr Shakespeares Sonette als Nachdichtung von Kraus erschienen waren wie auch eine tschechische Übersetzung von *Die letzten Tage der Menschheit,* brachte das Jahr 1933 abseits der persönlichen Verluste nicht zuletzt auch schwere finanziellen Einbußen von insgesamt 12.891,84 Schilling – das entspricht heute etwa 47.000 Euro. Durch den Wegfall des deutschen Marktes für seine Zeitschrift war Kraus, der auch immer noch Einkünfte aus den Vorlesungen und dem väterlichen Erbe bezog, zwar nicht verarmt, aber die Existenz der *Fackel*, die seit 1930 Verluste machte, stand ernsthaft in Frage.[56]

Berthold Viertel hatte einstweilen, nachdem er „eine Welt von tragischen Dingen erlebt"[57] hatte, den Frühsommer in Paris verbracht, wo sich die geflüchtete deutsche Filmindustrie versammelt hatte und er sich als „Exilierter" zu fühlen begann.[58] Über den Sommer kehrte er zu seiner Familie nach Santa Monica zurück, um „alles, ganz Europa, wie einen wüsten Traum hinter mir [zu] haben [...] – und werde froh sein zu leben, nur zu leben."[59] Salka Viertels Position als Drehbuchautorin für Greta Garbo-Filme – die sie auch ihrer persönlichen Freundschaft mit MGMs bestbezahltem Star zu verdanken hatte – war inzwischen für

---

51 T 1001 (16. August 1933), in: Pfäfflin, (Hg.): Karl Kraus, Briefe, 647.
52 F 889, Juli 1933, 1–3.
53 Vgl. Wagenknecht, Entstehung und Überlieferung, 336.
54 Vgl. Pfäfflin, (Hg.): Karl Kraus, Briefe, 648–650.
55 Vgl. Pfäfflin, Nähe, 301.
56 Vgl. Fischer, Widersprecher, 764–772 und Pfäfflin, Friedrich: Vom Verglühen der ‚Fackel'. Karl Kraus und sein Verlag 1930–1936, Warmbronn 2004.
57 Vgl. Berthold Viertel an Salka Viertel, 24. April 1933, 78.862/20, K34, A: Viertel, DLA.
58 Vgl. Berthold Viertel an Salka Viertel, 16. April 1933, 78.862/18, K34, A: Viertel, DLA.
59 Vgl. Berthold Viertel an Salka Viertel, 22. Mai 1933, 78.862/22, K34, A: Viertel, DLA.

das Auskommen der Familie mit drei Kindern am wesentlichsten. Doch auch Berthold Viertel konnte im September 1933 ein gutes Angebot aus London annehmen und ging für die nächsten drei Jahre als Regisseur der Gaumont British nach Großbritannien. Auf der Überfahrt nach Europa entstand ein rund 70-seitiger Romananfang mit dem Titel *Amalia oder die Hölle der Keuschheit*. Viertel schilderte darin autoritäre, patriarchalische Erziehungsstrukturen und unterdrückte Sexualität in (klein-)bürgerlichen Familien als gesellschaftliche Grundlagen des Faschismus in Deutschland.[60] Später begann Viertel auch an einem „Hitlerstück"[61] zu arbeiten, das Hitlers Werdegang und Wirkung zum Inhalt hatte. Und er schrieb jüdische Gedichte und Geschichten.

Viertel, der als junger Mann auch zionistisch fühlte und – ebenso bekennend jüdisch wie atheistisch – nie aus der Israelitischen Kultusgemeinde austrat, hatte sich hier schon immer anders als Kraus positioniert. Auch wenn rund 25 Jahre Austausch, Freundschaft und Zusammenarbeit mit Kraus Viertel geprägt hatten und bis in seine Wortwahl hineinwirkten, auch wenn die beiden Männer im März 1933 in der Beurteilung der Situation zu ähnlichen Schlüssen kamen, waren sie und ihre Texte doch völlig verschieden. Die Freundschaft hatte Widersprüche und Spannungen bisher immer ausgehalten, doch ab 1933 wirkten einige Unterschiede trennender als je zuvor: Viertels viel stärkere, intensiver gelebte Bindung an das Jüdische und die Linke, seine internationale Arbeits- und Lebensweise (während Kraus sein Zentrum Wien nie verlassen hatte) und sicher auch seine Pragmatik. Als Viertel Ende Mai 1933 eine Art Bestandsaufnahme seines bisherigen Lebens vornahm, rechtfertigte er sich gewissermaßen dafür, dass der Kraus-Kreis und Wien ihm nicht die einzige Instanz geblieben waren und er auch andere Gemeinschaften gesucht hatte, mit den Worten: „Wenn man erst anfängt in jedem Apfel den Wurm zu sehen, dann bleibt man zurück mit den Karl Kraus, Münz, Polgar […] – auf der Bank der Spötter, die ausrangiert sind."[62] Viertel betonte allerdings auch immer wieder, dass er von seiner „alte[n] Liebe"[63] für Kraus nie abgewichen war. Er hielt Kontakt mit Kraus und Münz – unter anderem telefonisch, wie aus etlichen Briefen hervorgeht – und so wusste er auch, dass Kraus etwas vorbereitete und er erfuhr auch:

---

60 Berthold Viertel, Amalia oder Die Hölle der Keuschheit, o. D., o.S., K10, A: Viertel, DLA.
61 Berthold Viertel, Die Weihe des Führers / Die Berserker. Ein historisches Satyrspiel, o. D., o.S., NK05, A: Viertel, DLA.
62 Vgl. Berthold Viertel an Salka Viertel, 22. Mai 1933, 78.862/22, K34, A: Viertel, DLA.
63 Berthold Viertel an Ludwig Münz, 14. November 1935, 78.849/4, K32, A: Viertel, DLA, in: Jansen, Berthold Viertel, 1992, 102.

„Münz hat, was ein Geheimnis ist, große Sorgen mit Kraus. Das Problem: soll Kraus schreiben, d. h. veröffentlichen, scheint ihn zu bedrücken. Wir Anhänger des Geistes sind in einer tragisch-komischen Position. Unsere Märtyrer funktionieren nicht, scheint ein Fehler in der Apparatur vorzuliegen."[64] Den „Fehler in Apparatur" – nämlich dass Kraus' satirische Methode angesichts der ungeheuerlichen Realität schon Anfang der 1930er-Jahre nicht mehr „funktionierte" – bemerkte und reflektierte Kraus selbst.[65] Das Wort „Märtyrer" ist schwerer einzuordnen – waren Münz und Viertel der Meinung, dass Kraus einfach zu feig war? Oder fanden sie, anders als Kraus, dass es eben diesmal „geistig-sittliche" Verantwortung sei, öffentlich gegen den Nationalsozialismus Stellung zu nehmen, auch wenn es „das tragische Opfer des ärmsten, anonym verschollenen Menschenlebens" bedeutete, das heißt die Verfolgung und Ermordung auch jener, die Kraus' Texte lasen.[66]

# Nachbeben 1934 / 1935 / 1936

Wenige Wochen später gab es andere Opfer und Märtyrer – und zwar jene aus den Kämpfen der österreichischen Arbeiterschaft zwischen 12. und 15. Februar 1934. Diesen blutig niedergeworfenen Aufstand, den der „österreichische Faschismus eines Dollfuß"[67] für Viertel herausgefordert hatte, bewertete er von London aus als ersten mutigen Widerstand gegen eines der faschistischen Regime in Europa. Dollfuß nutzte die dreitägigen Kämpfe, um mit überlegener Organisation und Ausrüstung die Arbeiterbewegung in Österreich niederzuschlagen. Polizei und Bundesheer beschossen Parteiheime, sozialdemokratische Einrichtungen und Gemeindebauten. Die sozialdemokratische Partei wurde verboten, ihre Führung floh, wurde brutal nach Standrecht hingerichtet oder eingesperrt. Wenige Wochen später wurde Dollfuß' „christlich-deutscher Ständestaat" ausgerufen, der sich als besserer deutscher Staat verstand.

Kraus veröffentlichte weiterhin nicht. Er zog sich Ende Februar zu Max Lobkowicz nach Raudnitz und Prag zurück, kehrte nur widerwillig und kurz nach Wien zurück. In Briefen an Sidonie Nádherný beschrieb er alles als trost- und ausweglos. Er kam auf den am Würgegalgen hingerichteten Schutzbündler Emil Swoboda als „armen Gehenkten" zu sprechen – Swobodas „letzter Brief" an seine Familie war am 1. März im der Zeitschrift *Sozialdemokrat* abgedruckt worden –, erklärte aber die sozialdemokratische Führung zum „eigentlichen Henker des Armen".[68] Der folgende Brief verrät, dass – „Ist das möglich?" – auch Sidonie Nád-

---

64 Berthold Viertel an Salka Viertel, 21. November 1933, 78.863/10, K34, A: Viertel, DLA.
65 Vgl. Kraus, Dritte Walpurgisnacht, 12; Fischer, Widersprecher, 754.
66 F 890–905, Juli 1934, 10.
67 Berthold Viertel, Die Heimkehr des verlorenen Sohnes, o. D., 240/a, K13, A: Viertel, DLA.
68 B 1015 (1. März 1934), in: Pfäfflin, (Hg.): Karl Kraus, Briefe, 652.

herný Kraus nicht verstand und dass auch „ein Lebenswerk, eine Lebenswirkung, von der niemand so lebendige Beweise empfangen hat wie Du [...] mich nicht schützen kann vor dem Verdacht, anders ‚gesinnt' zu sein als wo sie ‚gegen den Geist des Militärs, der Reichen, der Gewalt und der Ungerechtigkeit kämpfen'." Kraus erklärte eingangs auch, dass er keine Möglichkeit sah „hinein[zu]rufen" – weder in „dieses falsch gerichtete Pathos" noch „in das große Grauen jenes Orkans". Und so fühlte er sich unverstanden, einsam und „von vielen verlassen, auf die die Phrase stärker einwirkt als mein Werk, das keinen anderen Inhalt hatte, als ihr entgegenzuwirken." Von Nádherný verlangte Kraus, sie solle sich „zusammenraffen, mit mir die Dinge zu Ende zu denken." Dass viele andere nicht mehr mit ihm dachten, ihn „verrieten" und „abfielen", tat er verbittert ab.[69]

Obgleich die langjährige Liebesbeziehung zu Nádherný weiterbestand und sie sicher zu den für Kraus wichtigsten Menschen gehörte, waren es andere, die sich in diesen letzten Jahren alltäglich um Kraus kümmerten – und zwar vor allem der Kraus-Verehrer Karl Jaray, eigentlich Architekt aus einer einflussreichen Wiener Familie, und Helene Kann, die Berthold Viertel als Kraus' „Madame – jetzt hab ich ihren Namen vergessen – die mit dem grüngefärbten Haar" beschrieb: „Sie verwaltet jetzt das Kraus-Archiv, hat alle anderen Frauen in seinem Leben überlebt."[70] Auch Münz und Nádherný, die sich vom Wiener Kreis generell fernhielt, sahen Kann und Jaray sehr skeptisch. Sowohl Kann als auch Jaray wiederum sahen Engelbert Dollfuß und seine Ambitionen sehr positiv, und es war womöglich ihrem Einfluss zuzuschreiben, dass Kraus in dieser politischen Situation nicht nur die Option des Rückzugs wählte, sondern sie auf eine für viele erschreckende Weise mit einer politische Positionierung für Dollfuß und sein Regime verband, das er „frei von Anschlussgedanken, frei von Sympathien für den Nationalsozialismus und auch frei von Sympathien für die Sozialdemokratie" glaubte.[71] Während Dollfuß tatsächlich von Anfang an auf die Entmachtung seines politischen Hauptgegners, also der Sozialdemokratie, hinarbeitete, müssen die ersten beiden Annahmen jedenfalls aus heutiger Perspektive als Trugschluss gelten. Kraus konnte nicht wissen, dass es schon Anfang 1933 Geheimverhandlungen der Regierung Dollfuß mit dem nationalsozialistischen Deutschland gab, die darauf abzielten, eine gemeinsame antimarxistische Front aufzubauen. Sie scheiterten nicht an ideologischen Streitpunkten, sondern an pragmatischen Machtfragen – zwei Ministerposten, die die Regierung Dollfuß angeboten hatte, waren nicht genug. Was Kraus aber hören konnte, war etwa Dollfuß' Deklaration am 30. April 1933, dass das „deutsche Volk im Reiche [...]

---

69 B 1016 (6. März 1934), in: Pfäfflin, (Hg.): Karl Kraus, Briefe, 653–658.
70 Berthold Viertel an Salka Viertel, 21. Februar 1936, 78.866/9, K34, A: Viertel, DLA.
71 Fischer, Widersprecher, 790.

seine Verhältnisse gestalten [möge], wie es will. Wir sind gewillt, in aller Freundschaft mit der deutschen Regierung zusammenzuarbeiten." Auch in seiner programmatischen Trabrennplatzrede am 11. September 1933 betonte Dollfuß ausdrücklich, dass sein eigentlicher Feind nicht die Nationalsozialisten, sondern die Sozialdemokraten waren, und bedauerte, „dass der NS-Terror die österreichische Regierung zu einem Zweifrontenkrieg gezwungen habe."[72]

All das zeigt, dass Kraus auch bei den Christlichsozialen, für die er doch eigentlich durch die Erste Republik hindurch nur Verachtung gezeigt hatte, Vorwürfe und Verantwortung für die Beförderung des Nationalsozialismus hätte platzieren können, doch da waren nicht zuletzt Kraus' persönliche Sympathien für den „kleinen Retter aus großer Gefahr"[73] – wie er in Anlehnung an die zeitgenössische Huldigungspropaganda formulierte –, die sich in zahlreichen Zeugnissen nachweisen lassen und die von Jaray und Kann dezidiert unterstützt wurden.[74] Dollfuß war für Kraus jedenfalls nicht, wie viele es später darstellten, ein „kleineres Übel", sondern ein „Segen" und eine Hoffnung.[75]

Kann und Jaray waren – wohl auch durch politische Konformität – nicht zuletzt darum bemüht, Kraus nachhaltig in die österreichische Erinnerungskultur einzuschreiben. Sie organisierten im März 1934 eine Filmaufnahme in Prag, die Kraus als Vorleser überliefert, sie kümmerten sich um die Feierlichkeiten zum 60. Geburtstag mit Filmvorführung im Schwedenkino sowie um eine Festschrift, die verspätet im Herbst 1934 herauskam. Münz war an diesen Aktivitäten nicht beteiligt, obgleich er weiter für den zunehmend kranken Kraus da war, der es in diesem Frühjahr 1934 unternahm, in der umfangreichsten *Fackel*, die er jemals geschrieben hatte, der *Fackel* 890–905 zu erklären, *Warum die Fackel nicht erscheint*. Der erste Teil jenes Heftes mit einer ungewöhnlichen Struktur und einem ebenso seltsamen Tonfall enthielt zwar noch etwa 50 Seiten der *Dritten Walpurgisnacht,* doch der zweite Teil wandte sich mit heute befremdender Schärfe gegen die österreichische Sozialdemokratie, ihre Medien und ihre Intellektuellen, die Kraus vielfach auch gerichtlich verfolgte.[76] Die Taktiken, Phrasen und die Propaganda der eigent-

---

72 Vgl. Dreidemy, Lucile: „Ein leuchtend Zwerglein!" Karl Kraus' Bewunderung für Österreichs Diktator Engelbert Dollfuß. In: Katharina Prager (Hg.): Geist versus Zeitgeist: Karl Kraus in der Ersten Republik, Wien 2018, 86–99, 97.
73 F 890–905, Juli 1934, 14.
74 Vgl. Dollfuß-Postkarten aus dem Besitz von Karl Kraus. WBR, HS, H.I.N. 241200; Beileidstelegramm an Alwine Dollfuß, 27. Juli 1934, WBR, HS, H.I.N. 167357; Spende an die Vaterländische Front, 27. Juli 1935. WBR, HS, H.I.N. 241608; Kuvert mit Zeitungsausschnitten (u. a. Nachrufen) zu Engelbert Dollfuß aus dem Besitz von Karl Kraus, WBR, HS, H.I.N. 241202 - H.I.N. 241204; wie auch Zeugnisse von Helene Kann, Leopold Ungar und Karl Jaray in Pfäfflin, Nähe, 302–303.
75 Vgl. Fischer, Widersprecher, 804.
76 Vgl. Krieghofer, Menschheit, 206–219.

lichen Machthaber in Österreich sah er – der sonst in diesen Dingen so hellsichtig war – in diesem Fall nicht und manipulierte in diesem Kontext auch selbst Zitate.[77] Den „Nervenchok Intellektueller" angesichts seiner im Juli 1934 nun endlich öffentlich werdenden Haltung nahm Kraus „als das kleinste Übel hin".[78] Tatsächlich waren viele schockiert. Die sogenannte Dollfuß-Fackel „bekümmerte" Bertolt Brecht, sie „beschämte" den glühenden Kraus-Anhänger Elias Canetti, dem dieser zum „Monstrum" und „Hitler der Intellektuellen" wurde, und sie empörte zahlreiche sozialdemokratische Flüchtlinge im Exil, gegen deren anklagende Artikel Kraus wegen Ehrenbeleidigung prozessierte.[79]

Auch Viertel gehörte zu denen, die schockiert waren. Er, der der Arbeiterbewegung – nicht zuletzt durch seine Freundschaft zur Familie Adler – trotz aller Kritik immer nahegestanden hatte, verfolgte die Februarkämpfe von London aus in allen möglichen Medien und raste „vor Verzweiflung", wie sein junger Mitarbeiter Christopher Isherwood festhielt.[80] Als zwei Wochen nach dem Ende der Kämpfe ein Brief Jarays eintraf, der Viertel zur Mitarbeit an einer Festschrift zu Kraus' 60. Geburtstag einlud, begann er sofort, einen Aufsatz zu schreiben, in den all seine Empörung hineinfloss: Dass Kraus nun schweige, sei verständlich, schrieb er darin, denn der Februar 1934 habe ihn wieder einmal bestätigt. Viertel war sicher, dass Kraus wie damals beim Justizpalastbrand 1927 gegen den Staat, der auf seine Bürgerinnen und Bürger schoss, Stellung beziehen würde. Hier kam Viertel in seiner Aufregung etwas vom Thema Kraus ab und schrieb über den im Gefängnis sitzenden sozialdemokratischen Stadtrat Hugo Breitner, der „Häuser für die Arbeiter" gebaut hatte:

> Aber die Bourgeoisie der Stadt, deren [...] Leben er durch Luxussteuern erschwerte, liebte diese Häuser nicht. Und schließlich erlebten wir, dass Artillerie auffuhr und diese unbeliebten Wiener Häuser samt Inhalt an Frauen und Kindern beschoß." Fast beschwörend schloss Viertel seinen aktuellen Exkurs mit den Worten, dass Kraus „nie eine andere Partei genommen [habe] als die der Humanität" und „nicht gleichzuschalten" sei – „mit keinem politischen Programm, mit keiner Macht und Meinung.[81]

---

77 Vgl. Timms, Edward: Karl Kraus. Apokalyptic Satirist. The Post-War Crisis and the Rise of the Swastika, London 2005., 482–487 und Ganahl, Simon: Karl Kraus und Peter Altenberg. Eine Typologie moderner Haltungen, Konstanz 2015, 79–80.
78 F 890–905, Juli 1934, 294.
79 Vgl. Bertolt Brecht und Elias Canetti 1934, in: Pfäfflin, Nähe, 304–306; Timms, Kraus, 2005, 385–386 und Böhm, Karl Kraus contra, Bd. 4, 63–342.
80 Isherwood, Christopher: Praterveilchen, Hamburg 1998, 44/108; ders: Christopher and His Kind, 1976, 156–157.
81 BV, Zu Karl Kraus' sechzigstem Geburtstag, in: Kaiser/Roessler/Bolbecher (Hg.), Viertel, Überwindung, 1989, 16–19.

Jaray in Wien war über Viertels Beitrag entsetzt: Solche Sätze könnten zurzeit in Österreich nicht gedruckt werden. Zudem teilte er mit, dass Viertels Auffassung der „Februar-Ereignisse" der von Kraus, auf den es als Jubilar ja allein ankäme, „entgegengesetzt" sei.[82]

Wenige Tage später kam ein Brief von Ludwig Münz, den Viertel angerufen hatte und der Jarays Worte hatte bestätigen müssen: Karl Kraus sah in Dollfuß im Vergleich mit Hitler das „kleinere Übel". In „manchem Grundlegenden" habe er dabei sicher recht, erklärte Münz, der aus Angst vor Überwachung sehr verklausuliert formulierte: „Nur dort, wo im Gespräch manchmal das kleinere Übel zum höheren Wert wird, beginnt für mich die schwere Beklemmung. Es gibt Augenblicke, wo ich nicht Noahs Sohn sein will und wegschaue, wenn sich die Blöße mir zu offen darbietet."[83] Münz spielte hier offenbar auf Kraus' persönliche Sympathien für Dollfuß an, plädierte aber dafür, dass man den sehr isolierten Kraus gerade jetzt nicht im Stich lassen dürfe. Er hoffte zudem, dass Kraus' „unerträgliche" Äußerungen schriftlich einen „höheren Sinn" erlangen würden, und schlug vor, dass Viertel, wenn er „dem Geburtstagskind" eine Freude machen wolle, besser über ein anderes Thema – etwa über Kraus und das Theater – schreiben solle.[84] Schließlich eliminierte Münz in Absprache mit Viertel alle kritischen Stellen in dessen Beitrag und gab den Text für die Publikation frei.[85] Er bat Viertel auch, falls er mit Kraus telefoniere, seinen „Bedenken" keinen Ausdruck zu geben.[86]

Viertels „Bedenken" erreichten aber einen neuen Höhepunkt, als er Ende Juli die *Fackel* 890–905 las. Nun hatte er es schriftlich, dass Kraus Dollfuß' „Ordnungsstaat" verteidigte und „den Glauben an die Widerstandskraft der Demokratie, zu der er sich seit dem Ende des Weltkrieges bekannt hatte, verloren" hatte.[87] Dass Dollfuß fast zeitgleich mit dem Erscheinen der *Fackel* 890–905 im Zuge des nationalsozialistischen Juli-Putsches starb, zementierte Kraus' Parteinahme für ihn gewissermaßen. Zu all dem aber schwieg Viertel vorerst.

Etwa ein Jahr später, am 28. Juni 1935, wurde er 50 Jahre alt. Kraus schickte ein Glückwunschtelegramm. Mehrfach erinnerte Münz Viertel, darauf zu antworten, da Kraus sein Schweigen bereits für einen „Mangel an Teilnahme" halte und

---

82 Karl Jaray an Berthold Viertel, 26. März 1934, 69.2488/1, K41, A: Viertel, DLA.
83 Ludwig Münz an Berthold Viertel, 24. April 1934, 69.2616/2, K42, A: Viertel, DLA.
84 Ebenda.
85 Vgl. *Stimmen über Karl Kraus zum 60.Geburtstag*, herausgegeben von einem Kreis dankbarer Freunde im Verlag der Buchhandlung Richard Lányi, 1934.
86 Ludwig Münz an Berthold Viertel, 9. Mai 1934, 69.2616/3, K42, A: Viertel, DLA.
87 Berthold Viertel, Erinnerungen an Karl Kraus [Rede], o. D. [um 1948], 227, K13, A: Viertel, DLA.

er ihm nur mühselig klar machen könne, das dem nicht so sei.[88] Auch die neuen Nummern der *Fackel* erreichten Viertel nicht, da er seine Abreise nach Amerika dem Verlag nicht bekannt gegeben hatte. Da brach es aus Viertel heraus: Ludwigs Ermahnung sei sicher „lieb" gemeint, doch es sei immer noch seine Sache, ob und wann er an Kraus schreibe: „Glaube mir: ich ermahne mich oft genug selbst daran. Dass ich es noch immer nicht getan habe beruht weder auf Zeitmangel noch auf Nachlässigkeit. Die Hemmung sitzt tiefer." Telegrafisch habe er Karl ja bereits 1934 um ein aufklärendes Gespräch gebeten. Aber eine überstürzte Abreise nach Amerika kam dazwischen – und eben:

> Jene Nummer der Fackel, die sich mit den Februarkämpfen der Wiener Arbeiterschaft beschäftigt. Als ich sie las, wünschte ich, ich hätte nicht bis zu ihrem Erscheinen gelebt. Mir wurde physisch übel vor Traurigkeit. [...] Gewiss, es war sein Recht und seine Pflicht zu schreiben, wie er dachte und fühlte. Ich habe es auch seither so vielen Menschen gegenüber verteidigt. Aber ich höre nicht auf, es zu beklagen. [...] Ich habe nichts vergessen, ich bleibe Karl Kraus immer dankbar für die Lehre, die ich bei ihm genossen habe und die mein Leben und meine Arbeit beeinflusst hat. Ich liebe auch den Menschen immer noch. Aber es wird mir schwer ihm zu schreiben ohne dieser Fackel Erwähnung zu tun. [...] Was uns trennt, ist leider nicht eine Sache des Geistes, nicht eine Sache der Wahrheit und gewiss nicht eine Sache der Politik – es ist eine Herzenssache. Mein Herz mag Unrecht haben, aber es besteht auf seinem Gefühl. Es ist ohnehin nicht mehr weit bis zum Tod [...]. Nachher mag jener große Jom Kippur kommen, an dem wir uns gegenseitig alles verzeihen. Vielleicht werde ich mir dann auch verzeihen können, dass ich nie imstande war, klar zu sehen und klar zu urteilen; aber meinem Gefühl bin ich immer gefolgt, so gut ich konnte.[89]

So erklärte Viertel sein Schweigen, das „alte Liebe und viel neue Sorge" enthalte. Er sorgte sich um den gealterten, kränkelnden Kraus, dem er keinesfalls eine politische Meinung vorschreiben wollte, und er hatte Angst vor einem endgültigen Bruch:[90]

> Jetzt, da das Unglück über uns hereingebrochen ist, da wir alle – unsere Generation und erst recht die vorhergehende – mit heruntergelassenen Hosen und nacktem Hintern dastehen, da habe ich einfach Angst, dass ich mit dem besten Bestreben einen alten Mann verletzen werde, mehr als ihn mein Schweigen verletzt. Ich fürchte mich vor meinen eigenen Fehlern, die unausbleiblich sind. Ich bin ohnehin glücklich, dass ich nicht in Wien bin und sitzen bleiben muss, wenn er Leute auffordert, aufzustehen. Wenn er das ‚abgefallen sein' nennt, bin ich millionenfach abgefallen.[91]

---

88 Ludwig Münz an Berthold Viertel, o. D. und 5. November 1935, 69.2616/8 und 69.2616/9, K42, A: Viertel, DLA, in: Jansen, 97–98.
89 Berthold Viertel an Ludwig Münz, 12. November 1935, 78.849/3, K32, A: Viertel, DLA.
90 Berthold Viertel an Ludwig Münz, 14. November 1935, 78.849/4, K32, A: Viertel, DLA.
91 Berthold Viertel an Ludwig Münz, 27. November 1935, 78.849/5, K32, A: Viertel, DLA.

Viertel spielte hier auf Kraus' *Macbeth*-Vorlesung am 19. November 1934 an, mit der Kraus nach fast zwei Jahren erstmal wieder vor sein Wiener Publikum trat. Kraus hielt an diesem Abend einen verklärenden „Vorspruch und Nachruf" auf den „großen, kleinen, armen Schatten" Dollfuß und nahm, indem er sein Publikum aufforderte aufzustehen und so den Abend in das Zeichen seines „Glaubensheld[es] künftiger Freiheit" setze, Teil am Dollfuß-Kult des Regimes.[92] Karl Jaray hatte übrigens schon Anfang 1934 ein Rundschreiben an die Freundinnen und Freunde von Kraus verschickt, in dem er – nach dem „Abfall" so vieler – den „Nachweis der Treue wirklicher Anhänger" forderte.[93]

Angesichts eben dieser Praktiken empfand Viertel sich als „millionenfach abgefallen"[94] und doch kam er schließlich zu Weihnachten 1935 nach Wien, um mit Karl Kraus zu sprechen. Es ist unrichtig, wenn Jens Malte Fischer in seiner Kraus-Biografie behauptet, dass es nach der *Fackel* 890–905 „eigentlich keine einzige Reaktion von ernstzunehmender Seite [gab], die der Kompliziertheit der Lage, in der sich Kraus befand und der Ambivalenz des Textes, die der Ambivalenz der Situation entsprach, auch nur annähernd gerecht wurde."[95] Abseits von Nádherný, mit der Kraus sicherlich im Gespräch blieb, Brecht und wohl auch Walter Benjamin hatte sicherlich auch Viertel das 315 Seiten starke Heft „aufmerksam durchgelesen". Er hatte zudem, wie oben geschildert, „genug Berührung mit dem deutschen Reich und Einblick in die Vorgänge dort, um die Brutalität und Gefährlichkeit des neuen Regimes richtig einschätzen zu können", ja, er erfuhr durch die internationale Presse und den intensiveren Kontakt mit Flüchtlingen in Paris und London womöglich sogar mehr als Kraus in Wien.[96] Nicht zuletzt kannte, schätzte und liebte er Kraus und seine Arbeit aus großer Nähe seit über dreißig Jahren. Und er nahm sich Zeit für die „notwendige Auseinandersetzung mit Karl Kraus, die von ½ 12h Nacht bis ½ 6h morgens dauerte, nur wir beide und nur Politik – kaum ein paar persönliche Sätze, die Erkundigungen nach Dir [Salka Viertel] und den Kindern waren, von denen er Genaueres wissen wollte, als ich ihm sagen konnte."[97]

Im erinnernden Rückblick auf Kraus wurde Viertel immer wieder nicht nur der Komplexität der Lage, sondern auch der Ambivalenz des Textes und der Situation gerecht, und stellte die für ihn unauflöslich bleibenden Widersprüche in ebenso bleibender Freundschaft nebeneinander: „[In] langen Stunden hörte er

---

92 F 912–915, August 1935, 69–72; vgl. auch Gustav Kars 1991, in: Pfäfflin, Nähe, 310–311.
93 Vgl. Pfäfflin, (Hg.): Karl Kraus, Briefe, Bd. 2, 392 [Kommentar zu B 1016].
94 Berthold Viertel an Ludwig Münz, 27. November 1935, 78.849/5, K32, A: Viertel, DLA.
95 Fischer, Widersprecher, 881.
96 Als Entgegnung auf Fischer, Widersprecher, 809 und 874.
97 Berthold Viertel an Salka Viertel, 21. Februar 1936, 78.866/9, K34, A: Viertel, DLA.

sich meine Vorwürfe und Einwände, die rückhaltlos vorgebracht wurden, mit der sanftesten Geduld an und versuchte sie zu entkräften, ohne dass der eine von uns den anderen überzeugt hätte."[98] Und Viertel verteidigte Kraus nochmals: Nur die „tiefgefühlte Erfassung" der „Hitler-Katastrophe" habe ihn zur Fehleinschätzung von Dollfuß verleiten können:

> Während dieses Gespräches wurde mir immer banger bewusst, welche Hoffnungslosigkeit der Ausbruch der Barbarei in Karl Kraus bewirkt hatte. [...] Nur so erklärte sich die irrige Wahl des sogenannten kleineren Übels, das doch nur eine Angleichung an das größere war und ein Übergang dazu. Karl Kraus sah in Dollfuß einen Märtyrer, in den gefallenen Arbeitern dagegen die von einer falschen Politik verführten, vergeblichen Opfer. Ich sah es vom Ausland her anders, und ich konnte bei dem mir geistig Überlegenen die Blendung des Blickes nicht verstehen [...]. Was alles an zutiefst verbitterten Sprüchen und Widersprüchen in diesen dreihundertsechzig Seiten der Fackel [...] enthalten ist, ich habe es nie mit Ruhe aufnehmen können [...]. Hier stand der Apokalyptiker, der so vieles vorausgesehen [...] hatte, an der Grenze seiner Möglichkeit, zugleich der Mensch an der Grenze seines Lebens. [...] [E]r lehnte das freundliche Angebot eines Asyls in Kansas ab. Er wollte Wien nicht verlassen, was auch kommen möge.[99]

Bereits Anfang Dezember 1935 war es zum Zerwürfnis zwischen Kraus und Münz gekommen. Grund dafür war ein Streit zwischen Kann und Münz, der für eine Edition vorgesehene Briefe des verstorbenen Peter Altenberg sehr verspätet zurückgab. Kann warf ihm „jüdische Unverschämtheit" vor. Münz prozessierte und Viertels Versuche, ihn „von der Torheit dieser Aktion zu überzeugen", waren vergeblich:[100]

> Solch eine Gerichtsverhandlung – was für ein Schmutz! Eine Jüdin bezichtigt einen Juden einer jüdischen Untugend. Und darüber verhandelt ein österreichischer Richter. Der Vorfall selbst spielt in einem engen Kreise ältlicher Esoteriker [...]. Anlass des Streites sind die erotischen Briefe des armen Peter Altenberg. [...] [Kraus] ist doch ein Meister der Logik, die das Falsche in die Wahrheit umbiegt. An Verstandesschärfe uns allen turmhoch überlegen, besitzt er noch dazu eine infernalische Übung in diesen Dingen. Dagegen kannst du keinem Richter der Welt die komplizierten seelischen Bedingungen des Kraus Kreises plausibel machen [...].[101]

Noch hoffte Berthold Viertel auf Kraus' Vernunft, um die „ebenso läppische wie scheußliche Sache" zu beenden: „[...] das Ganze ist so tief neurotisch wie nur

---

98 Berthold Viertel 1947, in: Pfäfflin, Nähe, 312.
99 Ebenda.
100 Berthold Viertel an Salka Viertel, 21. Februar 1936, 78.866/9, K34, A: Viertel, DLA; vgl. auch Konvolut von Briefen, Ladungen, Sachverhaltensdarstellungen in der Privatklage Ludwig Münz gegen Helene Kann, H.I.N. 219574, HS, WBR.
101 Berthold Viertel an Ludwig Münz, 16. Februar 1936, 78.849/6, K32, A: Viertel, DLA.

möglich – und spielt in einem Grab, aus dem böse Düfte kommen."[102] Er selbst fühlte sich zu diesem Zeitpunkt schon sehr weit weg von Kraus, und Salka Viertel brachte die Sache auf den Punkt, als sie antwortete: „Es ist wirklich unglaublich was dieser Kraus-Kreis für Sorgen hat – die Welt bricht zusammen und diese Schmocks prozessieren wegen [...] idiotischen Angelegenheiten."[103]

Nur drei Monate nachdem diese Auseinandersetzungen begonnen hatten, starb Karl Kraus am 12. Juni 1936. Helene Kann hatte ihn in den letzten Tagen umsorgt und Münz konnte sich nicht mehr von seinem lebenslangen Freund verabschieden.[104] Die Viertels bezogen im „Kraus-Kreis" insofern Stellung, als sie Ludwig Münz telegrafisch ihr Beileid ausdrückten und nicht den „offiziellen" Erben, die sich an Kraus' Grab versammelten. In Kraus' Testament wurden Viertel und Münz nicht erwähnt.[105]

## Nachleben und Conclusion

Im Zusammenhang mit Kraus' Verarbeitung der politischen Ereignisse ab 1933 und seiner Positionierung dabei hat die Forschungsmonokultur um Kraus entweder diskret weggesehen[106] oder bis hin zur aktuellsten Kraus-Biografie immer wieder Kraus' Haltung zu verteidigen gesucht, in dem sie Dollfuß als Hitlers „einzigen entscheidenden Gegner" aufbaute.[107] Nur wenige haben die historischen Umstände genau(er) analysiert und zur Sprache gebracht.[108] So gut wie niemand aber versuchte, die lebensgeschichtlichen Ereignisse ernst zu nehmen.[109] Und doch sind gerade hier immer noch neue Quellen zu entdecken und einzubezie-

---

102 Berthold Viertel an Salka Viertel, 21. Februar 1936, 78.866/9, K34, A: Viertel, DLA. Sidonie Nádherný fand die Affäre um Kann und Münz übrigens ähnlich problematisch wie Viertel (Pfäfflin, Nähe, 315–316).
103 Berthold Viertel an Ludwig Münz, 16. Februar 1936, 78.849/6, K32, A: Viertel, DLA und Salka Viertel an Berthold Viertel, 11. März 1936, 78.866/9, K45, A: Viertel, DLA.
104 Ludwig Münz an Salka Viertel, 23. Juni 1936, H.I.N. 216660, HS, WBR.
105 Der Schriftsteller Hermann Hakel behauptete später, Viertel habe bei der letzten Zusammenkunft mit Kraus darauf verzichtet, „Erbverwalter und Mitverantwortlicher des Kraus'schen Nachlasses" zu werden. Vgl. Hakel 1981, in: Pfäfflin, Nähe, 314–315.
106 Vgl. Schick, Paul: Karl Kraus in Selbstzeugnissen und Bilddokumenten, Reinbek bei Hamburg 1965, 8–9.
107 Fischer, Widersprecher, 781 und 842.
108 Vgl. Timms, Kraus, 2005; Ganahl, Kraus, und auch (umstritten): Pfabigan, Alfred: Karl Kraus und der Sozialismus. Eine politische Biographie, Wien 1976.
109 Eine Ausnahme, die allerdings in der Forschung nach wie vor zu wenig beachtet wird, bildet hier die umfangreiche Editionspraxis von Friedrich Pfäfflin.

hen – auch diese Skizze kann nur einen weiteren Baustein aus den Nachlässen von Viertel und Münz liefern und den Weg aufzeigen. Der gründliche Blick etwa auf die Anwaltsakten von Kraus, die noch eine immense Fülle an Perspektiven bieten, oder auf Ludwig Münz, Helene Kann oder Karl Jaray, von denen noch immer viel zu wenig bekannt ist, steht weiterhin aus. Gerade die Stimmen der Frauen um Kraus müssten, so sie überliefert sind, auch noch viel stärker beachtet werden. Immerhin wird schon aus den hier vorgestellten Zeugnissen klar, dass Kraus' Arbeit an der *Dritten Walpurgisnacht* nicht so eine einsame Angelegenheit war, wie immer behauptet wurde, sondern im Zusammenspiel mit einem internationalen Netzwerk stattfand und ihm offenbar vieles zugespielt oder berichtet wurde.

Es ist auch nicht zutreffend, dass der Begriff „Austrofaschismus" beziehungsweise die „Beurteilung der Zeit von 1933 bis 1938 [in der (österreichischen)] Historiografie] dauerhaft außer Streit gestellt werden kann", wie Jens Malte Fischer behauptet.[110] Haltungen und Traditionslinien von Bezügen durchziehen die Kraus-Forschung ebenso wie die Geschichts- und Literaturforschung und sind daher sorgfältig auszuweisen und in ihrer Fülle gegeneinander zu stellen. Sigmund Freud, Robert Musil und auch Ernst Rüdiger Starhemberg sprachen vom Austrofaschismus; Kraus, weil es nicht in seine Argumentation gepasst hätte, tat das nicht.

Für Viertel wiederum war der „österreichische Faschismus eines Dollfuß und eines Schuschnigg, die die Garantien ihres weiteren Bestehens im Papst, in Mussolini, im katholischen Frankreich erblickten [...] die letzte und tragischste der österreichischen Illusionen."[111] Und Kraus, für Viertel der kritische „Niederreißer" aller österreichischen Illusionen, war ihr erlegen, war vom „Anti-Österreicher [...] zum Nur-Österreicher geworden, der nichts anderes mehr zu wünschen und zu hoffen wusste, als dass dieser Fleck Erde, zugleich der letzte Fleck deutschsprechender Kultur, durch welches Mittel auch immer von der Pest verschont werde."[112]

Es war allerdings nicht Viertel, der Kraus nach 1945 nach Europa zurückbrachte, sondern Kann, Jaray sowie Heinrich Fischer sowie Paul und Sophie Schick, die Kraus' Bild – aus wiederum nachvollziehbaren Gründen der besseren Vermittlung – einem konservativen Nachkriegsösterreich anpassen mussten. Zeitgeschichte, Rezeptionsgeschichte und nicht zuletzt die eigene Geschichte der ForscherInnen, die sich mit Kraus befassen, wurde und wird als ‚situated knowledge' (Donna Haraway) nach wie vor zu wenig reflektiert und mitgedacht. Genau hier aber bieten sich die aktualisierenden Zugriffe und neuen Erkenntnisse, die sich

---

110 Vgl. Fischer, Widersprecher, 797–799 und 840 und als Entgegnung darauf: Florian Wenninger https://tagebuch.at/politik/in-st-poelten-steht-ein-tempel-in-wien-ein-dixi-haeusl/.
111 Berthold Viertel, Die Heimkehr des verlorenen Sohnes, o. D., 240/a, K13, A: Viertel, DLA.
112 Berthold Viertel 1947, in: Pfäfflin (Hg.), Nähe, 2008, 312.

womöglich sogar aus der mit Walter Benjamin so oft konstatierten Lagerbildung in Adepten und Gegner herausbewegen können. Denn – so fand schon Berthold Viertel: „Das Bild des Mannes, gar das Erinnerungsbild [...] verändert sich in uns mit unserem eigenen Bilde."[113]

## Literaturverzeichnis

Bernhard Hachleitner, Alfred Pfoser, Katharina Prager, Werner Michael Schwarz (ed.), Die Zerstörung der Demokratie. Österreich, März 1933 bis Februar 1934. Wien/Salzburg: Residenz 2023.

Böhm, Hermann. *Karl Kraus contra ...: die Prozeßakten der Kanzlei Oskar Samek in der Wiener Stadt- und Landesbibliothek*, Bd. 1–4. Hrsg. von Herwig Würtz, bearbeitet von Hermann Böhm. Wien, 1995–1997.

Etzemüller, Thomas. *Biographien. Lesen – erforschen – erzählen*. Frankfurt am Main, 2012.

Dreidemy, Lucile: „‚Ein leuchtend Zwerglein!' Karl Kraus' Bewunderung für Österreichs Diktator Engelbert Dollfuß." *Geist versus Zeitgeist: Karl Kraus in der Ersten Republik*. Hrsg. v. Katharina Prager. Wien, 86–99.

Fischer, Jens Malte. *Karl Kraus. Der Widersprecher*. Wien, 2020.

Ganahl, Simon. *Karl Kraus und Peter Altenberg. Eine Typologie moderner Haltungen*. Konstanz, 2015.

Isherwood, Christopher. *Christopher Isherwood, Praterveilchen*. Hamburg, 1998.

Isherwood, Christopher. *Christopher and His Kind*. New York, 1976.

Jansen, Irene. *Berthold Viertel. Leben und künstlerische Arbeit im Exil*. Wien, 1992.

Kaiser, Konstantin, Roessler, Peter und Bolbecher, Siglinde (Hrsg.). „Berthold Viertel, Die Überwindung des Übermenschen. Exilschriften," *Berthold Viertel – Studienausgabe in 4 Bänden*, Band 1. Hrsg. v. Konstantin Kaiser, Peter Roessler und Siglinde Bolbecher. Wien, 1989.

Kaiser, Konstantin, Roessler, Peter und Bolbecher, Siglinde (Hrsg.). „Berthold Viertel, Kindheit eines Cherub. Autobiographische Fragmente," *Berthold Viertel – Studienausgabe in 4 Bänden*, Band 2. Hrsg. v. Siglinde Bolbecher und Konstantin Kaiser. Wien, 1990.

Köhne, Julia Barbara. *Geniekult in Geisteswissenschaften und Literaturen um 1900 und seine filmischen Adaptionen*. Wien/Köln/Weimar, 2014.

Kraus, Karl. *Die Fackel*, 992 Nummern in 37 Jahrgängen, Wien 1899–1936, zitiert nach: Die Fackel, AAC Digital Edition Nr. 1, http://www.aac.ac.at/fackel.

Kraus, Karl. *Dritte Walpurgisnacht*, zitiert nach: Karl Kraus: *Schriften*. Hrsg. v. Christian Wagenknecht, Bd. 12. Frankfurt a. M., 1989.

Krieghofer, Gerald. „‚Die Menschheit weiß immer noch nicht, was gesehen ist und jeden Augenblick geschieht' – Kraus nach 1933." *Geist versus Zeitgeist: Karl Kraus in der Ersten Republik*. Hrsg. v. Katharina Prager. Wien, 2018. 206–219.

Kuono, Eiji. *Die Performativität der Satire bei Karl Kraus. Zu seiner „geschriebenen Schauspielkunst"*. Berlin (= Schriften zur Literaturwissenschaft 38), 2015.

Pfabigan, Alfred. *Karl Kraus und der Sozialismus. Eine politische Biographie*. Wien, 1976.

Pfäfflin, Friedrich. *Vom Verglühen der ‚Fackel'. Karl Kraus und sein Verlag 1930–1936*. Warmbronn, 2004.

---

113 Berthold Viertel, Erinnerung an Karl Kraus (Fassung A), 13. August 1948, 227, K13, A: Viertel, DLA.

Pfäfflin, Friedrich (Hrsg.). *Karl Kraus, Briefe an Sidonie Nádherný von Borutin*, 2 Bd. Göttingen, 2005.
Pfäfflin, Friedrich. *Aus großer Nähe. Karl Kraus in Berichten aus Weggefährten und Widersachern.* Göttingen, 2008.
Prager, Katharina. *Berthold Viertel. Eine Biographie der Wiener Moderne.* Wien/Köln/Weimar, 2018.
Schick, Paul. *Karl Kraus in Selbstzeugnissen und Bilddokumenten.* Reinbek bei Hamburg, 1965.
Schick, Sophie (o. J.): *Karl Kraus. Fragmente einer Biographie*, Typoskript, B 268.365, Druckschriftensammlung, Wienbibliothek im Rathaus.
Stocker, Brigitte. *Rhetorik eines Protagonisten gegen die Zeit. Karl Kraus als Redner in den Vorlesungen 1919 bis 1932.* Wien, 2013.
Strigl, Daniela. „,Frauenverehrer', ,Liebessklave', ,Gott und Teufel' – zu Karl Kraus' erotischer Biographie." *Geist versus Zeitgeist: Karl Kraus in der Ersten Republik.* Hrsg. v. Katharina Prager. Wien, 2018. 166–181.
Timms, Edward. *Karl Kraus – Satiriker der Apokalypse. Leben und Werk 1874 bis 1918. Eine Biographie von Edward Timms.* Berlin, 1999.
Timms, Edward. *Karl Kraus. Apokalyptic Satirist. The Post-War Crisis and the Rise of the Swastika.* London, 2005.
Wenninger, Florian und Dreidemy, Lucile. *Dollfuß/Schuschnigg-Regime 1933–1938. Vermessung eines Forschungsfeldes.* Wien/Köln/Weimar, 2013.

www.ingramcontent.com/pod-product-compliance
Lightning Source LLC
LaVergne TN
LVHW090456180925
821343LV00002B/50